POVERTY
POLICY

T0328149

POVERTY POLICY

A COMPENDIUM OF
CASH TRANSFER PROPOSALS

Theodore R. Marmor
Editor

Routledge
Taylor & Francis Group

LONDON AND NEW YORK

First published 1971 by Transaction Publishers

Published 2017 by Routledge
4 Park Square, Milton Park, Abingdon, Oxon OX14 4RN
605 Third Avenue, New York, NY 10017

Routledge is an imprint of the Taylor & Francis Group, an informa business

Copyright © 1971 by Taylor & Francis.

Library of Congress Catalog Number: 2007027147

Library of Congress Cataloging-in-Publication Data
Marmor, Theodore R.
    Poverty policy : a compendium of cash proposals / Theodore R. Marmor, editor.
        p. cm.
    Originally published: Chicago : Aldine-Atherton, 1971.
    Includes bibliographical references and index.
    ISBN 978-0-202-36170-3 (acid-free paper)
    1. Economic assistance, Domestic—United States. 2. Income—United States. 3. Public Wefare—United States I. Marmor, Theodore R.

HC110.P63M35   2007
362.5'820973—dc22   2007027147

ISBN 13: 978-0-202-36170-3 (pbk)

Contributors

The President's Commission on Income Maintenance Programs, appointed by President Johnson in early 1968, submitted its report and recommended proposal in November, 1969.

Theodore R. Marmor is an Associate Professor of Political Science and Associate Director of the School of Public Affairs at the University of Minnesota.

The Advisory Council on Public Welfare was appointed in July, 1964 by the Secretary of Health, Education, and Welfare to review the administration of public assistance and child welfare services programs and to make recommendations for their improvement. The Council's report was submitted in 1966 and widely circulated.

Robert J. Lampman is a Professor of Economics at the University of Wisconsin and a staff member of the Institute for Research on Poverty.

Alvin L. Schorr is the Dean of Social Work at New York University.

Edward E. Schwartz is the George Herbert Jones Professor, School of Social Service Administration, at the University of Chicago.

Harvey E. Brazer is a Professor of Economics at the University of Michigan.

James G. Speth, Jr., Richard Cotton, Joseph C. Bell, and *Howard V. Mindus* were student editors of the *Yale Law Journal.* Their proposal incorporated suggestions by Professors Edward Sparer and Boris I. Bittker of the Yale Law School and Professors James Tobin and Peter Mieszkowski of the Yale Economics Department.

Earl R. Rolph is a Professor of Economics at the University of California, Berkeley.

Joseph A. Pechman is the Director of Economic Studies at the Brookings Institution.

Preface

The object and organization of this compendium require brief explanation. Its principal aim is to bring together in one accessible volume the most widely discussed plans for reducing financial poverty in the United States through cash transfers. Cash transfers are but one form of income supplementation, and a fuller presentation of antipoverty proposals would include both transfers in-kind (such as food, housing, and medical care) and human investment programs aimed at increasing the earning capacity of individuals. However, throughout the second half of the 1960s, much discussion has centered on how to reduce poverty by getting more cash income in the hands of poor people. This volume presents some of the widely diverse cash transfer proposals which have grown out of these reformist debates.

The proposals have been grouped to facilitate comparison. Readers who have tried to follow the American debate over cash transfers will undoubtedly have been struck by the confusing ways in which proposals are described and compared. Proposed beneficiaries sometimes provide the basis of comparison, as with proposals of old-age pensions or child allowances. In other cases, plans are described and compared as negative income taxes or welfare reforms by virtue of the administrative changes they imply or the mechanism for reducing benefits with respect to increased income. For reasons set out in the second chapter, I have found it most useful to group plans according to the social problems which they are intended to solve, the advantage being that discussion of means is not so likely to submerge awareness of the ends intended. Arranged in this way, the proposals in this volume are grouped as being primarily directed at the problems of welfare, Part II; at the problems of poverty, Part III;

or at the inequities in the tax system's treatment of poor persons, Part IV. These categories are not, of course, mutually exclusive. The problems are inter-related and the solutions to any one affect the others indirectly.

The first two chapters of the book were included to aid readers in intelligent discussion and comparison of the proposals. Chapter 1 offers what I believe is the most informed contemporary profile of financial poverty in the United States. The selection is taken from the November, 1969 report of the Heineman Commission (officially known as the President's Commission on Income Maintenance Programs). The reader will find here much of the background data on the poor and the dimensions of poverty which will be referred to unevenly by advocates of the various proposals. Chapter 2—an essay on how income supplementation plans might be most usefully compared—sets out the categories in which the plans will be grouped and defines six of the most prominent criteria by which plans might be evaluated. All of the compendium's proposals bear the imprint of having been directed towards different audiences at different points in the discussion of poverty issues. Applying a uniform set of criteria to them exposes both their characteristic features and the questions their authors did not explicitly raise. If Chapter 2 is used as intended, this volume will present not only the raw materials of policy discussion, but also a way of making sense of those materials. Financial poverty will, even under the most optimistic assumptions, continue to be an issue of concern in the foreseeable future; the systematic review of current proposals of reform should assist the intelligent discussion of future possibilities.

My interest in antipoverty policy proposals was stimulated and supported by the Institute for Research on Poverty at the University of Wisconsin. As a consultant to the President's Commission on Income Maintenance Programs, I was further encouraged to consider how various plans could be meaningfully evaluated. The Poverty Seminar of the American Academy of Arts and Sciences provided a forum for which the analytic scheme of Chapter 2 was first formulated. Time to bring together this compendium was made available in 1969–1970 by fellowships from two institutions concerned with questions of public policy: the Adlai Stevenson Institute of International Affairs in Chicago, and the John F. Kennedy Institute of Politics at Harvard. My research assistant, Carol Mermey, provided substantial aid at every stage in the formulation of this book.

Contents

Contents

PART ONE

The Analysis of Poverty and Poverty Policy

Poverty in America:
Dimensions and Prospects

The Poor

The postwar period has witnessed a remarkable improvement in the material welfare of most Americans. Even with the effect of inflation taken into account, median family income grew by 76 per cent between 1947 and 1967. The proportion of families enjoying a total income of $10,000 or more increased from 22 to 34 per cent during the same period. And, in recent years, we have taken justifiable satisfaction in the reduction of poverty from 22 per cent of the population in 1959 to 13 per cent in 1968. But the fact remains that 25 million persons are still poor.

Thousands of pages of statistics about the poor have been tabulated and published. The poor have been measured, surveyed, and sorted into numerous categories, some of which are summarized in Table 1–1 for 1966.[1] But in the end, the diversity of the poor overwhelms any simple attempt to describe them with statistics. What may be said simply is that millions of our fellow citizens are living in severe poverty, with few prospects for a better life, and often with little hope for the future.

To the poor, poverty is no statistical or sociological matter. Their condition exists as a daily fight for survival. This Commission has found their deprivation to be real, not a trick of rhetoric or statistics.[2] And for many

1. Aggregate poverty counts are available for 1968. The latest year for which detailed breakdowns are available is 1966.
2. In the course of our work, field investigations and public hearings were conducted in 17 areas. Transcripts of the hearings are available in the Archives.

Poverty Amid Plenty: The American Paradox, The Report of The President's Commission on Income Maintenance Programs. Washington: U.S. Government Printing Office, 1969, pp. 13–16, 23–32, 35–40.

3

Table 1–1.   Selected Characteristics of the
Poor and the Nonpoor, 1966

Characteristic	Number (millions)		Per Cent Distribution	
	Poor	Non-poor	Poor	Non-poor
Age				
Total	30.0	163.9	100.0	100.0
Under 18 years	13.0	57.4	43.5	35.0
18–21	1.6	10.4	5.3	6.4
22–54	7.4	68.7	24.7	41.9
55–64	2.5	14.7	8.5	9.0
65 and over	5.4	12.6	18.0	7.7
Race				
Total	30.0	163.9	100.0	100.0
White	20.4	150.2	68.3	91.6
Nonwhite	9.5	13.7	31.7	8.4
Family status				
Total	30.0	163.9	100.0	100.0
Unrelated individuals	5.1	7.6	17.1	4.6
Family members	24.9	156.3	82.9	95.4
Head	6.1	42.8	20.3	26.1
Spouse	4.1	38.5	13.5	23.5
Other adult	2.1	17.7	7.2	10.8
Child under 18	12.6	57.3	42.0	35.0
Type of residence				
Total	30.0	163.9	100.0	100.0
Farm	2.5	8.5	8.2	5.2
Nonfarm	27.5	155.4	91.8	94.8
Rural	11.2	46.7	37.3	28.5
Urban	18.8	117.2	62.7	71.5

SOURCE: Office of Economic Opportunity, unpublished tabulations from
the Current Population Survey and draft report, "Dimensions of Poverty,
1964–1966."

of the poor, their poverty is not a temporary situation, but an enduring
fact of life.

The Poverty Living Standard

Any discussion of the poor must begin by defining those who are poor
and those who are not. But it is obvious that any single standard or definition of poverty is arbitrary, and clearly subject to disagreement. The

standard which this Commission has employed is the widely used poverty index, developed by the Social Security Administration. This index is based on the Department of Agriculture's measure of the cost of a temporary low-budget, nutritious diet for households of various sizes. The poverty index is simply this food budget multiplied by three to reflect the fact that food typically represents one-third of the expenses of a low-income family. The resulting figure is the minimum income needed to buy a subsistence level of goods and services; the 25 million people whose incomes fall below the index are poor, while those above it are, officially at least, nonpoor. According to this poverty index, in 1968 a nonfarm family of four required a minimum income of $3,553 per year, or $2.43 per person per day to meet its basic expenses. Table 1–2 shows the poverty index for families of various sizes in 1968.

Table 1–2.   1968 Poverty Thresholds

| Family | Poverty Index | |
Size	Nonfarm	Farm
1	$1,748	$1,487
2	2,262	1,904
3	2,774	2,352
4	3,553	3,034
5	4,188	3,577
6	4,706	4,021
7 or more	5,789	4,916

How a typical poverty income might be spent can be seen in Table 1–3, which shows the standard of living available to the poor compared with that of a moderate-income family in 1967. In that year the poverty budget was $3,410. A moderate family budget developed by the Bureau of Labor Statistics required an income of $7,836 per year, or $1,300 less than the median family income of $9,120 for nonfarm families of four. Neither budget makes allowance for any costs of employment or taxes paid.

Clearly, the poor family must do without many of the things that families with an average income consider to be "necessities"—a car, an occasional dessert after meals, rugs, a bed for each family member, school supplies, or an occasional movie. Nothing can be budgeted for medical care or insurance.

This food budget requires more than a third of the poor family's income, but still allows only $1.00 a day for food per person. A family can buy a nutritionally adequate diet for this amount, using the Department of Agriculture's food plan, but it must eat considerably more beans,

Table 1–3. Monthly Budgets, Poor and Moderate-
Income Urban Families of Four, 1967

Consumption Item	Poor[a]	Moderate[b]
Total	$284	$653
Food	122	175
Housing	91[c]	199[d]
Transportation	6	77[e]
Clothing and personal care	57	82
Medical care	–	40
Gifts and contributions	–	21
Life insurance	–	13
Other consumption (recreation, education, tobacco, etc.)	9	46

[a] Based on budgeted need for an AFDC family of four in Los Angeles, California.
[b] Moderate living standard defined by the Bureau of Labor Statistics for a family of four.
[c] Renter.
[d] Homeowner.
[e] Automobile owner.

SOURCE: State of California, Assembly Committee on Social Welfare, *California Welfare: Legislative Program for Reform*, February 1969; and U.S. Department of Labor, Bureau of Labor Statistics, Bulletin No. 1570–5, *Three Standards of Living for an Urban Family of Four Persons, Spring, 1967.*

potatoes, flour and cereal products, and considerably less meat, eggs, fruits, and vegetables than the average family. Each member of the poor family may consume less than one-quarter pound of meat a day.

Unfortunately, the Department's food plan, the basis of the poverty index, is not very realistic. It is estimated that only about one-fourth of the families who spend that much for food actually have a nutritionally adequate diet.[3] The plan calls for skills in meal-planning and buying that are rare at any income level, and it requires extensive efforts by poor families to make the varied and appetizing meals which are ostensibly possible under the plan. Many of the poor lack common kitchen appliances. Moreover, the Department's plan assumes the shopper will buy in economical quantities and take advantage of special bargains, but this is particularly difficult for a poor family with inadequate storage and refrigeration facilities.

The poor family's budget has no provision for eating outside of the home. Any lunches bought by working members or school children will

3. U.S. Department of Agriculture, Consumer and Food Economics Division.

reduce funds available for eating at home, since few outside meals can be bought for the 33 cents per meal allotted to each family member. Many schools charge more than this for a Federally-subsidized lunch.

The poor family's budget provides only $91 a month for all housing costs—including rent, utilities, and household operation—for four persons. No allowance is included for the poor family to purchase household furnishings. In Head Start programs, for example, teachers found that many children never had eaten at a table. Thirty per cent of families on welfare live in homes where each family member does not have a bed.[4] A comparative breakdown of the housing allotments for poor and moderate-income families appears in Table 1–4.

Table 1–4. Monthly Housing Budgets, Poor and Moderate-Income Urban Families of Four, 1967

Housing Expenditures	Poor	Moderate
Total	$91	$199
Shelter cost	67[a]	159[b]
Household furnishing	—	22
Household operations	12	18
Utilities	12	—

[a] Renter.
[b] Homeowner; includes utilities and allowance for lodging away from home.
Source: See Table 1–3.

The money allotted to transportation for a poor family would not cover even daily transportation for a worker. The moderate-income family not only has more money to spend on recreation, but its automobile permits it to take the children on inexpensive outings, while poor children rarely have access to any form of transportation. Thus, many poor children have never left their own neighborhoods.

Clothing school children is a major problem in poor families. Many poor children wear hand-me-down clothes which they receive from relatives, neighbors, and even teachers. Some clothing may be purchased at second-hand stores. But many poor children have to go to school on rainy days with no boots or raincoats—or stay home.

The poor family has $108 annually—about $9 a month—to spend on "luxuries": reading matter, recreation, education, gifts and contributions, tobacco, alcohol. But it is likely that this money will be spent on necessi-

4. U.S. Department of Health, Education, and Welfare, National Center for Social Statistics, *1967 AFDC Study: Preliminary Report of Findings from Mail Questionnaire,* January 1969.

ties, supplementing the meager food, clothing, and housing allowances. There is no room in the budget for luxuries—or emergencies.

Technically, an income at the poverty level should enable families to purchase the bare necessities of life. Yet an itemized budget drawn at that level clearly falls short of adequacy. There are many items for which no money is budgeted, although those items may be needed. Funds for them can only come out of sums already allotted to the basic necessities of life. As one witness told the Commission, "I either eat good and smell bad, or smell good and don't eat."[5] When another witness was asked how he made ends meet, he simply replied, "They don't meet."[6]

Why They Remain Poor

The paradox of poverty in the midst of plenty causes many to ask why some people remain poor when so many of their fellow Americans have successfully joined the ranks of the affluent. It is often assumed that anyone who wishes to live well can achieve that objective by seeking and accepting work. It is often argued that the poor are to blame for their own circumstances and should be expected to lift themselves from poverty.

The Commission has concluded that these assertions are incorrect. Our economic and social structure virtually guarantees poverty for millions of Americans. Unemployment and underemployment are basic facts of American life. The risks of poverty are common to millions more who depend on earnings for their income. We all grow old. We all can fall victim to unemployment caused by technological change or industrial relocation. Any of us could become sick or disabled. And becoming unpoor is extraordinarily difficult. What does a disabled man, an elderly couple, or a child *do* to escape poverty? How does a woman with six children survive while she is hunting work or being trained? How does an unskilled, middle-aged laborer adjust to the loss of a job?

The simple fact is that most of the poor remain poor because access to income through work is currently beyond their reach.

The Aged

Old age is usually a period of nonemployment. Society neither expects nor assists the aged to work. Retirement at age 65 is common in both industry and government, and discrimination in hiring against the aged and aging is common among employers.

---

5. Witness before Commission, Seattle, Washington.
6. Witness before Commission, Quincy, Florida.

The aged possess limited earning potential. They generally are expected to live on pensions, savings, and Social Security benefits. Too frequently, savings and pensions deemed adequate at an earlier time become insufficient as inflation raises the cost of living. Millions of hard-working Americans, accustomed all their lives to paying their way, find themselves becoming unalterably and unavoidably poor in old age.

In 1966, 6.4 million aged persons and their dependents were in poverty. Over a million of these persons lived in families where the family head worked for at least part of the year, and almost half a million lived in families where the head worked 50–52 weeks. The average family income was more than $600 below the poverty line; this gap was about equal for low-income aged families whether the head worked or not. Average family income for poor households headed by the aged was below $1,200.[7]

In 1966, 65 per cent of the aged were over 70. Half of those over age 65 were 73 or older. The older a person is in the aged population, the less his total income is likely to be. Earning opportunities decline because advancing age often brings increasing infirmity. Moreover, the older a person is, the greater the likelihood that he has not earned high Social Security benefits or accumulated benefits in one of the newer private pension plans, and that he has exhausted his assets.

The poor will remain poor once they retire, and others who retire may become poor in their old age. Opportunities for the aged poor to make any improvement in their own lives are remote and unrealistic. Only public programs can make a difference in their incomes.

The Nonaged

While the aged apparently can do little about their poverty, what about the 24.6 million *nonaged* persons who were poor in 1966? Six per cent of these people were in families headed by aged poor persons, so their poverty can be linked to the elderly family heads on whom they depended. What possibilities do the remaining nonaged persons have to escape poverty through their own efforts? The unpleasant truth is that these possibilities are extraordinarily limited.

WORK EXPERIENCE

The work experience of the 4.5 million nonaged heads of poor families provides dramatic documentation of their limited ability to change substantially their circumstances on their own. In all, the heads of 1.9 million

7. U.S. Department of Health, Education, and Welfare, Office of the Assistant Secretary (Planning and Evaluation), *Poverty Status Tabulations, 1966.*

poor families—42 per cent of the total—worked full-time for more than 40 weeks of the year. Most of the remaining heads of families did some work.

• Of the 4.5 million nonaged heads of poor families, 3.3 million or 73 per cent worked for some period of time during 1966; 1.2 million did not work at all.

• Of the 3.3 million who worked, nearly 60 per cent worked full-time for most of the year. The rest worked either less than 40 weeks a year or less than 35 hours a week, because of illness, family responsibilities, inability to find sufficient work, or other reasons.

Table 1–5 summarizes the work experience of poor nonaged family heads and unrelated individuals for 1966. More than 70 per cent of the nonaged heads of poor families worked for some period, yet remained in poverty. The Commission considers the fact that 42 per cent of the nonaged heads of poor families worked full-time for most of the year to be as significant in understanding poverty as the fact that 58 per cent worked less than that, or did not work at all.

The different degrees of participation in the labor force among the poor seem due to chance more than to motivation or other factors. Unemployment or underemployment among the poor are often due to forces that cannot be controlled by the poor themselves. There are not two distinct categories of poor—those who can work and those who can not. Nor can the poor be divided into those who will work and those who will not. For many, the desire to work is strong, but the opportunities are not readily available. The opening or closing of a factory, ill health of the breadwinner, inability to find transportation, loss of a babysitter, weather conditions, and similar factors greatly affect employment opportunities.

Of the 1.2 million poor nonaged family heads who did not work at all in 1966:

• Nearly half were women with responsibilities for young children.

• Another third were unable to perform any work because of illness or disability.

• Of the remaining 230,000, 40 per cent were unable to work because they were attending school, and about 15 per cent reported that they were simply unable to find any work.

• A residual group of about 100,000 remains. It includes those who did not work at all during the year for reasons other than those listed.

Thus, less than 3 per cent of the nonaged heads of poor families might have freely chosen not to work at all. But many in this residual group actually may have had little choice between work and poverty. For exam-

Table 1–5. Work Experience of Poor Nonaged Family Heads and Unrelated Individuals, by Sex, 1966[a] *(in millions)*

Work Experience of Head	Families		Unrelated Individuals	
	Male Head	Female Head	Male	Female
Total	2.9	1.6	.7	1.4
Worked in 1966	2.4	.8	.5	.8
40 weeks or more	1.8	.4	.2	.4
Full-time	1.6	.3	.2	.3
Part-time	.2	.1	.1	.1
Less than 40 weeks	.6	.4	.3	.4
Full-time	.5	.3	.2	.2
Part-time	.2	.2	.1	.2
Did not work in 1966	.5	.7	.2	.6
Ill, disabled	.3	.1	.1	.2
Couldn't find work	°	°	°	°
Other reasons	.2	.6	.1	.4
In school	.1	°	°	°
Housekeeping	°	.6	°	.3
All others	.1	°	°	°

[a] Civilian noninstitutional population.
° Less than 50,000. Columns do not add to totals due to rounding.
SOURCE: Special Census Bureau tabulations from the Current Population Survey for the Office of Economic Opportunity.

ple, many poor individuals do not work because of disabilities which ordinarily are not recognized in official statistics, particularly disabilities of a mental rather than of a physical nature.

Factors Inhibiting Progress

Clearly, the experience of the poor indicates that work alone is no guarantee of escaping poverty. Why is it that employment—the basic source of income for most Americans—fails the poor?

Several factors account for this. Family size is relevant; the costs of supporting a large number of children can result in poverty for workers with even relatively high earnings. Low wages and/or lack of sufficient hours and weeks of work can account for a good deal of poverty. Disabilities prevent many from working. Poor preparation for working careers and discrimination affect many others. And, for large numbers of people, work is simply not available. Let us examine the impact of these factors more closely.

AN ECONOMY AT LESS THAN 100 PER CENT EMPLOYMENT

There is some unemployment even in the best of times, and it is not evenly distributed over the economy. A desire to avoid accelerating inflation has led policymakers to accept some unemployment. But it must be recognized that this policy has much to do with explaining poverty for many families. A 4 per cent unemployment rate—considered by many to be the lowest feasible, long-term unemployment rate—means that not everyone can work who wants to work. It also means that wages will be lower than they would be if there were greater competition for workers. It means that young people without work experience, people with low educational attainments, and members of minority groups subject to discrimination will be particularly handicapped in their search for employment. Moreover, official unemployment statistics do not reflect the number of persons who have withdrawn completely from the labor force because of long-term inability to find jobs.

Obviously, the state of the American economy and the consequent structure of opportunities at the local level can enhance or impede employability greatly. A fully employed person, earning good wages one day, can find himself suddenly unemployed and locally unemployable due to a work force reduction or plant closing. In the absence of strong aggregate demand, even well-planned efforts to find jobs can be ineffective.

> We were very much concerned with the fact that young people wanted to work and needed jobs; 2,782 screened applicants were approved. My Committee had a task of contacting private employers to try to develop jobs. We contacted all of the churches of the communities; we contacted approximately 350 private employers. We had the Governor of the State of Iowa coming in to kick it off by announcement. We had good radio, local press, and television coverage. We sent out a letter signed by the mayors of three central cities inviting people to get involved. The end result was that we got nine job offers. The amount of money that we realized from the nine jobs wouldn't pay for the postage and printing costs.[8]

The demand for labor also will affect the outcome of training programs. Many witnesses at Commission hearings expressed frustration at going through training programs which were not geared to jobs currently available or to the skills of the trainees.

> For instance, the Job Opportunity Center which was very effective, listened to some technician who had no feeling for the programs at all and trained 40 teacher's aides. But nobody alerted the school board or got any consideration

8. Witness before Commission, Waterloo, Iowa.

from them as to whether they would hire them. So these people are right back on the streets where they are more frustrated than ever because they know now that they have some training.[9]

The program put me into them (three different types of training for jobs.) What I was wondering is if they could put somebody in there who has been through the mill like I have and talk to the people, tell them what kind of a job they could get and what they would like . . . Because they sent me to Lowrey Field for sheet metal. Well, they say it pays pretty good but it takes four years to learn the trade and then $400 to join the union. And then you have to know too much math and algebra and all that.[10]

I have been trained . . . I was trained with my cane (for the blind). Training people for what, for sitting in the corner? They have given me the training of a king or queen and today I still sit in my corner with my knitting in my hand. . . . I have been trained to take dictaphone dictation and I have been trained to do answering services and I have been trained to do sewing . . . And what am I doing today? Sitting in my corner, waiting for the world to call me a leech. I am not willing to give any more time for any more training, thank you.[11]

Well . . . back in 1965, I went to the Bureau of Indian Affairs school . . . and they accepted me and I received my training in Chicago. The trouble was that I went out for welding and somehow when I got up there they had me down as a barber. (After completing barbering courses and finally receiving training as a welder) I tried to get a job and they throw the bit up to me about "Do you have any tools?" or "Do you have any experience?" And I said no. And I can't get no job, they won't hire me. I might as well go out and dig a ditch for Tom or Joe . . . because I am sick and tried of going to trade school.[12]

The whole system is bad . . . you start them on training full of hope and what guarantee? What job is there after the end of that training? Nothing but a waiting list.[13]

People are training for the jobs that they originally were hopeful of getting. But the problem has been that we haven't been able to locate them a job with industry because of the fact, as you probably are aware by now, there are no jobs in Albuquerque, New Mexico.[14]

9. Witness before Commission, Denver, Colorado.
10. Witness before Commission, Denver, Colorado.
11. Witness before Commission, Albuquerque, New Mexico.
12. Witnesses before Commission, Isleta Indian Pueblo, near Albuquerque, New Mexico.
13. Witness before Commission, Los Angeles, California.
14. Witness before Commission, Albuquerque, New Mexico (director of a training program).

When there are no jobs for the head of the family, then other members of the family may have to help support the family. One witness told the Commission:

> A poor family cannot put his child to work according to age, he puts him to work according to the needs of his family.[15]

In 1966 at least 160,000 male family heads were forced to work less than they desired because of an inability to find more steady employment. More than a million others were working part-time hours at low-paying marginal tasks.

One witness heard by the Commission, for example, spends part of the year raising cotton on a ten-acre plot in return for a share of the product. After paying all the costs associated with raising the crop, his net income from sharecropping is $400 annually. In addition, he earns $5 daily as a tractor operator when that work is available. During the winter, he sells firewood to supplement his income. He testified:

> Nine people live off of it. Just figure how could you do it with nine people; just one biscuit a day. A man with $5 can hardly cover that. And I only receive that through the summer. Winter time there ain't nothing to do. They give us a little something to do around and pay up what we owe; you don't get through paying what you owe. And if there were something to do, I would sure appreciate doing it. I wouldn't back off from no work.[16]

LOW EARNINGS

Full-time employment at the current Federal minimum wage of $1.60 an hour will provide a family of four or more with an annual income below the poverty line. In 1966, 3.1 million men working full-time, two-thirds of whom were family heads, earned less than $1.60 an hour. In 1967, almost half of the Nation's labor force was employed in occupations or industries not covered by the minimum wage provisions of the Fair Labor Standards Act. Many of the families of such workers are poor.

The sources of low wages can be found on both the demand and the supply sides of the labor market. The spread of complex automated industrial technology continually reduces the relative demand for workers in low-skilled occupations. Emigration from the agricultural sector, the growing number of youth, and increased participation of middle-aged women in the labor force add to the supply of low-wage job candidates.

In certain instances, however, low earnings reflect a breakdown in the market itself, either because of immobility of labor and capital resources

15. Witness before Commission, Quincy, Florida.
16. Witness before Commission, St. Joseph, Louisiana.

or because of discrimination in hiring. There is overwhelming evidence that the employment opportunities of nonwhite workers and female workers are more limited in number and lower in quality than those open to white male workers.

The fact that so many workers accept employment at very low wages indicates the basic strength of the work ethic in the economy. Although their jobs are often unpleasant and physically demanding, many workers have remained ready and willing to work for wages which cannot keep their families out of poverty.

LARGE FAMILIES

Large families need substantial incomes just to avoid poverty. According to the Social Security Administration's poverty index for 1968, a nonfarm family composed of two parents and five children would need at least $5,789 to maintain even the most basic standard of living. If the head worked full-time year-round, he would have to earn nearly $3.00 per hour to achieve this target. In 1966 over 40 per cent of the poor families with children headed by employed men under age 65 had more than three children to support. With an average family size of 4.6 persons, many working family heads are financially handicapped even when earning a relatively good annual income.

POVERTY AND EDUCATION

The association between education and income is a familiar one. Formal education not only enhances the quality of one's life, it also pays a high dividend in material rewards. Those with little education are at a disadvantage in the labor market. The heads of nearly three-quarters of all poor families in 1966 did not graduate from high school. Indeed, nearly one in five of the poor nonaged male and female family heads had completed less than six years of formal schooling—a level barely above functional illiteracy.

Limited education does not guarantee a life of poverty, but the income distribution is highly skewed in favor of the more educated. One fourth of those with less than eight years of schooling earned less than $3,000 while only 6 per cent of high school graduates had earnings that low. In 1967, the median income of families whose heads had completed less than eight years of schooling was about one-third that of families headed by college graduates. The gap between their median incomes was about $8,000.[17]

With a high proportion of the poor uneducated, it is unrealistic to

17. U.S. Bureau of the Census, *Current Population Reports*, Series P-60, No. 59, "Income in 1967 of Families in the United States," April 18, 1969, Table 14.

expect great upward mobility in terms of income. Those with low education levels receive the low-paying jobs that offer little opportunity for advancement. Once family responsibilities are acquired, this handicap is imposed on the entire family.

The effects of limited education are quite pervasive. For many of the undereducated, the most routine job-seeking activities may be difficult. People who are embarrassed by their inability to speak correctly, or to understand questions and the reasons behind them, or to fill out detailed forms quickly, or to grasp instructions, are particularly disadvantaged in securing a job. When a job opportunity is extended some of the uneducated do not take it because of their conviction that they cannot compete effectively. At an earlier point in our economic history, brawn and willingness to work would have been sufficient, but increasingly even menial jobs require high school diplomas. Many persons have been left out of the job market, not because they cannot do the work, but because employers would rather hire "over-educated" workers. One able-bodied male who did heavy manual farm work during the season testified that he could not move to the city and do more steady factory work because "Most jobs like that won't hire a guy without an education (who) can't fill out a form."[18]

POVERTY AND LOCATION

Two-thirds of the poor lived in urban areas in 1966. However, the risk of being poor was greater for those who resided in rural areas, whether they lived on or off the farm. Almost 20 per cent of the rural population was poor, compared with about 14 per cent for the urban population. Opportunities for earning are fewer in rural than urban areas, and work is more often seasonal.

The poor are somewhat concentrated geographically. Twenty per cent of Southern families were poor in 1966, while only 9 per cent of non-Southern families were poor. Half of all poor families lived in the South. Although nearly two-thirds of all poor nonwhite families lived in the South in 1966, Southern poverty was by no means confined to nonwhites. Close to 2 million white families—42 per cent of all poor white families— were residents of Southern States. The conditions that are conducive to poverty—low wages, low average education, seasonal employment, and declining opportunities for the unskilled—are especially prevalent in the South. These factors cross racial lines, although nonwhites are particularly affected.

Another focal point for poverty is the inner core of major cities, from

18. Witness before Commission, Mississippi County, Arkansas.

which it is often difficult, time consuming, and expensive to reach well-paying jobs in outlying areas.

We have one new employer who will employ 1600 people. A great many of these women will be trained by the employer. It is not essential that they have previous experience. But there is no transportation to this particular employer's place of business.[19]

In your core city, the jobs that are available will not pay a sustaining wage. They run from 80 cents per hour probably up to $1.30. A person who has a family to support cannot do it on this wage scale . . . Another thing is that jobs that do pay a sustaining wage are located in your suburban areas. There is no way of getting transportation to get to them. Transportation in Denver is inadequate. They don't run adequate buses to job sites. Most of the people don't have cars.[20]

In many American cities, the story is the same: There are no jobs where the poor live, the poor cannot afford—or are not allowed—to live where the jobs are opening up, and there is no transportation between these two places.

POVERTY AND THE FEMALE-HEADED FAMILY

The employment opportunities for women heading poor families are more limited than those for men. Because of their family responsibilities, women may be severely restricted from holding down even a part-time job. One in every two women heading poor families did not work in 1966.

Getting and keeping a job imposes certain conditions that are especially burdensome for women heading poor families. Working requires either that all children be old enough to care for themselves or that some day care provisions be made for the children. There are few such facilities available, even for those who can afford to pay. Many women heading families with children can work only at the expense of their family responsibilities.

I would like to state . . . that I do have a high school education; I have one year of college. I have ten years working experience behind me. The reason I am not employed at the present and am having to take AFDC is because of inadequate child care for my children.[21]

Many of the jobs available do not pay enough to cover the cost of child care and other employment expenses. Jobs for which the majority of

19. Witness before Commission, Atlanta, Georgia.
20. Witness before Commission, Denver, Colorado.
21. Witness before Commission, Seattle, Washington.

female heads of households qualify are at the lower end of the pay scale. In 1966 almost 50 per cent of all employed white women heading poor families and 75 per cent of nonwhite women heading poor families worked in service occupations, one of the lowest paid groups. For many such women, Public Assistance offers a more secure existence. It has been estimated that 70 per cent of mothers receiving Aid to Families with Dependent Children could not earn more money by working than they receive in assistance payments because of their low skill and educational levels.[22]

One witness told the Commission:

> I said that I was a New Careerist in the CEP, Concentrated Employment Program. I earn $1.60 an hour and I take home $242.22 every month for the support of myself and three children. My rent is $75 a month. The cost of my being employed far exceeds my income . . . By this I mean that it would be to my advantage to be on welfare. I am one of those people that are motivated, but is it worth it? I sometimes wonder.[23]

DISCRIMINATION AND POVERTY

At first glance it seems that poverty is a white problem—two-thirds of the poor are white, while one-third are nonwhite. However, 12 per cent of the white population is poor while over 40 per cent of the much smaller nonwhite population is poor.

The greater incidence of poverty among nonwhites reflects several factors: larger family size, lower average earnings, a greater proportion of female-headed families, lower educational levels, and the greater proportion of nonwhites living in the South. Yet, holding each of these factors constant and comparing across racial lines, nonwhites remain at a disadvantage.

Much of this differential is a result of direct or indirect discrimination. Many employers still are unwilling to hire members of minority groups. Others will employ them only in the most menial jobs. Some minority group members find themselves unable to compete for jobs because discrimination in public programs has provided them with inferior education or training.

> Our (Negro high) school is not up to the (white) standard. I remember a few days ago I visited our school and to my surprise—and this has been existing for several years—there were five classes in the gym going on at the same time, and one of these classes was a music class.[24]

22. U.S. Department of Health, Education, and Welfare, Office of the Assistant Secretary (Program Coordination), *Income and Benefit Programs*, October 1966, p. 58.
23. Witness before Commission, Albuquerque, New Mexico.
24. Witness before Commission, St. Joseph, Louisiana.

My check will run about $120 and his (a white) will run two something . . . He probably might be cleaning up. He is not doing the type of (heavy) work that I am doing.[25]

Ability testing is done in English. I would like to take all these English-speaking teachers and give them a test in Spanish and see how their ability is going to run. Terminology and pictures with which the child is not familiar are used. The Puerto Ricans have never seen a sleigh, because we never had snow.[26]

Mobility among the Poor

The little that is known about changes in income status over time is not heartening. Poverty persists in families headed by year-round, full-time workers. It persists in multiple-earner families. And it persists, to varying degrees, among the aged and nonaged, among families headed by men and women, and among blacks and whites.

Between 1965 and 1966, the number of households classified as poor declined by almost 3 per cent. This net change, however, obscures considerable movement of households into and out of poverty. Some 36 per cent of those households classified as poor in 1965 had, for one reason or another, left poverty by 1966. Of those classified as poor in 1966, 34 per cent were not poor in the previous year. These flows indicate that the risk of poverty is considerably more pervasive than has been imagined.

Finally, the 64 per cent remaining in poverty were disproportionately comprised of nonwhites, female-headed families, those in the South, and those families headed by a person with less than a high school education. For these groups, poverty is not a way station, it is a dead end.

DETERMINANTS OF POVERTY FLOWS

A move across the poverty line—in either direction—can be the consequence of a variety of uncontrollable changes in the household's circumstances. The addition or loss of an earner, a change in the size or composition of the family, a fluctuation in the wage level or hours worked by family members—all bear heavily on the probability that a family will experience a change in its economic status. Certain influences, however, stand out in bold relief.

Work, when available, can contribute significantly to a family's success in avoiding poverty. Over the 1965–1966 period, the rate of escape from poverty for families headed by a full-year worker was nearly twice as

25. Witness before Commission, St. Joseph, Louisiana.
26. Witness before a Commission, Philadelphia, Pennsylvania.

large as that for families whose head worked part-year or not at all. Conversely, the rate of entrance into poverty for the latter group was over seven times that of the former. The greater the amount of time the head spent working, the more likely the family was to have left or not to have entered poverty. This was true for whites and nonwhites, for male and female-headed families, and for the young and old. Indeed, in almost every conceivable comparison, those who worked fared better than those who did not.

More striking than the recorded successes are the failures. Of those families classified as poor in 1965 which were headed by a full-time, year-round worker, 43 per cent failed to escape poverty during the following year. In terms of absolute numbers there were nearly as many families leaving poverty whose heads worked less than 48 weeks as families whose heads worked 48 or more weeks. Clearly, work alone is no guarantee of leaving poverty.

EXTENT OF INCOME MOBILITY

Despite the way statistical indices are often used, poverty is not an either/or state. There are shades of poverty just as there are shades of wealth. This distinction is particularly important in discussing movements across a fixed poverty line. A person whose income is slightly below the poverty line can statistically move out of poverty by increasing his income by a small amount, but his standard of living will remain unchanged and he still will feel poor.

Of those persons who moved out of poverty between 1965 and 1966, a large number did not move far: one-eighth remained within $200 of the poverty line and one-quarter remained within $500 of the poverty line. For families such as these, it might be questioned whether the recorded change was significant. Of those falling into poverty, almost one-fifth fell less than $200 below the line and nearly half were within $500 of the line. Thus much of the movement into and out of poverty is really movement close to the line.[27]

The Future of Poverty

Getting ahead on a poverty income and becoming unpoor are problems whose solutions lie beyond the powers of most of the poor. They are also problems for which the formulation of meaningful and appropriate long-range solutions requires an undistorted view of the nature of poverty and of the Nation's economic system. Yet in many discussions of these topics, there are often implicit, unexamined assumptions and beliefs which must be questioned.

27. Unpublished tabulations from Current Population Surveys, 1965 and 1966.

• The Commission is concerned about the widespread belief that poverty will simply fade away. Will the enormous productivity and potential for growth of the American industrial system lead, inevitably, to the disappearance of poverty?

• The Commission is also concerned about the notion that poverty can be defined and dealt with as a fixed and timeless absolute concept. What does an absolute definition of poverty mean in an era of growing prosperity? Is it possible to grasp and to deal with the problems of *American* poverty without considering relative poverty and deprivation?

These questions must be asked even if final answers are not forthcoming immediately. Raising these questions gives us a better view of what is. Answering them will give us a better vision of what ought to be.

The Recent Decline in Poverty

During the 1960s the number of poor persons decreased sharply. From 1960 through 1968, the number of persons in poverty dropped from 39.9 to 25.4 million and the percentage of the population in poverty fell from 22 per cent to 13 per cent. This rate of decline can give rise to two misleading and dangerous views: that poverty will continue to decline at the same rate, thereby ultimately eliminating poverty, and that existing Government antipoverty programs have been solely responsible for the decline.

The decline in poverty came during a period of sustained economic expansion and extensive tightening of labor markets. The benefits of this economic growth were unevenly distributed among the poor. Those with labor force connections benefited considerably more than those outside the work force. In the early 1960s the number of poor families headed by nonaged working men fell by 9 per cent per year. By contrast, the number of aged poor households fell by only about one per cent per year, and for families headed by women the decline was imperceptible. This uneven pattern portends the pattern of the future.

Projections prepared by the Department of Health, Education, and Welfare show the overall incidence of poverty continuing to decline, but at a decelerating rate, with the composition of those remaining poor continuing to shift. It is estimated that by 1974 there still will be some 17 million poor persons living in nine million households if Gross National Product grows by 4 per cent per year in real terms. More than four million of these people will be in families headed by a nonaged working man.[28] Obviously, should we suffer a recession, or even a reduced rate of real economic growth, the projected number of poor families would be larger. Thus, despite the great productivity of the Nation's industrial system and

28. U.S. Department of Health, Education, and Welfare, *Toward a Social Report,* 1969, Chapter IV.

Table 1–6.   Poor Households, 1961, 1966, and 1974 (Projected) by Age, Family Status, and Sex of Family Head

Household Characteristic	Number of Households (in thousands)			Average Annual Per Cent Change	
	1961	1966	1974	1961–66	1966–74
Total	12,881	10,826	8,816	− 3.4	− 2.5
Nonaged households	8,360	6,591	3,936	− 4.6	− 6.2
Families	6,149	4,476	2,463	− 6.2	− 7.3
Male-headed	4,579	2,900	1,210	− 9.0	−10.3
White	3,416	2,102	833	− 9.5	−10.8
Worked	3,005	1,740	610	−10.7	−12.0
Didn't work	411	362	223	− 2.5	− 5.9
Nonwhite	1,163	797	377	− 7.5	− 8.9
Worked	1,060	691	282	− 8.4	−10.5
Didn't work	103	106	95	+ 0.6	− 1.4
Female-headed	1,570	1,576	1,253	°	− 2.8
White	939	934	751	− 0.1	− 2.7
Worked	451	460	301	+ 0.4	− 5.2
Didn't work	488	474	450	− 0.6	− 0.7
Nonwhite	631	642	502	+ 0.3	− 3.0
Worked	383	376	267	− 0.4	− 4.2
Didn't work	248	266	235	+ 1.4	− 1.5
Unrelated individuals	2,211	2,115	1,476	− 0.9	− 4.4
Male	815	712	451	− 2.7	− 5.5
White	567	534	351	− 1.2	− 5.1
Worked	421	386	201	− 1.7	− 7.9
Didn't work	146	148	150	+ 0.3	+ 0.2
Nonwhite	248	178	100	− 6.4	− 7.0
Worked	186	116	35	− 9.3	−13.4
Didn't work	62	62	65	0.0	+ 0.6
Female	1,396	1,403	1,025	+ 0.1	− 3.8
White	1,048	1,079	789	+ 0.6	− 3.8
Worked	590	571	354	− 0.7	− 5.1
Didn't work	458	508	435	+ 2.1	− 1.9
Nonwhite	348	324	236	− 1.4	− 3.9
Worked	204	199	116	− 0.5	− 6.2
Didn't work	144	125	120	− 2.8	− 0.5
Aged households	4,521	4,235	4,877	− 1.3	+ 1.8

° Less than 0.05 per cent.

Source: U.S. Department of Health, Education, and Welfare, *Program Memorandum on Income Maintenance and Social and Rehabilitation Service Programs of DHEW*, November 1968, and *Toward a Social Report*, 1969.

the increasing income which it generates for most Americans, the poor will remain with us in very large numbers for the foreseeable future.

Indeed, the composition of the poor is changing so that the poor more and more are those who gain least from economic growth: the aged, the disabled, female-headed families, and those whose limited skills seem unlikely to be demanded by an increasingly complex industrial system. Consequently, almost inevitably, there must be a slowing down of the rate of escape from poverty. The import of these projections, in the view of the Commission, is that public action is necessary to end absolute poverty in the United States. We cannot expect a significant portion of the future's affluence to flow automatically to the poor.

Moreover, these projections are based on a fixed poverty index—adjusted for price changes only—which may be misleading and obsolete in the context of the rapidly rising living standards of the general society.

Relative Poverty

Predictions, calculations, and prescriptions dealing with the problems of poverty rest on the Social Security Administration poverty index, a definition of poverty based on the cost of a fixed emergency food budget, adjusted annually only for price changes. No adjustments in the index are made to reflect changes in living standards enjoyed by the general population. This official poverty line purports to represent a level of survival income sufficient to buy bare necessities. Presumedly, it is based on scientifically determined standards of nutritional adequacy and other basic needs.

In fact, however, the objectivity of the absolute budget is illusory. Other poverty lines can be developed corresponding to lower or higher consumption standards. These can be bolstered with scientific surveys, but retain a large degree of arbitrariness. For, in the end, the choice of what must be included in the budget is made subjectively by the researcher.

The arbitrary quality of this sort of index was shown in August 1969 when the Government changed the price index and the ratio of farm to nonfarm incomes used in computing the poverty index. As a result of these strictly technical changes, the estimated number of poor persons in 1967 increased from 26 million to almost 28 million.[29]

THE CONCEPT OF A FIXED POVERTY LINE

The concept behind a fixed measure of poverty is itself subject to increasing criticism. It is argued that such a level merely allows the poor to survive at an unchanging, low level—while the nonpoor measure their well-being in terms of real income growth. The difficulty, of course, is

---

29. U.S Bureau of the Census, *Current Population Reports*, Series P–23, No. 28, "Revision in Poverty Statistics, 1959 to 1968," August 12, 1969, Table D.

not with the poverty index as a technical construct, but with changing subjective feelings about what standard of living is adequate and about the importance of relative deprivation.

Solely as a result of growing affluence, a society will elevate its notions of what constitutes poverty. Many factors account for this. All people tend to measure their well-being against some norm. When the median income is growing rapidly, those above it will perceive the poor differently, and the poor living on an unchanged income will view their lot differently.

But there are objective as well as subjective reasons for requiring poverty standards to rise with increases in the general level of prosperity. As affluence increases, community standards will constantly raise the level of income needed by the poor in order to exist. City housing codes will be upgraded, and the poor will have to improve their homes or pay more rent for their better buildings. When most of the community owns automobiles or moves to the suburbs, public transportation will probably deteriorate, leaving the poor with either inadequate or more expensive transportation. The city will enrich the public school curriculum, and poor students will have to pay for special assembly programs and field trips, or buy gym suits instead of just tennis shoes, or wear white shirts and neck ties instead of simpler clothing, or buy uniforms in order to belong to clubs. As economic advancement both allows and demands increasing education, children in families unable to provide money for higher education will fall further behind.

Clearly, as a society's general standard of living rises, increasingly expensive consumption patterns are forced on the poor, not in order to catch up, but in order to remain a part of that society. Moreover, as society's normal standard of living rises the poor will seek to emulate it—since they are part of society—and feel increasingly deprived if they cannot.

RELATIVE SHARES

A fixed definition of poverty leads to the conclusion that if income generated by future economic growth flows to the poor in the same proportions as in the past, then poverty will disappear. That is, if America's relative income distribution remains constant, or does not move against the poor, then eventually all might rise above the fixed poverty line.

The constancy of America's income distribution suggests that the poor consistently have received about the same percentage of the Nation's income. As Table 1–7 indicates, the bottom fifth of the population has received approximately the same proportion of aggregate income for over 20 years.

But this view of poverty and the use of a fixed definition implies a concept of absolute poverty unrelated to the growing American standard of living. Absolute poverty is difficult to define objectively. The notion of mere survival as a basis for defining poverty is unrealistic in an advanced industrial society which is daily growing richer. Poverty relative to some norm may be a more meaningful conception of this social problem. Despite all of our income and welfare programs, we have not altered appreciably the structure of this Nation's income distribution.

Table 1–7. Distribution of Money Income, Mean Income, and Share of Aggregate Received by Each Fifth and Top 5 Per Cent of Families and Unrelated Individuals, Selected Years, 1947–1966

| Year and Group | Mean Income before Tax (current dollars) | Percentage Distribution of Aggregate Income | | | | | |
		Lowest Fifth	Second Fifth	Middle Fifth	Fourth Fifth	Highest Fifth	Top 5 Per Cent
Families and unrelated individuals							
1947	$3,224	3.5	10.5	16.7	23.5	45.8	19.0
1957	4,861	3.4	10.8	17.9	24.8	43.1	16.7
1962	6,049	3.5	10.3	17.3	24.5	44.3	17.3
1966	7,425	3.7	10.5	17.4	24.6	43.8	16.8
Families							
1947	3,566	5.1	11.8	16.7	23.2	43.3	17.5
1957	5,483	5.0	12.6	18.1	23.7	40.5	15.8
1962	6,811	5.1	12.0	17.3	23.8	41.7	16.3
1966	8,423	5.4	12.3	17.7	23.7	41.0	15.3
Unrelated individuals							
1947	1,692	2.9	5.4	11.5	21.3	58.9	33.3
1957	2,253	2.9	7.2	13.6	25.3	51.0	19.7
1962	2,800	3.3	7.3	12.5	24.1	52.8	21.3
1966	3,490	2.8	7.5	13.2	23.8	52.7	22.5

SOURCE: Ida C. Merriam, "Welfare and its Measurement," Eleanor B. Sheldon and Wilbert E. Moore, eds., *Indicators of Social Change* (New York: Russell Sage Foundation, 1968), p. 735.

Most important of all, the gap between the living standards of the poor and the more affluent is increasing. This is true for everyone at the lower end of the income distribution scale, but obviously bears most on the very poor. When we use a specific income level such as the poverty index to define the poor, we find they are falling further behind the general population. Table 1–8 shows that the ratio of the poverty line to the median income has fallen significantly since 1959. The median income has risen by 57 per cent over this period, while the poverty line has increased by only 20 per cent.

Table 1–8. Median Income and Poverty Line For
a Nonfarm Family of Four, 1959 and 1968

Income Measure	1959	1968	Per Cent Increase
Median income	$6,355a	$9,948	57
Poverty line	2,973	3,553	20
Poverty line as per cent of median income	47%	36%	

a Median income for 1959 is for urban families.

SOURCE: U.S. Bureau of the Census, *Current Population Reports*, Series P–60, No. 35; Series P–23, No. 28; and Series P–60 to be released on December 1, 1969.

In the Commission's view, these are significant social facts. As the general American standard of living improves, the poor will become progressively worse off by comparison with some norm. The poor—defined by an unchanging scale—will be struggling for social survival even after the problems of physical survival have been solved.

Radically different consumption opportunities can be seen in traveling from the affluent suburbs of any large city into the deteriorating central core, or by driving from urban to rural America. These life styles are separated by a wide gulf and as the future brings larger incomes to some, those who remain even relatively poor will increasingly inhabit a different world than the affluent.

Controversial and difficult as the transition may be, our own affluence may force upon us a changed view of poverty. As citizens of the richest Nation in the world we may come to regard the social isolation of the poor from the standard of living and opportunities open to the rest of society to be as important as their low incomes.

We may view the consequences of living considerably below general standards—albeit above starvation—as real and significant, especially in a society which desires fluid class lines.

A relative view of poverty will obviously give a very different picture of the poor population. Table 1–9 presents recent trends in the incidence of poverty for families, as measured by an absolute and a relative standard. Using a fixed standard which defines poverty as an income of less than $3,000 a year, the percentage of poor families has decreased markedly between 1947 and 1965. Using, for purpose of illustration, a measure of relative poverty of one-half of the median income, the incidence of poverty has not fallen perceptibly since 1947. Commission staff estimates indicate a continued rough constancy through 1980.

Table 1–9.   Percentage of U.S. Families
Classified Poor by Changing and
Fixed Standards, 1947 to 1965
(in 1965 dollars)

Year	Percentage of Families	
	Income Less Than One-Half the Median	Income Less Than $3,000
1947	18.9	30.0
1948	19.1	31.2
1949	20.2	32.3
1950	20.0	29.9
1951	18.9	27.8
1952	18.9	26.3
1953	19.8	24.6
1954	20.9	26.2
1955	20.0	23.6
1956	19.6	21.5
1957	19.7	21.7
1958	19.8	21.8
1959	20.0	20.6
1960	20.3	20.3
1961	20.3	20.1
1962	19.8	18.9
1963	19.9	18.0
1964	19.9	17.1
1965	20.0	16.5

SOURCE: Victor R. Fuchs, "Comment on Measuring the Low Income Population," Lee Soltow, ed. *Six Papers on the Size Distribution of Wealth and Income* (National Bureau of Economic Research, 1969), p. 200.

In these trends is the potential for social division unparalleled in our Country. We already are seeing some of the results of this division in urban unrest. The Commission has been deeply disturbed by its contact, through field hearings, with many articulate poor persons who feel increasingly "left out" and helpless. This is a serious problem for National Government policy. The poor can do nothing to halt this growing division. As we have seen, the poor are unable to break out of absolute poverty. They will find it even further beyond them to close the widening gap of relative poverty.

Income Maintenance Alternatives: Concepts, Criteria, and Program Comparisons

Theodore R. Marmor is an Associate Professor of Political Science and Associate Director of the School of Public Affairs at the University of Minnesota. His major interests are in the field of social welfare policy, especially medical care and cash transfers, both within the United States and comparatively. Mr. Marmor began his evaluation and comparison of competing income maintenance schemes as a staff member of the Institute for Research on Poverty at the University of Wisconsin (1967–1970). He served as a special consultant to the President's Commission on Income Maintenance Programs (1968–1969). Marmor's essay sets forth criteria by which to compare cash transfer proposals that address similar problems and critically discusses the preoccupation of much of the American cash transfer debate with mechanisms of administration.

Introduction

Major social policy decisions in America are not made by intellectuals, particularly academic intellectuals. Nonetheless, social critics, particularly academic intellectuals, extensively discuss the problems of income distribution and poverty. The gross national discussion has grown so large,

Theodore R. Marmor, "Income Maintenance Alternatives: Concepts, Criteria, and Program Comparisons," Institute for Research on Poverty, University of Wisconsin, Discussion Paper No. 55–69, 1969. An earlier version of this paper was presented to the Conference on Income and Poverty, American Academy of Arts and Sciences, May 16–17, 1969. A somewhat different version of this paper appears in *The American Political Science Review*, March, 1971.

in fact, it appears we have a new service industry—one that does a lot of thinking about poverty. True, it has yet to do much about poverty, but "firms" within this industry write about poverty, argue about poverty, and generate papers for conferences at an accelerating rate and with escalating volume. The industry's growth has so expanded in the last ten years that some find it necessary to identify the division of this intellectual labor. Advocates of the negative income tax (NIT), for instance, are known by some producers of competing ideas as the "nit-wits."

No doubt, America's concern with its societal problems in the 1960s partly generated this proliferation of poverty research and researchers. But the output is not likely to be effective until it is recognized that a real dilemma exists: although intellectuals do not determine social policy, they do identify and define—perhaps more than the policy-maker—the problems associated with poverty and income maintenance. The net effect of research efforts has been to add yet more confusion to the thicket without really moving closer to finding a way out. There is some agreement that the eventual answer will be an income maintenance program, but there is less agreement about which plan is best. In the summer of 1968 at a joint congressional hearing on income maintenance, no less than two dozen intellectuals appeared before the committee to offer no less than two dozen different schemes on how the income of the poor might be maintained.[1]

Thus the larger question becomes: What can one usefully say about poverty, and particularly about means of relieving it? In turn, the question this paper addresses is: How can an intelligent discussion of the political and economic features of income maintenance proposals be framed?

Such a paper is called for because of the presently chaotic discussion of income maintenance alternatives. Discussion of family allowances, negative income taxes, and other cash transfer programs proceeds, as Lee Rainwater has said, ". . . either in the form of a catalogue of different proposals . . . or short-sighted polemics about the superiority of some one method."[2] Both professional and popular journals reflect this impasse. Alternative instruments for relieving poverty are compared in terms of

1. Income Maintenance Programs, *Hearings Before the Subcommittee on Fiscal Policy of the Joint Economic Committee*, Congress of the United States, Joint Economic Committee, 90th Congress, 2nd Session, Vol. I, June, 1968.

2. Lee Rainwater to author, May, 1968. An example of cataloguing income maintenance alternatives can be found in Christopher Green, *Negative Taxes and the Poverty Problem* (Washington, D.C., the Brookings Institution, 1967). James Vadakin, *Family Allowances* (Miami: University of Miami Press, 1968) illustrates special pleading for one mechanism of cash transfer, in this case one defined by the age characteristics of the recipients. Variations in the nature of family allowances are substantial; European nations have programs so different that little is gained by grouping them as if they served common ends with comparable efficiency. Milton Friedman has

how they work (administrative mechanisms), or whom they benefit (per cent and type of poverty population covered). Having made judgments about the political acceptability of an instrument, advocates then proceed to produce limited descriptions of cash transfer alternatives, concentrating

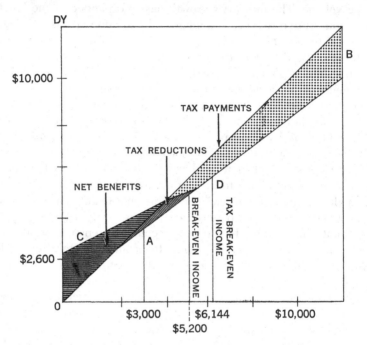

Figure 2–1. Negative Income Tax Plan for 4-Person Family

SOURCE: Tobin, Pechman, and Mieszkowski, "Is a Negative Income Tax Practical?" 77 *Yale Law Journal* 1 (1967), p. 7.

their attention on the mechanistic symbols of the programs they favor. Such analyses obscure differences in goals and, more importantly, differences in the social problems to which alternative programs might be addressed.

For example, negative income tax plans of vastly different scope and benefit levels are grouped under the same rubric even though they are clearly not alternative means to solving the same problem. The Tobin

disassociated his version of a welfare-replacing NIT from more generous negative tax plans such as James Tobin's. See *Time,* "Welfare and Illfare: The Alternatives to Poverty," December 13, 1968, and Figure 2–1. For support of the idea that concepts like NIT do not sufficiently describe a class of programs, see "Comment: A Model Negative Income Tax Statute," *Yale Law Journal* 78, No. 2 (Dec., 1968), p. 270, n. 6. The editors assert, " 'negative income tax' has no precise meaning," and add that, when they refer to "negative income tax," they mean their own proposal.

plan represented in Figure 2–1—with a $2600 guarantee level, universal eligibility, and a $5200 cut-off point—contrasts sharply with some low-level negative income tax plans. One such plan, formulated by Robert Lampman to supplement the wages of the working poor, calls for a $750 guarantee and a $1500 cut-off point for a four-person family.[3] The Tobin plan, because of its universal and high benefits, would cost approximately $26 billion, some three times more than the $7.5 billion cost of the Lampman plan. These two plans are alike in administrative mechanism but have little else in common, since they were designed as solutions to different problems.

There are proposals, however, which employ differing administrative mechanisms to solve similar problems. Consider the Brazer child allowance scheme described in Table 2–1. Although it is usually discussed as a child allowance plan, its effect is such that it could as properly be described as a negative income tax for families with children: it provides a guarantee of $1200 for a four-person family and a cut-off point of more than $10,000. Compared with the Tobin negative income tax scheme, it is apparent that both plans are substantial antipoverty measures and, as such, have more in common than either does with the low-level negative income tax plan which Lampman proposed as a device to supplement wages.

It is the thesis of this paper that administrative mechanisms are only one of several criteria by which income maintenance proposals ought to be compared; and that discussion of alternative proposals ought to proceed from the question, what problem(s) does each proposal set out to solve?

Criteria are specified by which alternative income maintenance programs might be compared, and those criteria are applied to two of the most prominently discussed income maintenance programs for welfare reform.

Various Problems of Poverty and Income Distribution

Three conceptions of social issues lie behind the variety of the poverty remedies now being bandied about in technical and nontechnical forums: the crisis of the welfare poor, the difficulties of all low-income Americans, and the inequities of the present distribution of income in the United States.

The first set of problems—identified with the crisis of the "welfare

3. Tobin *et al.*, "Is a Negative Income Tax Practical," *Yale Law Journal*, 77, No. 1 (November, 1967), and Robert Lampman, "Expanding the American System of Transfers to Do More for the Poor," *Wisconsin Law Review* 2 (1969), pp. 543–544.

Table 2-1. Net Change in Income after Tax Owing to Substitution of Children's Allowance for Exemptions, Taxing Allowances, and Applying the CARR, Selected Incomes, and Number of Dependent Children

Number of Dependent Children	Adjusted Gross Income							
	$ 0	$1000	$3000	$5000	$7000	$10,000	$15,000	$20,000
One	$ 600	$ 600	$ 339	$ 209	$ 124	$ 27	$ 13	$— 112
Two	1200	1144	618	355	218	39	— 45	— 211
Three	1800	1674	934	483	289	42	— 81	— 311
Four	2344	2008	1186	590	315	36	—124	— 410
Five	2874	2305	1377	684	313	21	—129	— 510
Six	3112	2562	1572	832	304	— 3	—226	— 610
Seven	3280	2700	1710	910	322	—45	—305	— 709

Source: Harvey Brazer, "Tax Policy and Children's Allowances," Children's Allowances and the Economic Welfare of Children, Report of a Conference (Citizen's Committee for Children of New York, Inc., 1968), p. 146.

poor"—involves persons currently receiving benefits and those eligible for them under federal and state assistance programs. The most controversial programs include Aid to Families with Dependent Children (AFDC)[4] and general assistance. Both hostile critics and sympathetic analysts of public assistance seem to agree that there is a "crisis." What this crisis consists of differs from analyst to analyst, but the following issues emerge:[5]

(a) inadequacy of payment levels;

(b) disparity of payments between one geographical area and another, and among various categories of public assistance recipients;

(c) administrative injustices and arbitrariness, including the alleged stigma of being on welfare, which also serves to deter eligible and deserving persons from applying;

---

4. Eligibility for AFDC requires that the family be needy, fatherless (or include an incapacitated father), and include children under 18; that the unemployed parent and/or mother accept a job or training for a job if offered (or else lose the benefits); and that, under the "Man in the House" Rule which applies in many states, the mother be moral. "Poverty, Income Sources and Income Maintenance Programs," *The President's Commission on Income Maintenance Programs* (Background Paper No. 2, May 18, 1968), p. 11. In 1961, the AFDC-UP program was instituted, permitting benefits to households headed by unemployed, able-bodied men. Only 25 states had adopted this program by 1969, and less than 100,000 families were receiving its benefits. *Poverty Amid Plenty: The American Paradox* (Washington, D.C.: U.S. Government Printing Office, 1969), p. 47.

5. For a typical example (a), see The Advisory Council on Public Welfare, *Having the Power, We Have the Duty*, Report to the Secretary of Health, Education, and Welfare (Washington, D.C.: Government Printing Office, 1966), p. 2, which asserts that "Public assistance payments are so low and so uneven that the Government is, by its own standards and definitions, a major source of the poverty on which it has declared unconditional war."

For (b) see the discussion of welfare's "inequitable treatment of marginal nonrecipients" in Jacobus ten Broek, "California's Dual System of Family Laws: Its Origin, Development, and Present Status," *Stanford Law Review* 16 (March, 1964), pp. 257–317; (July, 1964), pp. 900–981; Vol. 16 (April, 1965), pp. 614–682; and William A. Johnson and Robert Rosenkranz, "Public Assistance" in *Cities in Trouble: An Agenda for Urban Research*, Anthony H. Pascal, ed. (Memorandum RM-5603-RC, the Rand Corp., August, 1968), p. 87.

For (c) see Charles A. Reich, "Individual Rights and Social Welfare: The Emerging Issues," *Yale Law Journal*, 75 (June, 1965). This theme is understandably stressed by welfare rights' groups, and raised in almost all discussion of public welfare. See also *Having the Power, We Have the Duty*, Advisory Council on Public Welfare, p. 74, for the warning that "there is great urgency for the emphatic assertion of public welfare's accountability for the protection of individual rights, and for the scrupulous observance of the individual rights of the people it serves."

For (d) see the illustrative remarks by Congresswoman Griffiths in the 1968 *Hearings of the Joint Economic Committee, supra,* n. 1; and Daniel P. Moynihan, "The Crises in Welfare," *The Public Interest*, No. 10 (Winter 1968), p. 4.

For (e) see Herbert J. Gans, "The Negro Family: Reflections on the Moynihan Report," *The Moynihan Report and the Politics of Controversy*, Rainwater and Yancey, eds. Cambridge, Mass.: M.I.T. Press, 1967, p. 454.

For (f) see Moynihan, and the work by Lampman, among others, on how the American system of transfer payments affects the poor. Lampman, *supra,* n. 3.

(d) the financial costs of increasing the benefits and the number of eligibles who might seek benefits;

(e) the unfortunate effects of public assistance upon family cohesiveness and work behavior;

(f) the social divisiveness and inequity of welfare programs aiding only certain groups of the poor and excluding others, most notably the working poor.

This much is clear: the dimensions of these problems are not agreed upon; remedies to these various difficulties are not obviously compatible or complementary; yet, it is at least possible to begin discussion of alternative conceptions of and solutions to the problems of the welfare poor.

The second set of problems focuses on poverty in America, the number of persons with incomes below the poverty line, and the amount by which their incomes fall short of that standard (the poverty gap). The nonwelfare poor comprise the most obvious target group from this perspective. Nearly two-thirds of the poor do not qualify for public assistance, which limits benefits to widows, orphans, abandoned families, the aged, sick, and disabled. Most of those whose income falls below the poverty line are legally ineligible for assistance because of the restrictive categories now used. One substantial group of nonwelfare poor are the long-term unemployed who are by-passed because of ineligibility for unemployment insurance benefits, or the lack of universal coverage within public assistance.[6] However, most of the nonwelfare poor are from families in which at least one adult member is working.

Discussion of the nonwelfare poor has focused on how to expand or alter the existing categories in order to include those poor who are now ineligible for assistance; and, given the large number of working poor, how to build work incentives into cash transfers directed towards this group. Availability of work is central to discussion surrounding the long-term unemployed, but not the working poor, since that group already participates in the work force. Rather, aiding the working poor raises the issue of how to supplement income without reducing the incentive to work. Robert Lampman's low level version of the negative income tax may be considered one transfer plan to cope with this dilemma.[7]

The third set of problems involves the unequal distribution of wealth and income in contemporary America. Here the problem of poverty is

6. For data on the characteristics of the unemployed, see "Definition of Employability," *The President's Commission on Income Maintenance Programs*, Preliminary Draft (1.5.2), January 16, 1969, pp. 23, 27.

7. See outline in Robert J. Lampman, "Steps to Remove Poverty from America," paper prepared for delivery at the Wisconsin Symposium, January 13, 1968.

not simply that many Americans are unable to command a subsistence income, or that the public welfare system has built-in indignities and difficulties. Rather, poverty is viewed as relative deprivation, and the critical difficulties are those of an income distribution in which the relative gap between the very poor and the median wage-earner is widening, not narrowing. The ratios of the poverty line to median income has fallen considerably over the past decade. In 1959 the poverty line was 47 per cent of median income, in 1968, it was 36 per cent.[8]

Those interested in relative poverty are typically concerned with equity questions as well. Not only does the lower one-fifth in the national distribution of income control too small a proportion of the nation's wealth, but from this perspective the operation of the tax system also confers benefits which are socially unjustifiable. Two illustrations should make this point clearer. One equity issue is the way tax exemptions (such as child exemptions in the positive income tax) confer benefits in the form of savings whose value increases progressively with family income.[9] Another is the privileged treatment (through exemptions and other tax devices) of particular forms of income (the capital gains tax) and of certain forms

8. For a definition of poverty in relative terms, see Victor Fuchs, "Redefining Poverty," *The Public Interest*, No. 8 (Summer 1967), pp. 88–95. Martin Rein discusses the difficulties in absolutist, "bread-basket" conceptions of poverty in Louis Ferman *et al.*, eds., *Poverty in America* (2nd ed.), (Ann Arbor: University of Michigan Press, 1968), pp. 116–133. English social critics have recognized the problem of fixed poverty lines for some time. For a cogent critical view (directed against the views of Rowntree), see Peter Townsend, "The Definition of Poverty," paper presented at the Colloquium on Handicapped Families, Bureau de Recherches Sociales, held under the auspices of UNESCO (Paris, 10–12, February, 1964), pp. 6–10. For information on income distribution charges, see *Poverty Amid Plenty: The American Paradox* (Washington, D.C., U.S. Government Printing Office, 1969), pp. 38–39.

9. It is extraordinary how difficult it is to convince the skeptics that tax exemptions are functional equivalents of direct government expenditures. See H. Aaron, "Tax Exemptions—The Artful Dodge," *Trans-Action*, 6, No. 5 (March, 1969), pp. 4–6, for a statement of both the problem and the good reasons one has for treating tax exemptions and direct benefits as fiscal equivalents. It should be added that the *political process* affecting the two forms of transfers differs, and that there may be great differences in the legitimacy associated with particular forms. As Aaron says, suppose, "yesterday on the floor of Congress, Senator Blimp introduced legislation to provide cash allowances for most of the aged. Senator Blimp's plan is unique, however, in that it excludes the poor. The largest benefits, $70 per month, are payable to aged couples whose real income exceeds $200,000 per year. The smallest benefits, $14 per month, would be payable to couples with incomes between $1600 and $2600. Widows, widowers, and unmarried aged persons would receive half as much as couples. No benefits would be payable to those with very low incomes." Aaron remarks that "one can hardly imagine any public figure" introducing such legislation, for fear of being derided "in the press, by his constituency, and on the floor of the Congress. So one would think. But this system of 'old age allowances' has actually existed for many years, not as an expenditure program, but as a part of our tax system," through the double exemption granted aged couples.

of economic risk (the oil depletion allowance).[10] These illustrations of privileged tax treatment raise questions of equity which differ sharply from the issues of the welfare and nonwelfare poor. Accordingly, such a focus calls for a range of solutions quite different from those relevant to the problems of the welfare poor and low-income Americans.[11]

Alternative Income Maintenance Plans: Criteria for Comparison

There are criteria by which alternative means to a given poverty problem might be usefully compared. These criteria, while in no way exhaustive, represent a minimum list of considerations typically raised by American policy makers.

ADEQUACY

One of the most prominent standards of evaluation in any given income transfer program is the *adequacy of the benefit level*. Discussions of adequacy imply prior stipulation of the relevant standard against which benefits are measured. In other words, for any given conception of an appropriate standard of guaranteed income, the gap between that standard and the present income of the poor constitutes the "adequacy problem." Any transfer plan's benefits constitute some more or less adequate means to fill that gap.[12]

At least two indicators of adequacy should be used. The first is the proportion of the poverty gap filled by a given transfer program. This indicator provides an answer to the question, "how adequate an antipoverty program is a given plan?" This criterion may be referred to as

10. Tax reform was the subject of extended hearings before the House Committee on Ways and Means during the spring of 1969. For the range of reform proposals see *Tax Reform Studies and Proposals*, U.S. Treasury Dept., Joint Publication, Committee on Ways and Means, and Committee on Finance, 91st Congress, 1st Session, February 5, 1969 (Washington, D.C.: U.S. Government Printing Office).

11. The argument is not that programs related to one problem have no effect on other social ills; they do. But consider the difference between treating changes in children's tax exemptions as a tax reform issue and as an anti-poverty remedy. A more equitable treatment of children's tax exemptions would not necessarily involve enough money to relieve poverty substantially.

12. The differences between reforming welfare and eradicating poverty come out sharply in how analysts regard the adequacy criterion. Some, like the editors of the *Yale Law Journal*, take it as given that desirable programs will have a guarantee level set at the poverty line. Indeed, they question whether the "SSA poverty line—the 'minimum money income required to support an average family . . . at the lowest level consistent with the standard of living prevailing in this country'—"is adequate, even if it has gained wide acceptance." *Yale Law Journal* 78, No. 2 (Dec., 1968), p. 298, n. 91. On the other hand, welfare reforms costing approximately five billion dollars in 1970 were actively considered by the Congress. It is clearly possible to evaluate such low-adequacy alternatives by other criteria, and this may be very important if budgetary constraints rule out what the *Yale* editors so strongly seek.

aggregate program adequacy. The adequacy of grants to particular beneficiaries—*individual adequacy*—can be measured by guarantee levels.

Commonly, the Social Security Administration's poverty line ($3500 income for an urban family of four) is adopted as a reference point.[13] Those persons below the line are said to have less than minimally adequate income. The adequacy of a transfer program can then be evaluated from two perspectives: the degree to which benefits lift a recipient to the poverty line, and the extent to which total benefits fill the $12 billion gap between incomes of persons below and above the poverty line. Thus, the poverty line provides a basis for judging the adequacy of benefits directed to the welfare poor or, in a universal program, to all low-income Americans. The concern for adequacy may also be a criterion for tax reform if it focuses on the level of benefits for the poor in the form of more generous exemptions and deductions.

Although adequacy is not always the prime consideration in antipoverty efforts, it is the principal preoccupation of militant welfare rights organizations and welfare reformers, particularly social workers and welfare critics whose perspective is dominated by setting minimum floors of protection against various contingencies of living.[14]

STIGMA

The degree of stigma associated with the source, form and administration of income maintenance programs is the second criterion—one that has been emphasized in some criticisms of the current welfare system. Alvin

13. The poverty index set by the SSA is the minimum income per household of a given size, composition, and nonfarm status. In 1966 the Agriculture Department Economy Food Plan, which is the core of the poverty index, provided for total food expenditures of 75 cents a day per person (in an average four-person family). The index adds twice this amount to cover all family living items other than food. It has been adjusted for price changes since 1959, but has not kept pace with the increase in median income. Consequently, there was a larger absolute gap between median family income and the poverty line in 1969 than in 1959. Mollie Orshansky, "The Shape of Poverty in 1966," *Social Security Bulletin,* U.S. Department of Health, Education, and Welfare (Social Security Administration, March 1968), p. 5.

14. I am indebted to Robert Lampman for a suggested typology of poverty reformers. He distinguishes three perspectives: that of welfare (minimum floors of protection); of social insurance (security against *variability* of income over time through insurance); and of tax and public finance (equity of treatment, work incentives). Lampman emphasizes that each mentality directs attention selectively and ignores issues of great importance to the others. Thus, public finance experts are horrified by the inequitable treatment of welfare beneficiaries in different categories and in different states, and by the high marginal tax rates public assistance formally requires. Such considerations are less salient to welfare reformers who focus on adequacy of benefits, the speech with which destitution is relieved, etc. Social insurance advocates are more likely to evaluate transfers by the sense of entitlement they involve, the predictability of future benefits, and security they offer large classes of Americans, not especially the poor. This suggestive typology has yet to be worked out, but offers a way of comparing transfers that could be added to the approach I am suggesting.

Schorr has framed this concern in the telling phrase, "a means-tested program is a mean program."[15] Those like Schorr who are preoccupied with reducing stigma typically turn to social insurance programs as desirable alternatives.

The concern about stigma, however, is clearly relevant to groups other than the welfare poor. There is fear of stigma in programs that might be designed for the working poor. More generally, the U.S. Treasury, in evaluating tax reform proposals, typically worries about whether the reforms would require demeaning tax investigations.

Another aspect of this criterion is the economic function that stigma serves. Stigma may be viewed as a means of rationing government programs, of controlling the consumption of benefits in programs where conferring benefits to all those eligible would sharply increase government expenditures.[16]

Finally, one must say that knowledge about the extent of stigma and its causes is impressionistic. How obnoxious the "obnoxious means test" really is remains a question needing an answer before this criterion can be intelligently employed.[17] But the lack of knowledge in public policy is seldom a barrier to either strong views or policy action. And so it is in income maintenance debates that allegations about the causes, effects, and ways of eliminating stigma are presented and received as though stigma were precisely understood.

EQUITABLE EFFICIENCY

Weisbrod defines equitable efficiency as the degree to which "actual redistribution of income coincides with the desired redistribution." To illustrate, Weisbrod describes:

> a manpower retraining program which may be intended to benefit the hard core unemployed—those who cannot find regular employment even under 'full employment' conditions. But, as the program is actually administered, it

15. Alvin L. Schorr, *Explorations in Social Policy* (New York: Basic Books, Inc., 1968), p. 62.

16. The experience with the Kerr-Mills Medical Assistance law brings out this point. Generous in theory, only 32 states had workable programs by 1963, three years after enactment. Theodore R. Marmor, *The Politics of Medicare* (London: Routledge & Kegan Paul Ltd., 1970).

17. Some evidence has recently been gathered in Wisconsin indicating that the poor are not as hostile to the means test as commonly asserted. Handler and Hollingsworth found that "the clients reported very little evidence of hostility toward their caseworker or coercion in the administration of social services." Joel F. Handler and Ellen Jane Hollingsworth, "The Administration of Social Services in AFDC: The Views of Welfare Recipients," Institute for Research on Poverty, University of Wisconsin, Discussion Paper 37, p. 29.

may (1) miss many in the hard core group, while at the same time, (2) aids a number of less needy persons.[18]

Those concerned with efficiency argue that these effects reduce the desirability of a program. Considerations of equitable efficiency bring out how successfully (or unsuccessfully) a given program delivers benefits to a program's target population, and to no one else.

Weisbrod has introduced a useful distinction between two types of efficiency calculations. One efficiency consideration, he says, is the "degree to which programs intended to benefit group A also benefit group B." This might be termed *vertical efficiency*. The second issue is the degree to which "programs intended to benefit group A reach all of the group." Weisbrod refers to this as *horizontal efficiency*.

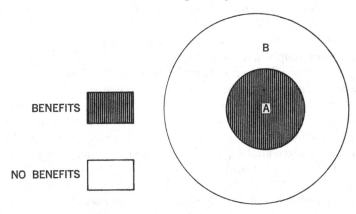

Figure 2–2. Illustration of Vertical Efficiency of 1

Vertical Efficiency. The vertical efficiency of a program may be defined as the ratio of benefits received by intended beneficiaries to total benefits distributed.[19] Consider two concentric circles, A and B (Figure 2–2). Circle A represents the target group, the intended beneficiaries. Circle B represents persons outside the target group. If payments, represented by the shaded areas, go only to those in A the vertical efficiency ratio of the program is 1.

18. Burton A. Weisbrod, "Collective Action and the Distribution of Income: A Conceptual Approach," *The Analysis and Evaluation of Public Expenditure: The PPB System*, Vol. 1, A Compendium of Papers, Subcommittee on Economy in Government, Joint Economic Committee, U.S. Congress, 91st Congress, 1st Session (Government Printing Office: Washington, D.C., 1969), p. 184.

19. As Weisbrod says, "a ratio of unity would thus indicate that all resources of the program are being devoted to the target group and do not benefit any others." *Ibid.*, p. 185.

Vertical efficiency can be conceived as a proxy for cost effectiveness: the greater the vertical efficiency ratio the smaller the per unit cost of benefits to the target group. Thus, between two programs that bring equal benefits to a given target group, the program having the higher vertical efficiency ratio, *ceteris paribus*, will be the least costly.

This conception of vertical efficiency implies that benefits to non-needy persons should be given a weight of zero. At least two objections can be made to this interpretation, as Weisbrod points out. First, there may be other than redistributional grounds for wanting to distribute benefits to the nonpoor (administrative simplicity, for example). Secondly, vertical efficiency may conflict with another criterion. For example, the extent to which a program limits benefits to those within the poverty class may contribute to stigma associated with such a program. This conflict is implicit in Schorr's comment about the meanness of means-tested programs.[20]

The problem of weighting benefits to non-needy persons is more complicated than simply avoiding stigma. A critical objection to programs with less vertical efficiency is that there may be resentment against windfall gains to those outside the target group. One of the objections to negative income tax proposals is that plans for transferring income to the poor must involve sizable payments to persons who are clearly not poor in order to provide a "meaningful floor of income and to avoid a very high tax on incremental income."[21] (Taxes here refer to the reductions in benefit payments per additional dollar of family income.) The magnitude of this difficulty would be revealed by the vertical efficiency ratio, though the revelation of the difficulty in no way resolves it.

Horizontal Efficiency. Horizontal efficiency may be defined as the "ratio of the number of beneficiaries in the target group to the total number of persons in the target group." An illustration of the sort provided in Figure 2-3 may clarify this point. The issue in horizontal equity is the absence of benefits for some persons within a designated group. The lower the value of this ratio, the smaller the proportion of the target group (all presumably deserving) being aided. The larger the shaded area of circle A—the target group—the greater the horizontal efficiency ratio, and the more it meets that standard of evaluation. It ought to be noted again, however, that the *horizontal efficiency* ratio is different from the adequacy standard. If all of the target group's members are regarded as equally deserving (and this need not always be the case), one's judg-

20. See also D. P. Moynihan's remarks about stigma and community reactions to transfer programs in his "Crises in Welfare," *The Public Interest*, No. 10 (Winter 1968), pp. 3–29.

21. See Weisbrod, *supra*, n. 18, p. 187.

ment as to the fairness of a program may well be an inverse function of the degree to which it has the effect—whether or not intentional—of discriminating among the target beneficiaries. Clearly inadequate payments could go to all persons within a target group and thus lead one to rank

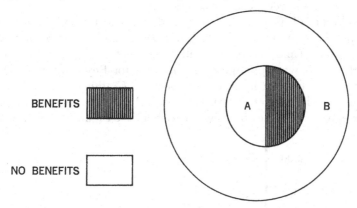

Figure 2–3. Illustration of Horizontal Efficiency of .5

a program high on horizontal efficiency and low on adequacy. The trade-off between these two criteria—at any given dollar cost of a program—is again a problem of weighting yet to be solved.

WORK INCENTIVES

The work incentive effects of cash transfers is a fourth criterion of importance. Regardless of the administrative mechanism, any transfer program must answer three different questions: What shall be the level of the income guarantee (the maximum benefit)? How shall that benefit be reduced as earnings vary from zero (the tax rate)? And what shall be the cut-off point (the earnings level at which no benefits are paid)?[22]

The appropriate level of taxation on cash transfers depends in part on the effect of the tax rate on the work behavior of various groups in the population. That information is not known in any precise way.[23] The result is that analysts work from rules of thumb of the following sort: any income guarantee will reduce some work effort if the marginal tax on earnings is more than zero; (or) the desire to work is so great in Ameri-

22. Outlined in Christopher Green, *op. cit.*, pp. 126–130.
23. In most of the literature proposing various income maintenance plans, guarantee levels are so low that to consider many heads of four-person families would give up higher incomes to loaf on $1500 or so per year is ludicrous and in violation of our common sense. Yet, for political reasons, there is still concern over incentive effects of such plans.

can society that the impact of a tax rate up to 50 per cent will not greatly reduce work-force participation. This latter view implies that, in considering the choice between increasing incentives to work (by lowering the tax rate) and reducing the guarantee level, one should worry a great deal about forcing a lower income guarantee.

The absence of information about work incentives is no bar to the issue being politically important. Indeed, the existence of strong feelings about what the poor (and near poor) will or will not do under various incentive schemes is what prompted the Institute for Research on Poverty at the University of Wisconsin to undertake the Graduated Work Incentive Experiment which involves testing of several negative tax schemes on the work responses of some 800 New Jersey families. Figure 2–4, representing

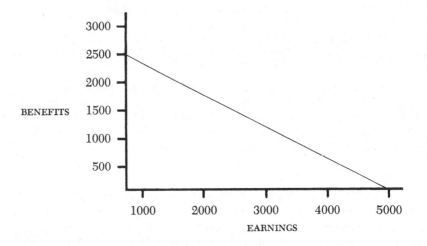

Figure 2–4.   A Negative Income Tax Plan

a moderately high negative income tax plan, illustrates the choices that must be made among (1) guarantee level, (2) tax rate, and (3) cut-off points.[24] A program guaranteeing $2500 when earnings are zero with a

24. David Wilkinson, "Foxtracks Across Ice," unpublished paper, University of Wisconsin, provides an illustration of this point. He visualizes the plan "as a line from a reel anchored to the top of an economic ladder. The line assures that the family won't drop below a certain rung. At the same time it assists a family moving up the ladder, though with decreasing payout as the family gets closer to the top. The reel and line represent an income assistance system working in conjunction with the family's own efforts to increase total income with earnings. The line won't lift the full weight of the family to the top, but it continues to be of assistance until the family gets there." The maximum vertical length of the line represents the level of support minimally guaranteed. The lift of the line represents the tax rate applied to earnings, with a smaller tax rate producing more lift than a larger rate. The break-even level corresponds to the top of the ladder, the point where all the line is reeled in.

"tax" rate of 50 per cent entails a cut-off point of $5000. If one specifies any two of the three variables, the value of the third variable is determined. The plan illustrated in Figure 2–4 sacrifices vertical efficiency for adequacy and substantial work incentives.

The concern about work incentives is part of the larger worry about the relation of transfer schemes to economic growth, productive efficiency, and allocative efficiency. Macroeconomic effects might be taken as another criterion of evaluation. In this paper, the work incentives issue is presented as a proxy for those broader concerns, as well as a salient political issue in its own right. All government redistribution affects what Musgrave calls the allocation and stabilization "functions" of the state.[25] The distribution of government goods and services between regions changes both the distribution of income and the allocation of productive resources. Giving money to the poor simply raises this issue more directly (and dramatically). What effect will given transfer schemes have on work performance, the mobility of labor, the process of automation in low-wage industries, or the price of labor? All such questions are called for in evaluating transfer programs.

PROGRAM COSTS

The costs of a transfer program may refer to total expenditures at all levels of government or the net increment to the federal budget, taking into account savings in other present federal, state, and local income transfer programs.

Program costs to any unit of government are very difficult to predict. Specifying the tax rate, cut-off point, and guarantee level does not tell how workers will behave. Consequently, the number of persons who will be in a specified income range cannot be unambiguously determined from present data on the poor. Nor can the amount of the poverty "gap" be precisely measured, except retrospectively. The best that can be done is to make reasonable assumptions (perhaps alternative assumptions) about the work response to various plans and estimate program costs on that basis.

The allocation of program costs involves both the governmental unit whose expenditures are affected and the taxpayers who finance the program. Minimum federal payment levels for public assistance, for example, are advocated by some as if the purpose is to increase the total payments to public assistance beneficiaries. But, in fact, the demand for such changes comes primarily from beleaguered state and local governments anxious to shift the burden of welfare payments to the federal govern-

---

25. R. Musgrave, *The Theory of Public Finance.* New York: McGraw-Hill, 1959, ch. 1.

ment. Hence, one of the cost issues is which level of the political system will finance what proportion of any given transfer scheme. Program costs can be treated as either a criterion or a constraint. That is, one may ask, what is the cost of plan X compared to plan Y? Or one may ask how plans compare on other dimensions, subject to the constraint that their program costs fall within a specified range.

POLITICAL SUPPORT

The relationship between political and economic costs and benefits is the "most talked about, least understood topic within the field of political economy."[26] As with program costs, political costs can be treated as a constraint or a variable. That is, given the political acceptability of two programs, they can be compared on the basis of the other criteria. Or, they can be compared according to the political support (and opposition) they will generate. The conceptual and measurement problems involved, however, are extraordinary.

Political support means the nature and extent of approval for a given program. One may speak of mass support and use polling data as an indicator of it. Public opinion polls recently have shown that more than a majority of those with opinions about income maintenance favored guaranteed employment plans, while less than a majority favored income guarantees.[27] More important for present purposes is support by governmental elites, particularly congressional elites. There are few ways one can accurately measure such support before decisive tests (like a vote) are taken. Votes on other redistributive issues are one indicator, but not a fully reliable one. Party positions on the questions offer another clue when combined with knowledge of the pattern of party cohesion on redistributive matters.

A good example of noting political costs and benefits, but not taking them into account systematically in comparing transfer programs, can be found in the *Yale Law Journal's* comment on

the relation between the [*Yale Law Journal's* model] NIT proposal and the increasingly urgent demands for a wholesale reform of public assistance. Any modification of public assistance programs that took into account all the serious criticisms of present welfare efforts—as, for example, do the recommenda-

---

26. Remark made to me by Professor Ira Sharkansky, University of Wisconsin.

27. In response to a question about guaranteeing every family an income of at least $3200 a year (for a family of four), with the government making up the differences, the following results were obtained: favor—36%; oppose—58%; no opinion—6%. Results of a question about providing enough work so that each family that has an employable wage earner would be guaranteed a wage of about $60 a week or $3200 a year were: favor—78%; oppose—18%; no opinion—4%. American Institute of Public Opinion, Gallup Opinion Index, Report No. 37, July, 1968, pp. 23–24.

tions of the U.S. Advisory Council on Public Welfare—would result in a system of distributing benefits strikingly similar to that outlined in the model statute. The NIT and public assistance reforms are not so much alternative ways of dealing with poverty as they are alternative ways of dealing with Congress, and the choice between them is chiefly one of political strategy. Since the NIT completely escapes the faulty concepts and spotted history of public assistance, it still ranks as the preferable approach.[28]

Evaluating Income Maintenance Alternatives: The Nixon Administration's Choice in Welfare Reform

Different welfare reform proposals proceed from different views of the present system of public assistance. Before comparing alternative welfare reforms, some preliminary remarks should be made about the demographic, administrative, and financial attributes of contemporary public assistance. Federal assistance goes to five state-federal programs: old age assistance (OAA), aid to families with dependent children (AFDC), aid to blind (AB), aid to the permanently and totally disabled (APTD), and aid to the medically indigent (Medicaid). There are residual relief programs in each state which are financed wholly by state and/or local funds. The later programs are collectively referred to as general relief or general assistance and do not receive federal supervision or funding.[29]

Federal participation in public assistance was originally designed to help states support persons who were unable to work because of age, blindness, or absence of a wage-earner. Since 1950, new groups and purposes have been included. Aid to the partially and totally disabled was enacted in 1950; in 1960, medical assistance for the aged was enacted as the Kerr-Mills program. In the early 1960s, an unemployed parent amendment permitted AFDC benefits to families where the father was in the home and unemployed (AFDC-UP, now operative in 21 states). Two other legislative developments in the 1960s were of importance: in 1962, rehabilitative services were provided under public assistance and, in 1967, new amendments were passed which sought to get AFDC recipients to work through incentives (job training, day care, financial inducements) and sanctions (denying aid to those considered able, but unwilling, to work). Categorical public assistance, in summary, was designed for the nonworking poor, and only recently has focused upon problems of rehabilitation and employment.

The number of persons receiving public assistance has grown sharply

---

28. *Yale Law Journal* 78, No. 2 (December, 1968), p. 282.
29. The following discussion draws on work of the staff of the President's Commission on Income Maintenance Programs which presented its final report *Poverty Amid Plenty: The American Paradox* in November, 1969.

since 1945. Part of the growth is attributable to the inclusion of new categories of assistance, but the AFDC program is clearly the source of most of the growth. The distribution of recipients for one month, by year and type of program, is presented in Table 2–2.

Table 2–2.   Number° of Public Assistance Recipients
(in thousands)

December of Year	Total	OAA	AFDC	AB	APTD
1945	3070.5	2056	943	71.5	–
1951	4963.2	2701	2041	97.2	124
1957	5274.0	2487	2398	108.0	281
1963	6642.9	2052	3930	96.9	464
1966	7410.7	2073	4666	83.7	588
1967	8111.0	2073	5309	82.6	646
1968	8896.0	2027	6086	80.7	702

°The Commission analysts note that the "number assisted in any one month is less than the total assisted during the year. One estimate would place the number of persons assisted in 1966 at over 10 million. Because of the lack of an unduplicated annual count and data on the financial circumstances of those assisted, the total number of poor persons helped is not known." Unpublished memorandum.

SOURCE: President's Commission on Income Maintenance Programs

The growth in AFDC has dominated much of the discussion of public welfare, or "illfare," as *Time* magazine recently put it. The distribution of poor persons *within* public assistance, however, does not point up the proportion of the poor excluded. Lampman has estimated that 20 million poor persons were ineligible for public assistance in 1966, representing approximately two-thirds of the total of 29.7 million poor.[30] Public assistance comprises programs for a minority of the poor. The crisis of welfare is thus only a part of the problem of American poverty.

Public assistance provides federal grants-in-aid to all states for cash payments to individuals and families in need. AFDC receives less federal assistance than the other programs, and the federal share under all the programs varies with the income level of the state. Of the $6 billion spent in 1966 on all public assistance programs, including administrative costs, about 60 per cent, or $3.5 billion, came from the federal government. The extent of federal participation over time is presented in Table 2–3.

The administration of public assistance is discretionary, local, and uneven. Eligible persons are "needy" by virtue of destitution. The definition

30. Robert J. Lampman, "Negative Income Taxation: A Challenge to Social Engineers," unpublished paper, Institute for Research on Poverty, University of Wisconsin, 1968, p. 9. See also Lampman, *supra*, n. 3, pp. 548–549.

Table 2–3. Federal Financial Participation in Public Assistance

Year	Total (millions of dollars)	Per Cent of Total		
		Federal	State	Local
1945	987.9	40.7	47.8	12.5
1951	2382.8	47.6	41.6	10.8
1957	3090.3	51.3	37.0	11.7
1963	4712.6	55.5	32.7	11.5
1966	6652.0	58.6	30.7	10.8

SOURCE: President's Commission on Income Maintenance Programs.

of destitution varies among the states. Moreover, state grants do not typically pay the difference between their definition of "need" and current income. In some states the "need" for a family of four is $280 per month and a family with no income gets that amount. In other states the "need" is $194, but the family with no income receives only $40. States vary in the requirements for granting assistance as well. In some states there were no residence tests; in others, a would-be recipient had to have lived in the state five of the past nine years and the year immediately preceeding assistance. However, the 1969 Supreme Court decision in *Shapiro v. Thompson* ruled such residency tests unconstitutional for federally assisted programs.

The above characterization of public assistance entails no obvious reformist perspective. One may applaud or denounce the extent to which states with unequal resources differently define and support their categorically poor. The extraordinary growth of AFDC might, in one view, be evidence that the states are discovering the needs that exist; in another view, it is a sign of moral decay in want of immediate attention. There are those who think the problem with welfare is that we have too much of it; some are worried about too much administration and others are upset about too many recipients. Then, there are those who see the problem as too little public welfare, either in the sense that too few of the poor are eligible or, within the current system, too little is provided the recipients both in cash and incentives to improve their income position.

Critics of welfare often proceed as if everyone agreed on the nature and ranking of these problems. That is simply not true. Despite the fact that most advocates of welfare reform begin with the same opening salvo of objections to public assistance (indeed the criticisms have become clichéd through endless listing), the classification of issues does not bring with it a decision rule. This failure occurs because a decision rule requires *both* a classificatory and a weighting scheme, and only the former is available. My thesis is that a weighting scheme also requires clear, explicit presentation of criteria to be weighted. I have tried to do that and will now apply those criteria to two welfare reform proposals and make a first step toward a systematic comparative evaluation.

The two proposals were the chief options under discussion by President Nixon's Urban Council during the spring of 1969. Both plans are directed towards reducing inequities within the present welfare system. One, popularly known as the Burns plan after presidential advisor Arthur Burns, proposes decreasing state variation in benefit levels through a national minimum standard for the present categories of public welfare, to be administered by the present federal-state welfare apparatus. This plan will be referred to as Uniform State Benefits (USB). The second proposal offers income assistance to poor families with children, which would be administered by the Social Security Administration, and will be referred to as Federal Family Benefits (FFB), though it is known more widely as the Finch-Moynihan proposal.

Both proposals seek to reduce inequities presently affecting individuals and states. The inequities for individuals arise from the fact that federal matching formulas are insufficient tools to reduce the variation in state treatment of similar welfare recipients. At the lower level, poor states are encouraged, but not required to provide minimum payments that satisfy the barest conception of subsistence income. The wealthier the state (in per capita income), the lower the proportion of federal support for more generous grants. Hence, welfare generosity is a heavy fiscal burden, one which some states (and state legislators) find intolerable.[31]

The similarities between proposals USB and FFB are striking. Both would cost the federal government under two billion dollars per year. Both would entail savings to financially hard-pressed states. Both provide for a national welfare minimum. The general income support program (FFB), while not universal, provides payments to all families with children and, thus, is much broader in scope than current AFDC and AFDC-UP programs. It is broader in that the income status of the family is the sole criterion of eligibility; this contrasts sharply with the father-less-family criterion in AFDC and the unemployed father standard of eligibility in AFDC-UP. Both programs establish minimum welfare standards nationwide, but distribution of the federal financial increment (less than two billion dollars) to the poor and to state treasuries differ. Both

31. One vivid illustration is the recent vote by the Wisconsin legislature to discontinue, because of cost, the state's AFDC-UP program, even though it comprised a small portion of Wisconsin's total welfare budget. This and other threatend retrenchments come at a time when the cost of living is rapidly rising and is thus exacerbating the welfare crisis.

the similarities and the differences are revealed clearly by evaluating the programs by the six criteria introduced in the second part of this paper, as shown in Table 2–4.

· Table 2–4. *Comparison of Two Welfare Reform Proposals: Uniform State Benefits (USB) and Federal Family Benefits (FFB)*

Criteria for Comparison	Indicators	USB	FFB
Adequacy	· 4-person family guarantee	$1500 or 42% of $3500 poverty line	$1500 or 42% of $3500 poverty line
	· Poverty gap filled	*1.5/12, .7/12	2/12, 1.3/21
Stigma		no improvement	some improvement
Efficiency Horizontal		.4	.8
Vertical	· Ratio of transfer benefits, poor to nonpoor	1	1
	· Amount of poverty gap filled to total benefits	7/15	13/20
Work incentive		$30 set aside + 67% tax rate	$50 bonus + 50% tax rate
Program cost**	· Federal cost	$1.5 billion	$2 billion
	· State saving	$800 million	$710 million
Political support	· Mass support for some reform	+	+
	· Bureaucratic support	—	+
	· Congressional support	uncertain	uncertain
Problem focus		disparity of payments by State and category (b)***	inequitable exclusion of the poor (the working poor especially) from public assistance (f)***

* The first ratio compares total federal program costs to the poverty gap; the second is a ratio of only the transfer amount to the $12 billion poverty gap.
**Excluding food and training programs.
*** See listings, pp. 33–34.

ADEQUACY

The first indicator in Table 2–4 measures the *individual adequacy* of benefit guarantees. By this standard there is no substantial difference between FFB and USB: both guarantee $1500 to a family of four (or about $31 per month for each family member). If one takes tax rate provisions into account, FFB appears more adequate than USB; since FFB "taxes" earnings less heavily than USB, it would provide higher average payments to recipients earning the same wages.

The second indicator provides two measures of *aggregate program adequacy:* (1) the ratio of total program costs to the $12 billion poverty gap, the ratio being approximately 1.5/12 under USB and 2/12 under FFB; and (2) the ratio of benefits for the poor to the poverty gap, by which standard FFB is somewhat more adequate.

It should be clear that although FFB ranks higher on adequacy than USB, both programs are inadequate when judged by the current poverty standard. The Social Security definition of minimum income for a family of four ($3500) is not approximated in either program. The $1500 guarantee represents only 42 per cent of the poverty line, while the higher FFB program costs ($2 billion) represent only one-sixth of the poverty income gap.[32] These points alone serve to demonstrate how welfare reform can proceed quite apart from serious efforts to eradicate financial poverty, either individual or aggregate.

STIGMA

Neither program represents a serious effort to reduce the stigma allegedly associated with public assistance. USB is an effort to make public assistance less inequitable among states and among different categories of beneficiaries. FFB is directed towards the inequitable exclusion of poor, male-headed families with an employed father. But neither program makes public welfare less selective in the sense of transferring income to the nonpoor. On the other hand, FFB proposes that the family benefit be administered by the Social Security Administration, an administrative system considered less stigmatized than welfare agencies. A qualified plus is given to FFB on this basis; a minus given to USB on the assumption that more stigma is attached to local welfare systems.

Vertical Efficiency. Both programs satisfy this criterion because the ratio of benefits received by the poor to total transfer benefits is 1. This is the case only for the transfer portion of the program. That is, nonpoor persons receive no benefits; no "leakage" of that kind takes place. But,

---

32. Estimates from Lampman, *Wisconsin Law Review* 2 (1969), p. 541.

taking into account the state "savings" changes the vertical efficiency ratio for each program. For USB, it is 7/75; for FFB, 13/20. Another way of expressing the relative poverty intensity is to compare poverty relief to state financial relief: the ratio of poverty relief to state relief in USB is 7/8; in FFB, 13/7.

On the first measure, both programs are vertically efficient. On the second, FFB is far more vertically efficient; 65 per cent of its costs represent direct expenditures for the poor, compared with 47 per cent of USB going directly to the poor. Since the two programs involve similar levels of federal expenditures, the efficiency ratio makes a useful distinction. Knowing that FFB is more vertically efficient than USB does not, however, tell us how important that criterion is—that is, what weight to give it. However, the comparison avoids difficulties that arise in describing two programs of vastly different cost. A $28 billion program with a vertical efficiency ratio of .5 may appear to be far more "efficient," from this perspective, than the $2 billion FFB program with a vertical efficiency ratio of .65. But this is the case only by mixing the adequacy and vertical efficiency criteria.

Horizontal Efficiency. Program USB is substantially less efficient, horizontally, than FFB. Indeed, increased horizontal efficiency in public welfare is the chief goal of the family benefit program. It is directed against what I termed problem (f) in the group of criticisms against the current welfare system (page 50). Since public assistance aids only about 40 per cent of the poor, its horizontal efficiency ratio is .4. Since families headed by a man who works account for the major portion of those excluded from assistance, FFB has a much higher horizontal efficiency ratio, approximately .8. Conversely, USB is relatively inefficient on this dimension, since it retains the current categories of public assistance.

USB subordinates horizontal efficiency to financial relief of states. FFB seeks greater horizontal efficiency at the price of somewhat less financial relief to states. However, this is true only when one looks at the transfer portion of the programs. The work and food programs would change these comparisons slightly, but, for present purposes, we will ignore that complication.

WORK INCENTIVES

USB provides for a continuation of the present Work Incentive Program (WIN) scheme under AFDC. Under WIN there is an earning exemption of $30, a 67 per cent tax rate on additional earnings, and a training-employment program exclusively for AFDC recipients. FFB provides more financial incentives to work than USB, but does not compel recipients to seek training or work. The FFB tax rate is 50 per cent, which means that the $1500 guarantee is combined with a cut-off point of $3000. In addition, individuals receive $50 per month as a special incentive for taking job training.

FFB also provides incentives to the state to *move* welfare clients into training. It does so because the trainee would continue to receive his family benefit, any amount he might be receiving from the state to supplement that payment, plus the bonus incentive of $50 per month. States giving families additional benefits under FFB (as would surely be the case in the larger industrial states) could gain substantially from widespread use of this training-payment provision. The training program would cost an additional $600 million if 150,000 training positions were created. Currently, there are 88,000 training positions budgeted under the WIN program, of which 35,000 are filled. At an average cost of $4000 per position, WIN would cost $352 million when fully utilized.

PROGRAM COSTS

The additional federal cost of FFB, including the adult categories but exclusive of food and training programs, is approximately $2 billion. Of this, approximately $710 million results in savings to the states. The estimated cost of USB is $1.5 billion, of which roughly $800 million represents dollar-for-dollar savings for the states. Neither estimate, of course, takes into account what the states might do with their "savings"; hence, no estimate of total governmental costs of the programs plus state supplementary schemes.

The program costs criterion is more difficult to apply than it appears. If we take only direct transfers into account, the programs involve comparable federal program costs: $1.5 billion for USB, $2 billion for FFB. Two complications arise, however. The first is the addition of training and food stamp programs which raise federal expenditures to approximately $4 billion. The comparison in Table 2–4 involves only the cash transfers, and this may confuse more than illuminate. But even for cash transfers, the program costs are very hard to gauge. It is impossible to know what the work response will be and, hence, the federal costs over time. The above estimates are made as if the poor tomorrow would act precisely as they do today. Nonetheless, there is reason to believe the costs are not markedly understated. Few heads of four-person families would voluntarily quit working to receive FFB's $1500 guarantee. And USB does not assist the working poor.

POLITICAL SUPPORT

Both programs share whatever diffuse political support exists for "doing something about welfare." FFB directs itself toward the AFDC problem and, through a sleight-of-hand name change, would, in the words of one promoter, "eliminate the much criticised AFDC program." USB directs itself to another aspect of the AFDC problem, the migration of welfare clients to large urban centers. FFB hopes to encourage families to leave welfare and also diminishes incentives for divorce and desertion presently found in AFDC programs. USB retains these unfortunate incentives but provides inducements for families in the less wealthy states to stay there. The support for stemming migration and discouraging desertion of fathers is, however, extremely hard to measure. Congressional committees with welfare jurisdiction are well represented with members declaring "widespread" support for doing something about the welfare mess. It is precisely the unspecified extent and nature of support for action that gives discretion to the congressional elites who manage, manipulate, and judge options like USB and FFB.

The mass public's opinions are equally distant from the legislative system. Whatever diffuse hostility exists towards AFDC in the larger public could be used to justify either USB or FFB. Where the two programs differ most sharply—as, for example, on the question of whether geographical inequity is less pressing than the exclusion of the working poor from public assistance—public opinion is unformed and unlikely to be crucial in the decision-making process. Both programs tap other widespread anxieties: the desire for making work more attractive for welfare clients; the financial problems of the states and localities in meeting welfare costs; and the current preoccupation with food programs. Referring back to our six criteria, it is clear that USB and FFB differ most sharply on the weight given to horizontal equity in a welfare reform that does not address itself to eradicating poverty.

The political costs and benefits from improving the horizontal efficiency of public assistance are easiest to estimate at the federal administrative level. The gains of substance are evident from either a welfare or public finance perspective. Professional reformers within the bureaucracy have for some years been asking universal public assistance based on income criteria rather than present categorical scheme which defines eligibility in terms of the *cause* of low income (blindness, disability, old age, etc.). If bureaucratic support is the only measure, then FFB without doubt ranks higher. Neither proposal proposes to do away with state administration of other adult programs; hence, one cannot contrast them in terms of the jurisdictional squabbles raised.

A measure of political costs, better than bureaucratic preferences, is the anticipated objections of Congress.[33] The political costs of USB arise from

33. All of the financial cost estimates are for Fiscal Year 1972. This postponement of program initiation reflects a number of considerations: the present administration's budget-cutting, the political gains of future as against present expenditures, and the assumption that passage of welfare reform would take perhaps two years.

its failure to deal with the problem of the working poor and its relatively lower horizontal efficiency. Its advocates, however, would argue that the congressional system directly represents the financial interests of states and localities, and that only a minority of the Congress stands for interests of the working poor and welfare efficiency. This argument rests, however, on the assumption that widespread congressional support for each feature of welfare reform is the precondition for enactment (the consensus view of political support). If, in contrast, one assumed sufficient general support for a large class of welfare reforms, the greater equity and efficiency of FFB would be decisive. Bureaucratic support for equity and efficiency would greatly assist in creating the minimum favorable coalition in the finance committees of the Congress. Only if it appeared that a determined majority would develop *against* FFB would one say that the political support criterion dictated selection of USB.

The politics of welfare reform provide a striking illustration of the characteristic political processing of redistributive policies.[34] The role of the bureaucracy in that arena is one of balancing the interests known to be involved in income redistribution. The Congress ratifies or refuses the bargains that are expressed in the legislative initiatives brought to it. The evaluative effort we have been making is an accurate representation of the comparative analysis that has already been made of USB and FFB within the Nixon Administration.[35]

Constrained by a $2 billion budgetary allowance for additional cash transfers, committed to welfare reform, concerned about the pressures to relieve the states of part of their welfare burden, uncertain about what will reduce welfare rolls, federal officials have had to compare programs by criteria whose weights are uncertain. If we have been unable to provide those weights and, hence, the basis for a simple decision rule, at least we have isolated some important criteria and discussed some of the issues involved in giving them weights.

---

34. For a characterization of the redistributive "political arena," see Theodore Lowi, "American Business, Case Studies and Political Theory," *World Politics, 16* (1963–64).

35. On Oct. 2, 1969, President Nixon sent to the Congress the Family Assistance Act of 1969, a plan modeled after FFB with the addition of a work requirement.

PART TWO

Welfare Reform Proposals

The proposals in this section focus on the character and difficulties of the contemporary American welfare system. The 1966 Report of the Advisory Council on Public Welfare (Chapter 3) is a striking example of how widely present practices are discredited. Concentrating on the inter-program and regional variations and the inadequate funding of public assistance, the report calls for a universal program of income guarantees, supervised by the federal government and administered by the states. Benefits that would assure a "modest but adequate budget" for all American families are recommended, but the report slights the problem of how to build in incentives to work. While insisting that welfare grants should be universally available "on a dignified basis as a matter of legal right," the Advisory Council leaves to the states the precise determination of budget needs and benefits. The report insists on the federal standards which have long been a demand of social work professionals, but it provides no clear estimate of what such an extensive reform of welfare would cost.

Both the Nixon and Lampman plans (Chapters 4 and 5) may be thought of as low benefit negative income taxes that would reform welfare by extending federal benefits to the currently unaided working poor. Both plans combine concern for expanding the coverage of public assistance with the insistence that beneficiaries have incentives (and, in the Nixon plan, sanctions) to work. The suggestion of providing work incentives through a 50 per cent tax rate on earnings is linked with income guarantees well below the poverty line. The projected costs—less than $5 billion—highlight the way these negative tax schemes address welfare reform, not the eradication of poverty.

55

Alvin Schorr's child allowance scheme (Chapter 6) is particularly directed at the stigma associated with the current AFDC program. Schorr suggests transferring $50 per month per child to those poor families (approximately two-thirds) who have children under six years of age. He too concentrates on extending cash assistance to the working poor, but emphasizes families with young children and an administrative mechanism that would not require demeaning income tests. At an estimated cost of $6 billion, the Schorr plan would involve substantial transfers to nonpoor families but exclude those poor without eligible children. This program, as with the others, proceeds from the dissatisfaction with public assistance, but represents a distinctive view of the proper trade-offs between such conflicting objectives as guaranteeing adequacy, reducing stigma, providing work incentives, expanding coverage, and insuring politically feasible program costs.

Public Welfare:
A Comprehensive Program
of Basic Social Guarantees

*The Advisory Council on Public Welfare was appointed in July, 1964,
by the Secretary of Health, Education and Welfare, acting under a Congressional directive included in the Public Welfare Amendments of 1962.
The purpose of the Council was to review the administration of public
assistance and child welfare services programs and to make recommendations for their improvement. The Council's report was submitted in 1966,
by which time public assistance had been widely discredited as inadequate, inefficient, inhumane, expensive, and administratively cumbersome. The report's version of a universal guaranteed income calls for
improvement on these issues, but commits itself to the present decentralized state-federal apparatus at the very time critics were insisting on shift-
ing welfare transfers to a less stigmatized administrative agency.*

The Present Situation

Public welfare is the only governmental program operating in the United
States today which has as its assigned task the provision of an ultimate
guarantee against poverty and social deprivation. Its role in society is to
assure to individuals, families, and communities the recognized basic

Advisory Council on Public Welfare, *"Having the Power, We have the Duty,"* Report
to the Secretary of Health, Education, and Welfare (Washington, D.C.: U.S. Government Printing Office, 1966), pp. xi–xix, 117–122.

essentials of living within a framework of related governmental and voluntary measures.

Its ability to carry out this function is necessarily governed by its legislative mandate and the financial resources it is given by the public. At the present time public welfare is desperately handicapped in both respects. But it is nevertheless to public welfare that people must look for aid when income from other sources falls short or the traditional protections of family and other forms of voluntary association do not adequately meet their social needs. All societies in order to survive must make provision for these needs within the limits of their resources and social pattern. The United States is, however, distinguished from other countries in the degree to which unprecedented resources combine with the unprecedented interdependence to make such basic protections both possible and essential.

The very concept of a guarantee requires that it be available to all it is intended to protect, be adequate to their needs, consistent with the standards of the society in which they live, and available on a dignified basis as a matter of legal right.

Today, despite legislative improvements and courageous administrative leadership, our public welfare provisions fall short on all these counts. They are expected to make up to individuals for all deficiencies of economic and social functioning in our society but are given limited resources in law and financing with which to do so. Approximately 8 million persons are today dependent on a precariously low level of assistance. But an additional 26 million are living below the income level which the Government defines as constituting poverty within American standards. Social services for the protection of children, aid to families, and facilitating help for the aged, the disabled, the isolated, the uprooted or other individuals overburdened by problems beyond their powers of personal solution are so spotty as to constitute a token of help for some rather than a true guarantee for all. Public welfare is not the only or always the best answer to all these problems but in the realities of today's situation it is caught between overwhelming needs and inadequate resources with which to meet them.

Congress recognized the inadequacy of our present public welfare provisions when it authorized in 1962 the creation of an Advisory Council on Public Welfare to review the present Federal provisions for public assistance and child welfare services and to submit recommendations for their improvement.

The Advisory Council on Public Welfare has diligently pursued this assignment since its appointment in 1964. It has met a total of 18 days in Washington. It has studied all available documents, reports, and statistics. It has conferred with responsible officials from all the operating bureaus charged with the administration of these programs at the Federal level. It has conducted six open hearings in various sections of the country at which the opinions and recommendations of almost 350 interested persons were solicited, heard, recorded, and analyzed. Witnesses including spokesmen for State governments, members of the legislatures, State and local public welfare administrators, experts from voluntary social welfare agencies and universities, representatives of business and labor organizations, and persons representing the public welfare beneficiary groups.

On all counts and from all sources the weight of the evidence is incontestable: a major updating of our public welfare system is essential if it is to fulfill its assigned task of assuring a basic floor of economic and social security for all Americans. The remedies must match these indictments:

• Public assistance payments are so low and so uneven that the Government is, by its own standards and definitions, a major source of the poverty on which it has declared unconditional war.

• Large numbers of those in desperate need, including many children, are excluded even from this level of aid by arbitrary eligibility requirements unrelated to need such as those based on age, family situation, degree of disability, alleged employability, low earnings, unrealistic requirements for family contribution, durational residence requirements, and absence of provisions for emergency assistance.

• The methods for determining and redetermining eligibility for assistance and the amount to which the applicant is entitled are, in most States, confusing, onerous, and demeaning for the applicant; complex and time consuming for the worker; and incompatible with the concept of assistance as a legal right.

• The lack of adequate social services for families, children, young people, and individuals isolated by age or disability is itself a major factor in the perpetuation of such social evils as crime and juvenile delinquency, mental illness, illegitimacy, multigenerational dependency, slum environments, and the widely deplored climate of unrest, alienation, and discouragement among many groups in the population.

• Neither the war on poverty nor achievement of the long range goals implicit in a Great Society concept can succeed so long as the basic guarantees of a practical minimum level of income and social protection are not assured for all.

The Council's Recommendations

Only comprehensive nationwide protections can meet this challenge. The Council, therefore, recommends the addition of a title to the Social Security Act to provide, in cooperation with the States, a new nationwide program of basic social guarantees on the following basis:

1. GENERAL PROPOSAL

The new program would require that adequate financial aid and social services be available to all who need them as a matter of right. To make this possible a new pattern of Federal-State cooperation is proposed. The Federal Government would set nationwide standards, adjusted by objective criteria to varying costs and conditions among the States, and assume the total cost of their implementation above a stipulated State share. The States would thus be freed to concentrate their efforts on meeting human needs, relieved of the present multiple Federal program requirements and the constant pressure to find new sources of State financing. The required components for participation in this new program are described below.

2. ASSISTANCE STANDARDS

A floor of required individual or family income would be established for each State in terms of the cost of a modest but adequate family budget for families of various sizes and circumstances as established by objective methods of budget costing. This would constitute the minimum level of assistance which must prevail in that State.

3. ELIGIBILITY FOR AID

All persons with available income falling below this established budget level would be entitled to receive aid to the extent of deficiency. Need would be the sole measure of entitlement and irrelevant exclusions such as those based on age, family composition or situation, degree of disability, presumption of income not actually available to the applicant, low earning capacity, filial responsibility, or alleged employability would not conform with requirements of this program. Provision for immediate emergency aid when needed would also be required.

4. ELIGIBILITY DETERMINATION

Applicants for aid would establish their initial eligibility by personal statements or simple inquiry relating to their financial situation and family composition, subject only to subsequent sample review conducted in such manner as to protect their dignity, privacy, and constitutional rights.

5. CHILD AND YOUTH WELFARE SERVICES

The Federal Government would also specify the required components for child and youth welfare services to be included within the comprehensive new program. These would include protective and social services for children in a vulnerable situation, foster care placement in homes and institutions at reasonable rates of reimbursement, adoptive placement services, services to unmarried mothers, homemaker services, day care, other types of group service, provisions for specialized institutional care, probation and school social service (where not otherwise available), special programs for young people, and services related to the licensing of nongovernmental programs. Special provisions would be required for young people coming to the attention of authorities for unlawful or antisocial acts or believed to be vulnerable to such activity.

It is the goal of the Council that adequate child welfare services should be available to all children in need of them as a matter of enforceable legal right. Recognizing, however, the practical difficulty of assuring the universal availability of a full range of services immediately, it is recommended that the Federal Government distinguish between services which must be available to all eligible children and those which may be included in the comprehensive program on a progressively expanding basis within the same financing pattern.

6. OTHER SOCIAL SERVICES

The comprehensive State plan would also include other specified social services for families, older persons, individuals with special problems relating to health or other handicaps, and for a better ordering of community social resources. Again a distinction would be made between those to which individuals would be entitled by legal right on the basis of universal availability and those approved for inclusion within the State plan on a basis of progressive coverage. Examples of such social services would include the following: neighborhood advice and referral centers; services to assist the aged and homebound in meeting their medical, housing, recreational, social and activity needs; supportive services for mothers with special problems; social services related to health needs including family planning; services to advance employability—including aid in moving to new locations promising employment opportunity; and community planning services.

7. LEGAL RIGHTS

Entitlement to all benefits and services within this program would be protected by the following legally enforceable rights: (1) the right to apply and receive prompt, objective, and impartial determination of eligibility for and provision of benefit or service, (2) the right to be given a fair hearing against unacceptable judgments, by an impartial appeals agent, (3) the right to representation in appeals, by an attorney whose services and costs would be compensated by the agency if not otherwise provided for, (4) the right to court review, and (5) the obligation on the agency to publicize the conditions of entitlement to all benefits and services. The right to services would be conditioned on the need for service rather than income level.

8. PERSONNEL

Because the fulfillment of all these objectives depends upon a dramatic increase in the present limited national pool of professional social workers, social work aides, and related auxiliary personnel, special legislation for Federal financial aid to encourage and expand the training of such workers is essential to this plan.

9. STATES' SHARE

The State's share in the financing of this comprehensive program would be established each year on a total dollar basis determined by objective criteria related to its fiscal capacity and effort.

10. FEDERAL SHARE

For States operating under this program of basic social guarantees the Federal Government would assume the full financial responsibility for the difference in cost between the State's share and the total cost of the new program. This constitutes in effect a revolutionary reversal of roles of the Federal and State governments in the financing pattern. Under the present system it is assumed that the primary responsibility for determining the scope, level of benefits, and financing of the various components of a public welfare program rests with the States. Under the new proposal national standards of performance would be recognized as calling for an equivalent national assumption of financial responsibility by the Federal Government. Within this pattern, since no differentials would be applied among types of expenditures, Federal auditing would be limited to actual expenditures and program performance in terms of required Federal standards. States would, of course, be required either to finance their share by State funds or to make comparable financial arrangements with their political subdivisions to assure equitable and universal standards throughout the State.

11. INTERIM OPTION

States not yet prepared to participate in the new nationwide program could continue on a transitional but limited interim basis to operate under the existing titles. States' rights and State options would thus be protected during the period of accommodation but the fiscal, policy, and administrative advantages to the States of a plan which fixes and limits their total financial obligation in relationship to their fiscal capacity would be a powerful incentive to cooperate in this new plan of partnership. The simplification of accounting, reporting, and audit procedure alone would eliminate many of the complexities and confusions that presently plague Federal-State relationships.

Answers to Some Basic Questions

CAN WE AFFORD THIS PROPOSAL?

America is not only a country of actual, advancing, and virtually unlimited potential material prosperity, it is also a country committed to high social aspirations. The elimination of poverty and the achievement for all its people of social justice, basic security, and opportunities for self-realization are the announced goals of the Great Society. We have the resources in productivity and institutional adaptability to realize these aspirations for our own people without sacrificing our obligations to the peace and development of the rest of the world. It is not only our present national income and growth rate that justify this assumption; it is also our faith in America's capacity to make continuing advances in the most effective development and use of its vast resources.

Public welfare, as the ultimate source of protection against poverty and social deprivation, has its unique role to play in this great national undertaking. But it is one of many measures through which we are seeking to reduce the extent of such economic and social hardships. At present it is expected to do too much in some situations and too little in others. This is so because we have not yet sufficiently expanded those other measures that can prevent poverty before it occurs and thus free public welfare for its essential social service task. It should not be expected to serve either as a universal panacea or a universal scapegoat for all the ills of society. Measures to prevent poverty should reduce its burden and thereby bring the cost of doing its own job within manageable proportions.

Much of the cost of an adequate program of basic guarantees against poverty and social deprivation can and should be reduced by measures to assure adequately paid jobs to all who can and should work, an adequate system of replacement income through the proven mechanism of social insurance for those no longer able to work, an adequate network of educational and health measures, and adequate legal protections for those vulnerable to discrimination and exploitation. Others are intrinsic to the social task of public welfare and must be met if the promise of a Great Society is to be achieved. For the very complexity of the social organization, on which our vaunted prosperity depends, demands an equivalent assumption of social responsibility toward its individual members. Not only can we well afford the costs involved, but we can *not* afford to ignore the responsibility to further this adaption at all levels of our community life. This is the core job of public welfare to the achievement of which the Advisory Council's recommendations are directed.

WHY A NATIONAL PROBLEM?

The United States is a single Nation, operating within a nationwide economic system, and committed to a single set of social values. The mobility of its population is not only necessary to the functioning of the economy but is guaranteed by the Constitution. Its citizens have the right to expect comparable protections wherever they live and wherever they may move in the interests of their own and the Nation's welfare. Only through the leadership of the Federal Government, agent of all the American people, can this goal be achieved. Not only does it require a national program standard but a plan of financing which recognizes that the costs and burdens of such a standard tend to fall most heavily on those areas of the country least able to bear them. Experience has shown that the Federal Government must be prepared to carry the additional cost to the States of the standards it imposes if they are to be effective. A guarantee which is not supported by adequate nationwide requirements and financing is—in the realities of modern America—no guarantee at all.

WHY A PLAN OF FEDERAL-STATE COOPERATION?

Public welfare has by tradition and Constitutional interpretation been an administrative responsibility of the States and their political subdivisions. There are many advantages in building on this existing nationwide institutional base and the Council believes its proposal would successfully reconcile the values of national program standards with decentralized administration. Alternative plans for Federal administration of minimum income guarantees seem to assume that we will never be able to prevent or greatly reduce poverty by other measures and must, therefore, retool our assistance program on a depersonalized basis to carry a major part of the load. The Council's recommendation, on the other hand, assumes that a reduction in the extent of preventable poverty will serve to emphasize the individualizing service role of public welfare as a comprehensive program of aid and services functioning at a neighborhood level.

Recognizing, however, that the success of any innovation depends upon its acceptability to those with the means and authority to make it work, the Council recommends a limited transitional period during which the States would have the option to continue under the existing assistance and child welfare titles of the Social Security Act. Frequently time is required for States to evaluate the full advantages of a new proposal and make the necessary legislative and administrative changes. The Council's recommendation in this respect follows the precedent of optional alternatives already adopted by the Congress with respect to titles XVI, XIX and the provisions for social service reimbursement but offers an unprecedented incentive in its financial and administrative advantages to the States as described below.

WHY THE NEW PATTERN OF FINANCIAL SHARING?

Under the Council's proposal, which is the very essence of simplicity, the States would be offered a new kind of relationship to the Federal program: basic Federal financing on a lump sum residual basis in return for (1) the adoption of minimum national program standards and (2) the investment of a fixed State share which would be predetermined according to objective criteria related to fiscal capacity and effort. States wishing to use their own funds to move above the prescribed national minimum would, of course, be encouraged to do so. But within the prescribed national standards the responsibility of the States would be fixed.

There are clear advantages to both the Federal and State administering agencies in such a plan. It would obviate much of the elaborate paperwork now made by after-the-fact auditing of individual expenditures to meet complex reimbursement formulas. It would overcome the differentials in Federal matching which have discriminated so severely against children under both the AFDC and child welfare programs. It would give the States great freedom in the internal organization of their programs and the distribution of their resources.

But the principal advantage is that it would clearly implement the concept of minimum national standards by placing on the Federal Government the full responsibility for the additional costs of the policies and levels of benefit it prescribes.

WHY A NATIONAL FLOOR
UNDER ASSISTANCE PAYMENTS?

Present variations in the levels and scope of income guarantee are unconscionable by any measure. Once the practical limitation of State fiscal capacity has been eliminated by the plan of financing proposed by the Council the logic of nationwide Federal standards becomes incontestable. Just as minimum wage legislation places a floor under most wages so such a standard would place a practical floor under the American level of living. Differentials in the costing of such a level of living could be objectively determined by periodic spot checks such as those now made by the Labor and Agriculture Departments.

There are many advantages to the States themselves in such a national floor. For the States where standards are now low it would act as a powerful lever in upgrading the economic level of the whole population. For the States where standards are higher it removes the argument for residence restrictions based on the assumption that assistance serves as an incentive to migration. But the greater long run advantage lies in the fact that people who are in fact moving under the inexorable pressure of labor-market changes would not bring with them the accumulated handicaps imposed by prior economic deprivation.

For the Nation as a whole a floor under income constitutes a clear declaration of conscience and of practical intention to move above that level. All our experience has shown that it is the practical minimum which acts as a lever on other sources of income in the total dynamic of income policy. The Council does not recommend a floor under income on the defeatist assumption that millions of Americans must settle for a minimum level of living dependent for its financing on the more affluent majority. Its advocacy of this step is based on the positive belief that this is a practical step toward minimizing that depressed minority by assuring a guaranteed level of living and service.

WHY ARE SERVICES ESSENTIAL TO A PROGRAM
OF BASIC SOCIAL GUARANTEES?

The goal of the Great Society assumes a social setting in which all individuals and families are able to realize their full potential for self-realization and participation in community life. This means that every child should be assured the supportive care necessary to his growth and development, that every individual should have available to him necessary help when age, disability, or isolation creates need beyond the scope of his personal or family resources, that no one should feel lost in the present day variety of specialized programs, and that no community should lack a focus of responsible leadership in assuring that existing needs are met and new services developed as new needs emerge. This is the essential service task.

The Council's recommendations assume that the program of basic social guarantees must combine provision for these services with those for assuring minimum income and that these services should be available as a matter of legal right to all who need them. From the point of view of individuals and families experiencing difficulty or needing help, their problems do not appear in neatly segmented categories; their need is for a single source of aid or guidance. The overburdened mother suddenly left with several children may need day care or other services as much as income. The chronically ill older person requiring constant care needs help in locating as well as paying for a nursing home or other suitable arrangements. But within the proposed comprehensive financing pattern the responsible public welfare agency would have much wider freedom than at present in organizing the actual administration of specialized services in such a way as to make the best use of available resources in meeting actual need.

The Council proposes that the concept of legal entitlement to specified services be extended as rapidly as universal availability can be assured. This challenge is nowhere more apparent than in the area of our oldest social service responsibility, that of child welfare services. The vitality of any society can be measured by the way it treats the children on whom its own future health depends. Adults who in childhood have failed to receive the physical and emotional nourishment necessary for their own best development become, in their turn, inadequate parents, poor citizens, and economic misfits, incapable of the adaptations required by our technological society. Somewhere this cycle must be broken and this is the task of those social services broadly covered by the term "child welfare." The Council proposes that these services be extended to all who need them on the basis of a legally enforceable right.

Historically child welfare services have been centered on the most obviously vulnerable child: the child left without adequate adult protection because of death, illness, desertion, neglect, abuse, or inadequacy on the part of one or both parents. Substitute care has been provided in the form of placement in a foster home or institution or through adoption. Recently the concept of child welfare has widened to include measures to improve the situation of the child in his own home through the counseling of parents, the provision of ancillary services, such as day care and other group activities, specialized services for children with particular physical or psychological handicaps, etc., and the provision of homemaker service when the mother is ill or absent or otherwise unable to meet her basic responsibilities to the family. The potential scope for services of these kinds is almost unlimited and offers a new frontier in our increasingly service oriented economy.

The existing program of child welfare services has pioneered in all these areas but coverage is so spotty both geographically and in scope of benefits that it offers little guarantee of protection to the Nation's children. Some of the most vulnerable, especially children in minority groups, have had the least protection where they need the most. Adapting to these needs and deprivations as best they can, today's neglected children become tomorrow's social problems. The Council believes that a nationwide guarantee of protection and help to these children should have a top priority in the Great Society program.

While child welfare services have the longest history among the social services, the role of services generally in our society is currently experiencing an explosive growth in extent and variety. On all sides new developments and experiments are responding to the demands of an increasingly complex, changing, and urbanized environment in which the traditional role of family and neighborly mutual aid requires these supports and supplementation of organized measures. Some of these services are highly specialized requiring the competence of professional social workers while others, under professional supervision and organization, can be effectively rendered by individuals with special but subprofessional training. For example, the family of small children temporarily deprived by illness of a mother's care or the homebound elderly person of limited strength and mobility can be helped to maintain his accustomed way of life by a homemaker trained for that particular function, working under professional supervision.

Services are important not only in assisting families and individuals in situations of special crisis and continuing need; they also become increasingly essential as the inescapable specialization of community services confronts people with a complex and often baffling maze of benefits and services. People need a readily accessible source of advice and counsel in negotiating the complexities of finding the best answer to all requirements and desires. Neighborhood centers should be universally available as a source of advice, help, and service to people of all income levels. For while poverty compounds the difficulties that create a need for social services, the pressures of modern life do not limit this need to the poor.

Helping individuals is, however, only one side of the social service job. As the need and demand for social services grow so does the complex task of organizing community resources—governmental, voluntary, and the traditional method of neighborhood self-help—in a way that creates a coherent network of answers to those needs and demands. Provision must be assured not only for this kind of coordinated approach to social services but for one in which all elements of the local community, including those who need and benefit from such services, have a voice in the way they are provided.

The service functions of public welfare, while less conspicuous than those of assistance in the present scene, stand on the frontier of a new phase in American social development. Already a majority of those in our working force are engaged in service occupations. As technological developments increasingly turn over to machines the traditional jobs of producing and distributing material goods, the expansion of needed services opens up new careers for those whose labor is freed from these ancient imperatives. Social services, like those in education, health and recreation, are not only needed by people in their role as consumers but are also a necessary development in furnishing them with outlets to serve their society in the role of workers.

WHY EMPHASIZE LEGAL RIGHT AND ENTITLEMENT?

All social welfare programs are based on the recognition of a social risk which warrants social remedy in the form of special benefits and protections. Public assistance is a remedy for the risk of economic deprivation and child welfare a protection against the risk to a child of failure of normal parental care. But a protection which is not available to all who incur the risk under a rule of enforceable law is a gratuity subject to elements of chance or the caprice of prejudices of those who determine its policies or control its administration.

The federally aided programs of public assistance under the Social Security Act are the one area of social protection against the risk of actual poverty which carries built-in provisions for legally enforceable entitlement. Recently the concept of legal entitlement to public assistance has rceived new emphasis through rulings of the Federal department and the growing interest of the legal profession. The Advisory Council wishes to give its full support to this development and recommends its further extension to all areas of public assistance and social services.

The very concept of a guarantee assumes objectively determinable rights for all those who are eligible for the benefit or protection. Two conditions are essential if such a right or guarantee is to become a practical reality: (1) the benefits must be available in sufficient quantity, quality, and distribution to meet the need toward which they are directed on the basis of a "reasonable classification" and (2) the practical means must be provided to assure their equitable availability to all those entitled to them. While the latter requirement is best served by a mechanism for appeal outside the line of administration with an ultimate recourse to the court system in cases of ambiguity, it also requires clearly and publicly stated policies toward which the appeal may be directed and the services of a professional—typically an attorney—in marshalling the facts and arguments in behalf of his client.

There are many today who express a sincere anxiety or alarm lest the growing interdependence of people in the modern world, reflected in turn in their growing dependence on the instrumentalities of government, throw into imbalance the carefully designed weighting of rights reserved to the individual and powers assigned to the State. These people fear that a beneficent State may become, in effect, an oppressive State. But again there is little value in closing one's eyes to the practical needs of the day or mourning for the different conditions of an earlier time. The only practical remedy for this legitimate anxiety is to accompany each new assignment of responsibility to governmental programs with equivalent protections for the rights of those affected by those programs. In this sense the Advisory Council's emphasis on rights and guarantees to the citizen in his most vulnerable situations follows the highest tradition of American democracy.

Summary of Recommendations

In setting forth a comprehensive program of Basic Social Guarantees, the Advisory Council on Public Welfare has presented its central recommendations as follows:

The Advisory Council on Public Welfare Recommends a Minimum Standard for Public Assistance Payments Below Which no State May Fall.

The Advisory Council on Public Welfare urges prompt, decisive action to bring the amounts of public assistance payments throughout this Nation up to a minimum American standard of health and decency.

The Advisory Council on Public Welfare Recommends a Nationwide Comprehensive Program of Public Assistance Based Upon a Single Criterion: Need.

The Advisory Council on Public Welfare strongly urges legislation that will make possible comprehensive public assistance programs based upon the only relevant eligibility requirement—need.

The Advisory Council on Public Welfare Recommends a Uniform and Simple Plan for Federal-State Financial Sharing in Costs of All Public Welfare Programs: The Plan Should Provide for Equitable and Reasonable Fiscal Effort Among States and Should Recognize the Relative Fiscal Capacity of the Federal and State Governments to Finance Adequate and Comprehensive Programs.

It is the conviction of the Advisory Council on Public Welfare that the adoption of a single uniform formula, which reverses the responsibilities of the Federal and State governments for basic financial support and which recognizes varying State fiscal capacities and effort, is essential.

The Advisory Council on Public Welfare Recommends Prompt Extension of Coverage and Liberalization of Benefits Under the Social Insurance Programs.

The Advisory Council on Public Welfare is of the opinion that the adequacy of social insurance benefits should not remain static but be kept in proper relationship to living costs and wage levels.

The Advisory Council on Public Welfare Recommends That Social Services Through Public Welfare Programs Be Strengthened and Extended and Be Readily Accessible as a Matter of Right at All Times to All Who Need Them. The Advisory Council Considers It Urgent That Public Welfare Programs Be Structured to Provide Ever More Effective Social Services, Medical Assistance, and Income Maintenance in Readily Accessible Local Centers, Properly Staffed and Organized. Increasingly, They May Become Associated with a Complex of Special Services.

The Advisory Council on Public Welfare recognizes that child welfare services constitute a major component in the proposed comprehensive program of social guarantees.

The Advisory Council on Public Welfare believes that child welfare and youth services, as well as other services of public welfare agencies, should be available as a right, subject to enforcement in the courts.

The Advisory Council on Public Welfare Recommends That the Present Work Training Programs Be Strengthened and Become Permanent Parts of the Public Welfare Structure.

The Advisory Council on Public Welfare Recommends That One Consolidated Program Within the Welfare Administration for the Prevention, Treatment, and Control of Juvenile Delinquency Be Established.

The Advisory Council on Public Welfare urges that existing gaps in the medical assistance program be closed through Federal sharing in the cost of medical assistance for the medically needy between 21 and 65 years of age.

Although it is not required until July 1, 1975, the Advisory Council on Public Welfare believes it is not only feasible, but necessary, to advance the provision of dental services, particularly for children, to a much earlier date. The Advisory Council on Public Welfare calls upon the Welfare Administration to exert strong leadership for the States in the development of family planning services part of their medical and social services.

The Advisory Council on Public Welfare Recommends That All Public Welfare Programs Receiving Federal Funds Be Administered Consistent With the Principle of Public Welfare as a Right.

The Advisory Council on Public Welfare further emphasizes that to achieve this recommendation Federal law and policy must be explicit in requiring that all Federally supported public welfare programs provide for:

A readily available and understandable application process for aid, whether for financial assistance of social services, including readily available and conveniently located public welfare offices in areas where people live;

Promptness in all administrative actions within specifically stated time limits;

A method or mechanism to assure legal representation for all who wish it, including payment for necessary costs of such representation;

An independent appeals system, with procedures and mechanisms so devised that decisions on appeals are truly independent judgments even when made within the framework of the administering agency;

An opportunity for aggrieved individuals to test the reasonableness of policies of the agency as well as the application of policies through the appeals process;

A positive program for informing recipients and applicants of their rights, utilizing all appropriate means of communication.

The Advisory Council on Public Welfare believes that there is great urgency for the emphatic assertion of public welfare's accountability for the protection of individual rights, and for the scrupulous observance of the individual rights of the people it serves.

The Advisory Council on Public Welfare Recommends Prompt Action To Enable the Welfare Administration To Expand Its Support of All Phases of Recruitment, Education and Training for Welfare Personnel, Including Pre-Professional, Professional, and Advanced Social Work Education; Vocational Training for Sub-Professional Aides and Technicians; and Research and Development in More Effective Use of Available Personnel.

The Advisory Council on Public Welfare urges that sharply increased Federal support of social work education be made available so that the knowledge and skills of social work can contribute fully to our National effort to assure the welfare of all the people.

The Advisory Council on Public Welfare Recommends That the Welfare Administration Be Enabled To Mount a Social Welfare Research Effort Commensurate in Size and Scope With the National Investment in Its Programs.

The Advisory Council on Public Welfare urges that the present Division of Research be greatly strengthened as rapidly as possible so that it becomes a national social welfare research center which provides (a) a setting for research and development in the area of human resources, (b) a center for the dissemination of social information, (c) a facility for collection, storage, and retrieval of social statistics and other relevant information, (d) a stimulus to creativity and innovation in the monitoring and solving of social problems, and (e) a vehicle for continuing assessment of the social state of the Nation.

The Advisory Council on Public Welfare Recommends That the Resources of Staff and Administrative Funds for the Welfare Administration and for State Public Welfare Agencies Be Expanded Commensurate With Needs for Staff and Facilities Necessary to Improve and Update Program Administration.

It is the belief of the Advisory Council on Public Welfare that significant improvements in administration can be made by immediately furnishing the Welfare Administration adequate resources to exert maximum leadership within the framework of the existing structure.

The Advisory Council on Public Welfare Recommends That the International Office of the Welfare Organization Be Given Necessary Authority and Resources to Strengthen its Role As a Major Participant in International Social Welfare Programs.

The Advisory Council on Public Welfare Recommends That Public Welfare Agencies Continuously Seek Greater Public Understanding of Their Programs, Methods, and Objectives Through All Appropriate Means.

It is the opinion of the Advisory Council on Public Welfare that a clearly defined program of public interpretation and enlistment of wide community advice on and understanding of the public welfare program is fundamental and essential to more effective administration.

Pending full achievement of the recommended comprehensive public welfare program, the Advisory Council on Public Welfare makes the following recommendations:

Temporary Legislation, Enacted in 1961, Which Extends the Aid to Families With Dependent Children Program to Include Needy Families With an Unemployed Parent, Should Be Made Permanent and Mandatory Upon the States, and Provision Made for Covering More of the Unemployed Than Many of the States Now Include.

Temporary Legislation, Enacted in 1962, Providing AFDC Payments in Nonprofit Private Child Care Institutions for Children Whose Placement and Care is the Responsibility of the Public Welfare Agency, Should Be Made Permanent.

Temporary Legislation, Enacted in 1962, Providing for Protective Payments to a Qualified Individual Interested in the Welfare of an AFDC Family When States Have Evidence That There is Inability To Manage Money and That Continued Money Payments Would Be Contrary to the Benefit of the Child, Should Be Made Permanent.

The Authorization for the Expenditure of Appropriated Funds, Provided in 1962 and Limited to Fiscal Years Prior to July 1967, To Support Demonstration Projects in State and Local Public Assistance Agencies So That New Methods, Techniques, and Practices Can Be Tested, Should Be Made Permanent and Substantially Increased.

The Legislation, Enacted in 1961, Authorizing Temporary Assistance for United States Citizens and Their Dependents Returned From Foreign Countries, Should Be Made Permanent.

Temporary Legislation, Enacted in 1962, Which Provides Federal Participation in Certain Costs of Community Work and Training Programs Designed To Conserve and Develop Work Skills of the Unemployed Parent Receiving AFDC, Should Be Improved and Made Permanent. To build into the public assistance program resources that will assure training or retraining of all employable recipients or potential recipients, the Advisory Council on Public Welfare further recommends that:

a. a training component be required as part of the work program;

b. Federal financial participation be provided in the costs of project materials, supervision, training, and in associated costs; and

c. children 18 to 22 years of age be included where the State's AFDC program does not include this age group.

With the Expiration of Public Law 87–274, as Amended, New Legislation Should Provide Authorization to the Welfare Administration for Grants-in-Aid and Project Funds for the Prevention, Treatment, and Control of Juvenile Delinquency.

In Their State Plans for Public Assistance, States Should Be Required to Include All Types of Persons Eligible Under Federal Law.

Financial Aid Should Be Available to a Low Income Family Otherwise Eligible Whose Earnings From Employment Are Insufficient to Provide the Basic Essentials of Living.

Exemption of a Reasonable Proportion of Earnings of Children and Relatives Caring for Them in an AFDC Family Should Be Mandatory Upon the States; and Earnings Exemptions Should Be Made Consistent for All Assistance Programs.

The APTD Program (Title XIV) Should Be Broadened by Deleting the Eligibility Requirement of "Permanent and Total" Disability and by Extending the Program to Include Needy Disabled Children Under 18 Years of Age.

The Age Requirement for Old Age Assistance and Medical Assistance for the Aged (Title I) Should Be Lowered From the Present 65 Years of Age to 60 Years of Age.

The Age Requirement Under the AFDC Program Should Be Extended to Include Children up to 22 Years of Age if They Are Regularly Attending a School, College, or University, or a Course of Vocational or Technical Training, and Should Be Made Mandatory Upon the States.

No Liens Should Be Permitted to Be Placed Against the Real Property of Any Recipient of Federally Aided Public Assistance. Rather, All Federal Legislation in This General Area Should Be Made Consistent With the Provisions of Title XIX.

Relatives Should Not Be Required to Support Those Needing Public Assistance Beyond Spouses and Parents of Minor Children.

Without Any Change in the Present Grants-in-Aid Under Title V, Part 3, Costs of Certain Expenses in the Administration of Child Welfare and Youth Services (Including Professional Staff and Their Immediate Supporting Clerical Staff, and Costs of Professional Education) Should Be Financed Immediately on the Same Open-Ended Matching Basis as Provided for Comparable State Costs in the Administration of Title IV of the Social Security Act (Aid to Families With Dependent Children) and the Federal Governemnt Should Establish Adequate Standards for All Such Services.

Provision Should Be Made for Increased Staff in Both the Headquarters and Regional Offices of the Welfare Administration Commensurate With the Increased Federal Responsibility Placed Upon It by Recent Legislation.

To Accelerate the Trend Toward Comparability and Equity Among Public Welfare Programs From State to State, Any New Monies or Released Funds Due to Changes in Any Title of the Social Security Act, Prior to the Full Adoption of the Proposed New Method of Financing Described in This Report, Should Contain a Maintenance of State Effort Provision Comparable to That in the 1965 Amendments to the Social Security Act.

The Nixon Administration's
Welfare Reform:
The Family Assistance Plan

The Family Assistance Plan (FAP) is a legislative expression of the effort to reform welfare by applying the principles of negative income taxation to an expanded system of public assistance. (See Lampman proposal, Ch. 5). Justified as a plan for structural change, FAP expands the coverage of welfare through a low-level negative income tax for families with children, seeks to reduce the geographical variation of present welfare benefits, and, as a bid for political support, emphasizes work incentives and sanctions. FAP, introduced in 1969, culminates the discrediting of welfare without fully taking on the larger and more expensive task of eradicating poverty.

To the Congress of the United States:

A measure of the greatness of a powerful nation is the character of the life it creates for those who are powerless to make ends meet.

If we do not find the way to become a working nation that properly cares for the dependent, we shall become a Welfare State that undermines the incentive of the working man.

"Welfare Reform: A Message from the President of the United States," House Document No. 91–146, *Congressional Record*, Vol. 115, No. 136, The House of Representatives, 91st Congress, First Session, H7239–7241.

The President's Proposals for Welfare Reform and Social Security Amendments, Hearings Before the Committee on Ways and Means, House of Representatives, 91st Congress, 1st Session, Part 1 of 7 (October 15 and 16, 1969), (Washington, D.C.: U.S. Government Printing Office, 1970), pp. 103–109, 49–63.

The present welfare system has failed us—it has fostered family breakup, has provided very little help in many States and has even deepened dependency by all too often making it more attractive to go on welfare than to go to work.

I propose a new approach that will make it more attractive to go to work than to go on welfare, and will establish a nationwide minimum payment to dependent families with children.

I propose that the Federal government pay a basic income to those American families who cannot care for themselves in whichever State they live.

I propose that dependent families receiving such income be given good reason to go to work *by making the first sixty dollars a month they earn completely their own, with no deductions from their benefits.*

I propose that we *make available an addition to the incomes of the "working poor,"* to encourage them to go on working and to eliminate the possibility of making more from welfare than from wages.

I propose that these payments be made upon certification of income, with demeaning and costly investigations replaced by simplified reviews and spot checks and with *no eligibility requirement that the household be without a father.* That present requirement in many States has the effect of breaking up families and contributes to delinquency and violence.

I propose that all employable persons who choose to accept these payments be required to register for work or job training and *be required to accept that work or training,* provided suitable jobs are available either locally or if transportation is provided. Adequate and convenient day care would be provided children wherever necessary to enable a parent to train or work. The only exception to this work requirement would be mothers of pre-school children.

I propose *a major expansion of job training and day care facilities,* so that current welfare recipients able to work can be set on the road to self-reliance.

I propose that we also *provide uniform Federal payment minimums for the present three categories of welfare aid to adults*—the aged, the blind and the disabled.

This would be total welfare reform—the transformation of a system frozen in failure and frustration into a system that would work and would encourage people to work.

Accordingly, we have stopped considering human welfare in isolation. The new plan is part of an overall approach which includes a comprehensive new Manpower Training Act, and a plan for a system of revenue sharing with the States to help provide all of them with necessary budget relief. Messages on manpower training and revenue sharing will follow this message tomorrow and the next day, and the three should be considered as parts of a whole approach to what is clearly a national problem.

NEED FOR NEW DEPARTURES

A welfare system is a success when it takes care of people who cannot take care of themselves and when it helps employable people climb toward independence.

A welfare system is a failure when it takes care of those who *can* take care of themselves, when it drastically varies payments in different areas, when it breaks up families, when it perpetuates a vicious cycle of dependency, when it strips human beings of their dignity.

America's welfare system is a failure that grows worse every day.

First, it fails the recipient: In many areas, benefits are so low that we have hardly begun to take care of the dependent. And there has been no light at the end of poverty's tunnel. After four years of inflation, the poor have generally become poorer.

Second, it fails the taxpayer: Since 1960, welfare costs have doubled and the number on the rolls has risen from 5.8 million to over 9 million, all in a time when unemployment was low. The taxpayer is entitled to expect government to devise a system that will help people lift themselves out of poverty.

Finally, it fails American society: By breaking up homes, the present welfare system has added to social unrest and robbed millions of children of the joy of childhood; widely varying payments among regions, it has helped to draw millions into the slums of our cities.

The situation has become intolerable. Let us examine the alternatives available:

—We could permit the welfare momentum to continue to gather speed by our inertia; by 1975 this would result in 4 million more Americans on welfare rolls at a cost of close to 11 billion dollars a year, with both recipients and taxpayers shortchanged.

—We could tinker with the system as it is, adding to the patchwork of modifications and exceptions. That has been the approach of the past, and it has failed.

—We could adopt a "guaranteed minimum income for everyone," which would appear to wipe out poverty overnight. It would also wipe out the basic economic motivation for work, and place an enormous strain on the industrious to pay for the leisure of the lazy.

—Or, we could adopt a totally new approach to welfare, designed to assist those left far behind the national norm, and provide all with the motivation to work and a fair share of the opportunity to train.

This Administration, after a careful analysis of all the alternatives, is committed to a new departure that will find a solution for the welfare problem. The time for denouncing the old is over; the time for devising the new is now.

People usually follow their self-interest.

This stark fact is distressing to many social planners who like to look at problems from the top down. Let us abandon the ivory tower and consider the real world in all we do.

In most States, welfare is provided only when there is no father at home to provide support. If a man's children would be better off on welfare than with the low wage he is able to bring home, wouldn't he be tempted to leave home?

If a person spent a great deal of time and effort to get on the welfare rolls, wouldn't he think twice about risking his eligibility by taking a job that might not last long?

In each case, welfare policy was intended to limit the spread of dependency; in practice, however, the effect has been to increase dependency and remove the incentive to work.

We fully expect people to follow their self-interest in their business dealings; why should we be surprised when people follow their self-interest in their welfare dealings? That is why we propose a plan in which it is in the interest of every employable person to do his fair share of work.

THE OPERATION OF THE NEW APPROACH

1. *We would assure an income foundation throughout every section of America for all parents who cannot adequately support themselves and their children.* For a family of four with income of $720 or less, this payment would be $1,600 a year; for a family of four with $2,000, this payment would supplement that income by $960 a year.

Under the present welfare system, each State provides "Aid to Families with Dependent Children," a program we propose to replace. The Federal government shares the cost, but each State establishes key eligibility rules and determines how much income support will be provided to poor families. The result has been an uneven and unequal system. The 1969 benefits average for a family of four is $171 a month across the Nation, but individual State averages range from $263 down to $39 a month.

A new Federal minimum of $1,600 a year cannot claim to provide comfort to a family of four, but the present low of $468 a year cannot claim to provide even the basic necessities.

The new system would do away with the inequity of very low benefit levels in some States, and of State-by-State variations in eligibility tests, by establishing a Federally-financed income floor with a national definition of basic eligibility.

States will continue to carry an important responsibility. In 30 States the Federal basic payment will be less than the present levels of combined Federal and State payments. These States will be required to maintain the current level of benefits, but in no case will a State be required to spend more than 90 per cent of its present welfare cost. The Federal government will not only provide the "floor," but it will assume 10 per cent of the benefits now being paid by the States as their part of welfare costs.

In 20 States, the new payment would exceed the present average benefit payments, in some cases by a wide margin. In 10 of these States, where benefits are lowest and poverty often the most severe, the payments will raise benefit levels substantially. For 5 years, every State will be required to continue to spend at least half of what they are now spending on welfare, to supplement the Federal base.

For the typical "welfare family"—a mother with dependent children and no outside income—the new system would provide a basic national minimum payment. A mother with three small children would be assured an annual income of at least $1,600.

For the family headed by an employed father or working mother, the same basic benefits would be received, but $60 per month of earnings would be "disregarded" in order to make up the costs of working and provide a strong advantage in holding a job. The wage earner could also keep 50 per cent of his benefits as his earnings rise above that $60 per month. A family of four, in which the father earns $2,000 in a year, would receive payments of $960, for a total income of $2,960.

For the *aged, the blind and the disabled,* the present system varies benefit levels from $40 per month for an aged person in one State to $145 per month for the blind in another. The new system would establish a minimum payment of $65 per month for all three of these adult categories, with the Federal government contributing the first $50 and sharing in payments above that amount. This will raise the share of the financial burden borne by the Federal government for payments to these adults who cannot support themselves, and should pave the way for benefit increases in many States.

For the *single adult* who is not handicapped or aged, or for the *married couple without children,* the new system would not apply. Food stamps would continue to be available up to $300 per year per person, according to the plan I outlined last May in my message to the Congress on the food and nutrition needs of the population in poverty. For dependent families there will be an orderly substitution of food stamps by the new direct monetary payments.

2. *The new approach would end the blatant unfairness of the welfare system.*

In over half the States, families headed by unemployed men do not qualify for public assistance. In no State does a family headed by a father working full-time receive help in the current welfare system, no matter how little he earns. As we have seen, this approach to dependency has itself been a cause of dependency. It results in a policy that tends to force the father out of the house.

The new plan rejects a policy that undermines family life. It would end the substantial financial incentives to desertion. It would extend eligibility to *all* dependent families with children, without regard to whether the family is headed by a man or a woman. The effects of these changes upon human behavior would be an increased will to work, the survival of more marriages, the greater stability of families. We are determined to stop passing the cycle of dependency from generation to generation.

The most glaring inequity in the old welfare system is the exclusion of families who are working to pull themselves out of poverty. Families headed by a non-worker often receive more from welfare than families headed by a husband working full-time at very low wages. This has been rightly resented by the working poor, for the rewards are just the opposite of what they should be.

3. *The new plan would create a much stronger incentive to work.*

For people now on the welfare rolls, the present system discourages the move from welfare to work by cutting benefits too fast and too much as earnings begin. *The new system would encourage work by allowing the new worker to retain the first $720 of his yearly earnings without any benefit reduction.*

For people already working, but at poverty wages, the present system often encourages nothing but resentment and an incentive to quit and go on relief where that would pay more than work. The new plan, on the contrary, would provide a supplement that will help a low-wage worker—struggling to make ends meet—achieve a higher standard of living.

For an employable person who just chooses not to work, neither the present system nor the one we propose would support him, though both would continue to support other dependent members in his family.

However, a welfare mother with pre-school children should not face benefit reductions if she decides to stay home. It is not our intent that mothers of pre-school children must accept work. Those who can work and desire to do so, however, should have the opportunity for jobs and job training and access to day care centers for their children; this will enable them to support themselves after their children are grown.

A family with a member who gets a job would be permitted to retain all of the *first $60 monthly income*, amounting to $720 per year for a regular worker, *with no reduction of Federal payments*. The incentive to work in this provision is obvious. But there is another practical reason: going to work costs money. Expenses such as clothes, transportation, personal care, Social Security taxes and loss of income from odd jobs amount to substantial costs for the average family. Since a family does not begin to *add* to its net income until it surpasses the cost of working, in fairness, this amount should not be subtracted from the new payment.

After the first $720 of income, the *rest* of the earnings will result in a systematic reduction in payments.

I believe the vast majority of poor people in the United States prefer to work rather than have the government support their families. In 1968, 600,000 families left the welfare rolls out of an average caseload of 1,400,000 during the year, showing a considerable turnover, much of it voluntary.

However, there may be some who fail to seek or accept work, even with the strong incentives and training opportunities that will be provided. It would not be fair to those who willingly work, or to all taxpayers, to allow others to choose idleness when opportunity is available. Thus, they must accept training opportunities and jobs when offered, or give up their right to the new payments for themselves. No able-bodied person will have a "free ride" in a nation that provides opportunity for training and work.

4. *The bridge from welfare to work should be buttressed by training and child care programs.* For many, the incentives to work in this plan would be all that is necessary. However, there are other situations where these incentives need to be supported by measures that will overcome other barriers to employment.

I propose that *funds be provided for expanded training and job development programs* so that an additional 150,000 welfare recipients can become jobworthy during the first year.

Manpower training is a basic bridge to work for poor people, especially people with limited education, low skills and limited job experience. Manpower training programs can provide this bridge for many of our poor. In the new Manpower Training proposal to be sent to the Congress this week, the interrelationship with this new approach to welfare will be apparent.

I am also requesting authority, as a part of the new system, to provide child care for the 450,000 children of the $150,000 current welfare recipients to be trained.

The child care I propose is more than custodial. This Administration is committed to a new emphasis on child development in the first five years of life. The day care that would be part of this plan would be of a quality that will help in the development of the child and provide for its health and safety, and would break the poverty cycle for this new generation.

The expanded child care program would bring new opportunities along several lines: opportunities for the further involvement of private enterprise in providing high quality child care service; opportunities for volunteers; and opportunities for *training and employment in child care centers of many of the welfare mothers themselves.*

I am requesting a total of $600 million additional to fund these expanded training programs and child care centers.

5. *The new system will lessen welfare red tape and provide administrative cost savings.* To cut out the costly investigations so bitterly resented as "welfare snooping," the Federal payment will be based upon a certification of income, with spot checks sufficient to prevent abuses. The program will be administered on an automated basis, using the information and technical experience of the Social Security Administration, but, of course, will be entirely separate from the administration of the Social Security trust fund.

The States would be given the option of having the Federal government handle the payment of the State supplemental benefits on a reimbursable basis, so that they would be spared their present administrative burdens and so a single check could be sent to the recipient. These simplifications will save money and eliminate indignities; at the same time, welfare fraud will be detected and lawbreakers prosecuted.

6. *This new departure would require a substantial initial investment, but will yield future returns to the Nation.* This transformation of the welfare system will set in motion forces that will lessen dependency rather than perpetuate and enlarge it. A more productive population adds to real economic growth without inflation. The initial investment is needed now to stop the momentum of work-to-welfare, and to start a new momentum in the opposite direction.

The costs of welfare benefits for families with dependent children have been rising alarmingly the past several years, increasing from $1 billion in 1960 to an estimated $3.3 billion in 1969, of which $1.8 billion paid by the Federal government, and $1.5 billion is paid by the States. Based on current population and income data, the proposals I am making today will increase Federal costs during the first year by an estimated $4 billion, which includes $600 million for job training and child care centers.

The "start-up costs" of lifting many people out of dependency will ultimately cost the taxpayer far less than the chronic costs—in dollars and in national values—of creating a permanent under-class in America.

FROM WELFARE TO WORK

Since this Administration took office, members of the Urban Affairs Council, including officials of the Department of Health, Education, and Welfare, the Department of Labor, the Office of Economic Opportunity, the Bureau of the Budget, and other key advisers, have been working to develop a coherent, fresh approach to welfare, manpower training and revenue sharing.

I have outlined our conclusions about an important component of this approach in this message; the Secretary of HEW will transmit to the Congress the proposed legislation after the summer recess.

I urge the Congress to begin its study of these proposals promptly so that laws can be enacted and funds authorized to begin the new system as soon as possible. Sound budgetary policy must be maintained in order to put this plan into effect—especially the portion supplementing the wages of the working poor.

With the establishment of the new approach, the Office of Economic Opportunity will concentrate on the important task of finding new ways of opening economic opportunity for those who are able to work. Rather than focusing on income support activities, it must find means of providing opportunities for individuals to contribute to the full extent of their capabilities, and of developing and improving those capabilities.

This would be the effect of the transformation of welfare into "workfare," a new work-rewarding system:

For the first time, all dependent families with children in America, regardless of where they live, would be assured of minimum standard payments based upon uniform and single eligibility standards.

For the first time, the more than two million families who make up the "working poor" would be helped toward self-sufficiency and away from future welfare dependency.

For the first time, training and work opportunity with effective incentives would be given millions of families who would otherwise be locked into a welfare system for generations.

For the first time, the Federal government would make a strong contribution toward relieving the financial burden of welfare payments from State governments.

For the first time, every dependent family in America would be encouraged to stay together, free from economic pressure to split apart.

These are far-reaching effects. They cannot be purchased cheaply, or by piecemeal efforts. This total reform looks in a new direction; it requires new thinking, a new spirit and a fresh dedication to reverse the downhill course of welfare. In its first year, more than half the families participating in the program will have one member working or training.

We have it in our power to raise the standard of living and the realizable hopes of millions of our fellow citizens. By providing an equal chance at the starting line, we can reinforce the traditional American spirit of self-reliance and self-respect.

Richard Nixon

The White House,

August 11, 1969.

Appendix

Proposed Benefit Schedule
(*excluding all state benefits*)

Earned Income	New Benefit	Total Income
$ 0	$1600	$1600
500	1600	2100
1000	1460	2460
1500	1210	2710
2000	960	2960
2500	710	3210
3000	460	3460
3500	210	3710
4000	0	4000

(For a four-person family, with a basic payment standard of $1600 and an earned income disregard of $720.)

Explanation of the Bill:
Statement of Secretary of Health,
Education, and Welfare Robert H. Finch
in Explanation of the
Family Assistance Act of 1969

The Family Assistance Plan is a revolutionary effort to reform a welfare system in crisis. With this program and the Administration's proposed Food Stamp plan, the Federal Government launches a new strategy—*an income strategy*—to deal with our most critical domestic problems. For those among the poor who can become self-supporting, this strategy offers an avenue to greater income through expanded work incentives, training, and employment opportunities. For those who cannot work, there is a more adequate level of Federal support.

If the Family Assistance and Food Stamp proposals are enacted, we will have reduced the poverty gap in this country by some 59 per cent. In other words, these two programs taken together will cut by almost 60 per cent the difference between the total income of all Americans and the total amount they would have to earn in order to rise out of poverty. In one particular category of the poor, that of couples over 65 years of age, the Family Assistance Plan will in fact raise recipients' incomes above the poverty line altogether. This income strategy includes an Administration proposal for a 10 per cent increase in Social Security benefits, coupled with an automatic cost of living escalator. This is a real war on poverty and not just a skirmish.

The Failure of Welfare

On August 8 the President addressed the nation and called the present welfare system a failure. He said:

"Whether measured by the anguish of the poor themselves, or by the drastically mounting burden on the taxpayer, the present welfare system has to be judged a colossal failure. . . .

"What began on a small scale in the depression 30s has become a huge monster in the prosperous 60s. And the tragedy is not only that it is bringing States and cities to the brink of financial disaster, but also that it is failing to meet the elementary human, social and financial needs of the poor."

The failure of the system is most evident in the recent increases in welfare costs and caseloads. In this decade alone, total costs for the four federally-aided welfare programs have more than doubled, to a level now of about $6 billion.

In the Aid for Families with Dependent Children program (AFDC), costs have more than tripled since 1960 (to about $4 million at the present time) and the number of recipients has more than doubled (to some 6.2 million persons). Even more disturbing is the fact that the *proportion* of persons on AFDC is growing. In the 15 years since 1955, the proportion of children receiving assistance has doubled—from 30 children per 1,000 to about 60 per 1,000 at present.

Prospects for the future show no likelihood for relief from the present upward spiral. By conservative estimates, AFDC costs will double again by Fiscal Year 1975, and caseloads will increase by 50 to 60 per cent. Yet, the great irony is that despite these crushing costs, benefits remain below adequate levels in most States.

Moreover, the present AFDC program is built to fail. It embodies a set of inequities which help to cause its own destruction. First, it is characterized by unjustifiable discrepancies as between regions of the country. With no national standards for benefit levels and eligibility practices, AFDC payments now vary from an average of $39 per month for a family of four in Mississippi to $263 for such a family in New Jersey.

Second, it is inequitable in its treatment of male-headed families as opposed to those headed by a female. In no State is a male-headed family, where the mother is also in the home and the father is working full time for poverty wages, eligible for AFDC. In half the States, even families headed by unemployed males are still not eligible under the AFDC-UF program. On the other hand, families in poverty headed by women working full or part-time are almost universally covered. The result of this unfortunate discrimination is the creation of a powerful economic incentive for the father to leave home so that the State may better support his family than he can. For example, if a father employed full time in a low wage job is able to earn only $2000 per year, and welfare in the State would pay a fatherless family $3000 per year, his wife and children are financially 50 per cent better off if he leaves home. And this financial incentive has taken its toll. In 1940, only 30 per cent of the families on AFDC had absent fathers, but today the figure stands at over 70 per cent.

Third, AFDC imposes inequities between those who work and those who do not. Because families in poverty headed by working men are not covered, it is easily possible for such a working family to be less well off than the welfare family. And what could be more debilitating to the motivation to work to see the opportunity for one's family to be better off on welfare? Moreover, the present system further undercuts the incentive to work by reducing welfare payments too rapidly and by too much as the head of the household begins to work.

The Family Assistance Plan

This Administration began its formal inquiries into welfare reform even before the inauguration. From the report of the Transition Task Force on Welfare to the present time, a number of reform proposals have been considered. The final result reflects the best efforts of many different people in and out of government and in different Federal agencies.

This analysis led us to the conclusion that revolutionary *structural reform* in the system is required. The first priority of the Family Assistance Plan has been to remove, or at least minimize the inequities of present welfare policies. It is designed to strengthen family life and incentives for employment. This strategy may not pay off immediately, but unless this investment is made now, fundamental reform will be even more expensive in the future.

The Family Assistance Plan provides fiscal relief for hard pressed States and at the same time raises benefit levels for recipients in those areas where they are lowest. Of the $2.9 billion made available in new funds under the plan for benefits to families and to aged, blind and disabled adults, an estimated $700 million will have the effect of providing fiscal relief for the States and about $300 million will be for benefit increases for present recipients. But these goals, it must be said, cannot be our first priority at the present time. There are others who would invest more of our available resources in benefit increases or in a federalization of the program designed to provide maximum fiscal relief to the States. These are not easy priorities to weigh and balance, but we have concluded that —while those other approaches might be politically more popular in many respects—they only pour more Federal money into a system doomed to failure. The *system* must be changed, not just its payment levels or the division of labor between the Federal and State governments within it.

The technical operation of the Family Assistance Plan is described in the attached summary. This memorandum will review its major purposes.

First, it combines powerful work requirements and work incentives for employable recipients. By including the working poor—families in poverty headed by men working full time—the new plan much reduces and in many cases eliminates the inequity of treatment between those who work and those who do not. Second, by making it possible for a family to earn $60 per month without any reduction of benefits, a recipient will have a strong financial incentive to enter employment and will be able to recoup his expenses of going to work without a drop in total income. Third, the program includes a strong work requirement: those able bodied persons who refuse a training or suitable job opportunity lose their benefits. For this reason, the program is not a guaranteed annual income. It does not guarantee benefits to persons regardless of their attitudes; its support is reserved to those who are willing to support themselves. The work requirement is made effective by a new obligation of work registration. In order to be eligible for benefits, applicants must first register with their employment service office so that training and job opportunities can be efficiently communicated to them. Mothers with children under six are, however, exempted from this requirement of work and work registration and may elect to stay at home with their children without any loss in benefits.

Second, the Family Assistance Plan treats male and female-headed families equally. All families with children, whether headed by a male or female, will receive benefits if family income and resources are below the national eligibility levels. From this structural change in coverage flows one of the key advantages of the program in terms of family stability. No longer would an unemployed father have to leave the home for his family to qualify for benefits. In fact, the family is better off with him at home since its benefits are increased by his presence. And for employed men, the system greatly reduces and in some cases reverses the financial incentive to desert. In the example cited above of the father earning $2000 in a State where his family would receive $3000 on welfare, the Family Assistance Plan would supplement his wages by $960, giving the family $2960 in income and eliminating the financial incentive for the father to leave home.

Third, the program establishes a national minimum payment and national eligibility standards and methods of administration. For a dependent family of four, the Federal benefit floor will be $1600 per year. *When benefits under the President's Food Stamp proposal are also taken into account, the assistance package for such a family is about $2350 per year, or more than two-thirds of the poverty line as it has been most recently redefined.* This is not, of course, a sufficient amount to sustain an adequate level of life for those who have no other income; it is, nevertheless, a substantial improvement and can be made more adequate as budget conditions permit. As a result of the establishment of the Federal benefit floor of $1600, payment levels will be raised in 10 States and for about 20 per cent of present recipients.

For the aged, blind, and disabled, a nationwide income floor would be set at $90 per month per person of benefits plus other income. This comes on a yearly basis to $2160 for two persons, an amount which is actually above the poverty line for an aged couple. This represents an important change which we have made in the program since the President announced it on August 8; when the minimum for the adult categories was set at $65.

Perhaps at least as important as the establishment of national minimum benefit levels, however, is the provision of national eligibility standards and administrative procedures to govern the Family Assistance and State supplementary payment programs. For the first time, a single set of rules will apply throughout the nation, although the States will remain free to administer their supplementary payment programs under these uniform rules if they so desire. (The pre-existing State standards of need and payment levels will still continue to control in the supplementary payment programs with regard to eligibility and amount of benefits.)

States will be given the option, for both the supplementary payment and the adult category programs, to contract with the Social Security Administration for Federal assumption of some or all of the administrative burdens under these programs. In this way, we should be able to move toward a single administrative mechanism for transfer payments, taking advantage of all the economies of scale which such an automated and nationally administered system can have. The eventual transfer of the Food Stamp Program to the Department of Health, Education, and Welfare—as previously proposed by the Administration—should further enhance this administrative simplification.

Fourth, the plan includes over $600 million for a major expansion of training and day care opportunities. Some 150,000 new training opportunities will be funded under the legislation, which, when combined with the proposed Manpower Training Act in a simplified and decentralized framework, should greatly broaden the opportunities for self support for recipients. Some 450,000 quality child care positions are also funded in a new and flexible program which further extends the Administration's commitment to the first five years of life.

Fifth, the Family Assistance Plan provides major fiscal relief for the States. An estimated $700 million of the $2.9 billion in new Federal money being made available for expanded cash assistance will go to the States in the form of savings on their existing welfare costs. For five years from the date of enactment, every State is assured fiscal relief at least equal to 10 per cent of what its costs would have been under the old welfare program. When these savings are combined with the new money going to the States through the training and child care components and through the separate revenue sharing program, major relief for State governments is produced. In particular, by including the working poor within the Family Assistance Plan, we are establishing a wholly Federal responsibility for a category of potential recipients which an increasing number of States are beginning to assist at their own initiative. Some 7 States now have Statewide programs of relief for the working poor and another 8 States have local or experimental programs directed to these people— all entirely at State expense. By establishing a Federal program to cover the working poor, we are relieving the States of what seems to be the next likely increase in costs and coverage.

Impact on Other Programs

The Family Assistance Plan has a major impact on several other Federal programs bearing on the poor.

First, we have changed the treatment of unearned income compared to the present welfare system so that the recipient of Family Assistance benefits loses only 50 cents from his benefit for each dollar of unearned income received. This results in the elimination of an important inequity which, for example, would make a female-headed family of four ineligible for Family Assistance benefits if it received $1700 per year in alimony or support payments, but would pay that family a benefit if the husband were at home and earning $1700 per year. It also has an important impact on other Federal programs such as Old Age, Survivors and Disability Insurance, and Unemployment Insurance by eliminating the dollar-for-dollar loss in benefits under welfare as income from these other programs is received.

Second, this legislation amends Title XIX (Medicaid) to extend mandatory coverage under that program to the AFD-UF category. It is not possible at this time to include the working poor adults in Medicaid even though they are added to public assistance coverage under Family Assistance.

Third, Family Assistance has been carefully harmonized with the Food Stamp Program. As has already been stated, the benefits under these two programs are additive, so that a family of four receives a package of Family Assistance and Food Stamp subsidies totalling about $2350. Moreover, the eligibility ceilings have been set at virtually the same point—$4000 for a family of four—and both programs would now extend coverage to the working poor.

Finally, certain changes in the programs of services for AFDC recipients under Title IV of the Social Security Act are necessitated as a result of the Family Assistance Plan. The Department of Health, Education, and Welfare will be submitting more comprehensive amendments on the service program shortly. These amendments will include an expanded program of assistance to the States for foster care. In the meantime, however, we are leaving the present AFDC services provisions intact and retaining the 75 per cent Federal matching for the financing of these programs.

Summary of
Family Assistance Act of 1969

Title I—Family Assistance Plan
Establishment of Plan

Section 101 of the bill adds new parts D, E, and F to title IV of the Social Security Act, establishing a new Family Assistance Plan providing for payment of family assistance benefits by the Secretary of Health, Education, and Welfare and supplementary payments by the States.

ELIGIBILITY AND AMOUNT

The new part D of title IV of the Social Security Act authorizes benefits to families with children payable at the rate of $500 per year for each of the first two members of a family plus $300 for each additional member.

The family assistance benefit would be reduced by non-excluded income, so that families with more non-excludable income than these benefits ($1600 for a family of four) would not be eligible for any benefits.

A family with more than $1500 in resources, other than the home, household goods, personal effects, and other property essential to the family's capacity for self-support, would also not be eligible.

Countable income would include both earned income (remuneration for employment and net earnings from self-employment) and unearned income.

In determining income the following would be excluded (subject, in some cases, to limitations by the Secretary):

95

(1) all income of a student;

(2) inconsequential or infrequent or irregular income;

(3) income needed to offset necesary child care costs while in training or working;

(4) earned income of the family at the rate of $720 per year plus ½ the remainder;

(5) food stamps and other public assistance or private charity;

(6) special training incentives and allowances;

(7) the tuition portion of scholarships and fellowships;

(8) home produced and consumed produce;

(9) ½ of other unearned income.

Veterans pensions, farm price supports, and soil bank payments would not be excludable income to any extent and would, therefore, result in reduction of benefits on a dollar for dollar basis.

Eligibility for and amount of benefits would be determined quarterly on the basis of estimates of income for the quarter, made in the light of the preceding period's income as modified in the light of changes in circumstances and conditions.

DEFINITION OF FAMILY AND CHILD

To qualify for Family Assistance Plan benefits a family must consist of two or more related individuals living in their own home and residing in the United States and one must be an unmarried child (that is, under the age of 18, or under the age of 21 and regularly attending school).

PAYMENT OF BENEFITS

Payment may be made to any one or more members of the qualified family. The Secretary would prescribe regulations regarding the filing of applications and supplying of data to determine eligibility of a family and the amount for which the family is eligible. Beneficiaries would be required to report events or changes of circumstances affecting eligibility or the amount of benefits.

When reports by beneficiaries are delayed too long or are too inaccurate, part or all of the resulting benefit payments could be treated as recoverable overpayments.

REGISTRATION FOR WORK AND
REFERRAL FOR TRAINING

Eligible adult family members would be required to register with public employment offices for manpower services and training or employment unless they belong to specified excepted groups. However, a person in an excepted group may register if he wishes.

The exceptions are: (1) ill, incapacitated, or aged persons; (2) the caretaker relative (usually the mother) of a child under 6; (3) the mother or other female caretaker of the child if an adult male (usually the father) who would have to register is there; (4) the caretaker for an ill household member; and (5) full-time workers.

Where the individual is disabled, referral for rehabilitation services would be made. Provision is also made for child care services to the extent the Secretary finds necessary in case of participation in manpower services, training, or employment.

DENIAL OF BENEFITS

Family Assistance benefits would be denied with respect to any member of a family who refuses without good cause to register or to participate in suitable manpower services, training, or employment. If the member is the only adult, he would be included as a family member but only for purposes of determining eligibility of the family. Also, in appropriate cases, the remaining portion of the Family Assistance benefit would be paid to an interested person outside the family.

ON-THE-JOB TRAINING

The Secretary would transfer to the Department of Labor funds which would otherwise be paid to families participating in employer-compensated on-the-job training if they were not participating. These funds would be available to pay the training costs involved.

State Supplementation of Family Assistance Benefits

REQUIRED SUPPLEMENTATION

The individual States would have to agree to supplement the family assistance benefits under a new part E of title IV of the Social Security Act wherever the family assistance benefit level is below the previously existing Aid to Families with Dependent Children (AFDC) payment level. This supplementation is a condition which the State must meet in order to continue to receive Federal payments with respect to maternal and child health and crippled children's services (title V) and with respect to their State plans for aid to the aged, blind, and disabled (title XVI), medical assistance (tilte XIX), and services to needy families with children (part A of title IV). Such "supplementation" would be required to families eligible for family assistance benefits other than families where both parents are present, neither is incapacitated, or the father is not unemployed. The States would thus be required to supplement in the case of individuals eligible under the old AFDC and AFDC-UF provisions; they would not have to supplement in case of the working poor.

AMOUNT OF SUPPLEMENTATION

Except as indicated below and, except for use of the State standard of need and payment maximums, eligibility for and amount of supplementary payments would be determined by use of the rules applicable for Family Assistance Benefits.

In applying the family assistance rules to the disregarding of income under the supplementary payment program—

(1) in the case of earned income of the family, the State would first disregard income at the rate of $720 per year, and would then be permitted to reduce its supplementary payment by 16⅔ cents for every dollar of earnings over the range of earnings between $720 per year and the cutoff point for family assistance (that is, $3920 for a family of four), and could further reduce its supplementary payments by an amount equal to not more than 80 cents for every dollar of earnings beyond that family assistance cutoff point.

(2) in the case of unearned income, these same percentage reductions would apply, although the initial $720 exclusion would not apply.

REQUIREMENTS FOR AGREEMENTS

Some of the State plan requirements now applicable in the case of Aid and Services to Needy Families with Children would be made applicable to the agreement. These include the requirements relating to:

(1) statewideness;

(2) administration by a single State agency;

(3) fair hearing to dissatisfied claimants;

(4) methods of administration needed for proper and efficient operation, including personnel standards, training, and effective use of subprofessional staff;

(5) reporting to Secretary as required;

(6) confidentiality of information relating to applicants and recipients;

(7) opportunity to apply for and prompt furnishing of supplementary payments.

PAYMENTS TO STATES

A State agreeing to make the supplementary payments would be guaranteed that its expenditures for the first 5 full fiscal years after enactment would be no more than 90 per cent of the amount they would have been if the Family Assistance Plan amendments not been enacted. This would be accomplished by Federal payment to each State, for each year, of the excess of—

(1) the total of its supplementary payments for the year plus the State share of its expenditures called for under its existing State plan approved under title XVI plus the additional expenditures required by the new title XVI, over

(2) 90 per cent of the State share of what its expenditures would have been in the form of maintenance payments for such year if the State's approved plans under titles I, IV(A), X, XIV, and XVI had continued in effect (assuming in the case of the part A of title IV plan, payments for dependent children of unemployed fathers).

On the other hand, any State spending less than 50 per cent of the State share, referred to in clause (2) above, for supplementary payments and its title XVI plan would be required to pay the amount of the deficiency to the Federal treasury.

A state would also receive ½ of its cost of administration under its agreement.

Administration

AGREEMENTS WITH STATES

Sufficient latitude is provided to deal with the individual administrative characteristics of the States. Provision is made under which the Secretary can agree to administer and disburse the supplementary payments on behalf of the States. Similarly the States can agree to administer portions of the family assistance plan on behalf of the Secretary, with respect to all or specified families in the States.

EVALUATION, RESEARCH, TRAINING

The Secretary would make an annual report to Congress on the new Family Assistance Plan, including an evaluation of its operation. He would also have authority to make periodic evaluations of its operation and to use part of the program funds for this purpose.

Research into and demonstrations of better ways of carrying out the purposes of the new Plan, as well as technical assistance to the States and training of their personnel who are involved in making supplementary payments, would also be authorized.

SPECIAL PROVISIONS FOR PUERTO RICO, THE VIRGIN ISLANDS, AND GUAM

There are special provisions for these areas under which the amount of family assistance benefits, the $720 of earned income to be disregarded, and several other amounts under the Family Assistance Plan and the new title XVI of the Social Security Act (aid to the aged, blind, and disabled) would be reduced to the extent that the per capita income of these areas is below that of that one of the 50 States which had the lowest per capita income.

Training, Employment, and Day-Care Programs

Section 102 of the Administration bill would replace part C of title IV of the Social Security Act in its entirety.

PURPOSE

The purpose of the revised part C is to provide manpower services, training, and employment, and child care and related services for individuals eligible for the new Family Assistance Plan benefits (new part D) or State supplementary payments (new part E) to help them secure or retain employment or advancement in employment. The intent is to do this in a manner which will restore families with dependent children to self-supporting, independent, and useful roles in the community.

OPERATION

The Secretary of Labor is required to develop an employability plan for each individual required to register under the new part D or receiving supplementary payments pursuant to the new part E. The plan would describe the manpower services, training, and employment to be provided and needed to enable the individual to become self-supporting or attain advancement in employment.

ALLOWANCES

The Secretary of Labor would pay an incentive training allowance of $30 per month to each member of a family participating in manpower training. Where training allowances for a family under another program would be larger than their benefits under the Family Assistance Plan and supplementary State payments, the incentive allowances for the family would be equal to the difference, or $30 per member, whichever is larger.

Allowances for transportation and other expenses would also be authorized.

These incentive and other allowances would be in lieu of allowances under other manpower training programs.

Allowances would not be payable to individuals participating in employer compensated on-the-job training.

DENIAL OF ALLOWANCES

Allowances would not be payable to an individual who refuses to accept manpower training without good cause. The individual would receive reasonable notice and have an opportunity for a hearing if dissatisfied with the denial.

UTILIZATION OF OTHER PROGRAMS

In order to avoid the creation of duplicative programs, maximum use of authorities under other acts would be made by the Secretary of Labor in providing the manpower training and related services under the revised part C, but subject to all duties and responsibilities under such other programs. Part C appropriations could be used to pay the cost of services provided by other programs and to reimburse other public agencies for services they provided to persons under part C. The emphasis is on an integrated and comprehensive manpower training program involving all sectors of the economy and all levels of government to make maximum use of existing manpower and manpower related programs.

APPROPRIATIONS AND ADMINISTRATION

Appropriations to the Secretary of Labor would be authorized for carrying out the revised part C, including payment of up to 90 per cent of the cost of training and employment services provided individuals registered under the Family Assistance Plan. The Secretary would seek to achieve equitable geographical distribution of these funds.

In developing policies and programs for manpower services, training and employment for individuals registered under the Family Assistance Plan, the Secretary of Labor would have to first obtain the concurrence of the Secretary of Health, Education, and Welfare with regard to all programs under the usual and traditional authority of the Department of Health, Education, and Welfare.

CHILD CARE AND SUPPORT SERVICES

Appropriations to the Secretary of Health, Education, and Welfare would be authorized for grants and contracts for up to 90 per cent of the cost of projects for child care and related services for persons registered under the Family Assistance Plan and in manpower training or employment. The grants would go to any public or non-profit private agency or organization, and the contracts could be with any public or private agency or organization. The cost of these services could include alteration, remodeling, and renovation of facilities, but no provision is made for wholly new construction. The Secretary of Health, Education, and Welfare could allow the non-federal share of the cost to be provided in the form of services or facilities.

These provisions (unlike other provisions of the bill) would become effective on enactment of the bill.

ADVANCE FUNDING

To afford adequate notice of available funds, appropriations for one year
to pay the cost of the program during the next year would be authorized.

EVALUATION AND RESEARCH

A continuing evaluation of the program under part C and research for
improving it are authorized.

ANNUAL REPORT AND ADVISORY COUNCIL

The Secretary of Labor is required to report annually to Congress on the
manpower training and related services.

Elimination of Present Provisions on Cash Assistance for Families with Dependent Children

Section 103 of the bill revises part A of title IV of the Social Security Act
which relates to cash assistance and services for needy families with children. The new part A is called Services to Needy Families with Children,
reflecting the elimination of the provisions on cash assistance. The cash
assistance part is no longer necessary because of the Family Assistance
Plan in the new part D of title IV.

The revised part A provides for continuation of the present program of
services for these families. Foster care for children and emergency assistance, as included under existing law, are also continued.

REQUIREMENTS FOR STATE PLANS

Section 402 of the Social Security Act which sets forth the requirements
to be met by State plans before they are approved and qualify the State
for federal financial participation in expenditures, would be revised as
appropriate in the light of the elimination of the cash assistance provisions.

PAYMENTS TO STATES

The provisions on payments to States for expenditures under approved
State plans remain the same as existing law with respect to services,
emergency assistance, and foster care. The matching formulas continue
to vary, as in existing law, according to the kinds of services involved.

DEFINITIONS

The definitions of "family services" and "emergency assistance to needy
families with children" have not been substantially changed.

The definitions of "dependent child", aid to families with dependent children", and "relative with whom any dependent child is living" have been replaced (as no longer applicable) by definitions of

(1) "child"—which refers to the definition in the new part D, establishing the Family Assistance Plan; this in effect substitutes a requirement that the child be a member of a "family" (as defined in the new part D) instead of having to live with particularly designated relatives;

(2) "needy families with children" (and "assistance to such families")—this being defined as families receiving family assistance benefits under the new part D, if they are also receiving supplementary State payments pursuant to the new part E or would have been eligible for aid under the existing State plan for aid to needy families with children if it had continued in effect.

FOSTER CARE AND EMERGENCY ASSISTANCE

The provisions on payments for foster care of children and emergency assistance remain virtually the same as under existing law.

ASSISTANCE BY INTERNAL REVENUE
SERVICE IN LOCATING PARENTS

The provision on this subject remains the same and allows use of the master files of the Internal Revenue Service to locate missing parents in certain cases.

Title II—Aid to the Aged, Blind, and Disabled

This title revises the current title XVI of the Social Security Act and sets forth the revised title XVI in its entirety. One of the major changes is the removal of the provisions relating to medical assistance for the aged which, under existing law, would terminate at the end of calendar 1969. All medical assistance for which the Federal government shares costs will now be provided under approved title XIX State plans.

REQUIREMENTS FOR STATE PLANS

Few changes are made in this section (sec. 1602), aside from deleting the provisions relating to medical assistance for the aged. The section retains, without substantial change, the requirements relating to:

(1) administration by a single State agency (except where a separate agency is permitted for the blind as under existing law);

(2) financial participation by the State;

(3) statewideness;

(4) opportunity for fair hearing;

(5) methods of administration, including personnel standards, training, and effective use of subprofessional staff;

(6) reporting to the Secretary as required;

(7) confidentiality of information relating to recipients;

(8) opportunity for application and furnishing of asisstance with reasonable promptness;

(9) establishment and maintenance by the State of standards for institutions in which there are individuals receiving aid;

(10) description of services provided for self-support or self-care; and

(11) determination of blindness by an ophthalmologist or an optometrist.

The present prohibition against payment to persons in receipt of assistance under title I, IV, X, or XIV would be applicable instead to cases of receipt of family security benefits under the new part D of title IV.

The provision on inclusion of reasonable standards for determining eligibility and amount of aid would be replaced by one requiring a minimum benefit of $90 per month, less any other income, and by another requiring that the standard of need not be lower than the standard applied under the State plan approved under the existing title XVI or (in case the State had not had such a plan) the appropriate one of the standards of need applied under the plans approved under titles I, X, and XIV.

While the requirement relating to the determination of need and disregarding of certain income in connection therewith has been continued (although without the authorization to disregard $7.50 per month of any income, in addition to other income which may or must be disregarded), it has been expanded in a manner parallel to family assistance benefits to include disregarding as resources the home, household goods, personal effects, other property which might help to increase the family's ability for self-support, and, finally, any other personal or real property the total value of which does not exceed $1500. There would also be a new requirement for not considering the financial responsibility of any other individual for the applicant or recipient unless the applicant is the individual's spouse or child under the age of 21 or blind or severely disabled, and a prohibition against imposition of liens on account of benefits correctly paid to recipients.

Other new requirements relate to provision for the training and effective use of social service personnel, provision of technical assistance to State agencies and local subdivisions furnishing assistance or services, and provision for the development, through research or demonstrations, of new or improved methods of furnishing assistance or services. Also added is a requirement for use of a simplified statement for establishing eligibility and for adequate and effective methods of verification thereof.

Finally, there are new requirements for periodic evaluation of the State plan at least annually, with reports thereof being submitted to the Secretary together with any necessary modifications of the State plan; for establishment of advisory committees, including recipients as members; and for observing priorities and performance standards set by the Secretary in the administration of the State plan and in providing services thereunder.

The present prohibitions against any age requirement of more than 65 years and against any citizenship requirement excluding U.S. citizens would be continued.

In place of the present provision on residency, there is a new one which prohibits any residency requirement excluding any resident of the State. Also there would be new prohibitions against any disability or age requirement which excludes a severely disabled individual aged 18 or older, and any blindness or age requirement which excludes any person who is blind determined under criteria by the Secretary.

PAYMENTS

In place of the present provision on the Federal share of expenditures under the approved State plan there is a new formula which provides for payment as follows with respect to expenditures under State plans for aid to the aged, blind, and disabled approved under the new title XVI:

With respect to cash assistance, the Federal Government will pay (1) 100 per cent of the first $50 per recipient, plus (2) 50 per cent of the next $15 per recipient, plus (3) 25 per cent of the balance of the payment per recipient which does not exceed the maximum permissible level of assistance per person set by the Secretary (which may be lower in the case of Puerto Rico, the Virgin Islands, and Guam than for other jurisdictions).

With respect to services for which expenditures are made under the approved State plan, the Federal Government would pay the same percentages as are provided under existing law, that is, 75 per cent in the case of certain specified services and training of personnel and 50 per cent in the case of the remainder of the cost of administration of the State plan.

PAYMENT BY FEDERAL GOVERNMENT TO INDIVIDUALS

The revised title XVI includes authority for the Secretary to enter into agreements with any State under which the Secretary will make the payments of aid to the aged, blind, and disabled directly to individuals in the State who are eligible therefore. In that case, the State would reimburse the Federal Government for the State's share of those payments and for ½ the additional cost to the Secretary of carrying out the agreement, other than the cost of making the payments themselves.

DEFINITION

The new title XVI defines aid to the aged, blind, and disabled as money payments to needy individuals who are 65 or older or are blind or are severely disabled.

TRANSITIONAL AND RELATED PROVISIONS

Titles I, X, and XIV of the Social Security Act would be repealed.

Provision is made for making adjustments under the new title XVI on account of overpayments and underpayments under the existing public assistance titles.

Provision is also made for according States a grace period during which they can be eligible to participate in the new title XVI without changing their tests of disability or blindness. The grace period would end for any State with the June 30 following the close of the first regular session of its State legislature beginning after enactment of the bill.

CONFORMING AMENDMENTS

The bill also contains a number of conforming amendments in other provisions of the Social Security Act in order to take account of the substantive changes made by the bill. Thus, the changes in the medicaid program (title XIX of the Social Security Act) would require the States to cover individuals eligible for supplementary State payments pursuant to the new part E of title IV or who would be eligible for cash assistance under an existing State plan for aid to families with dependent children if it continued in effect and included dependent children of unemployed fathers.

EFFECTIVE DATE

The amendments made by the bill would become effective on the first January 1 following the fiscal year in which the bill is enacted. However, if a State is prevented by statute from making the supplementary payments provided for under the new part E of title IV of the Social Security Act, the amendments would not apply to individuals in that State until the first July 1 which follows the end of the State's first regular session of its legislature beginning after the enactment of the bill—unless the State certified before this date that it is no longer prevented by State statute from making the payments. In the latter case the amendments would become effective at the beginning of the first calendar quarter following the certification.

Also, in the case of a State which is prevented by statute from meeting the requirements in the revised section 1602 of the Social Security Act, the amendments made in that title would not apply until the first July 1 following the close of the State's first regular session of its legislature beginning after the enactment of the bill—unless the State submitted before this date a State plan meeting these requirements. In the latter case the amendments would become effective on the date of submission of the plan.

Another exception to this effective date provision is made in the case of the new authorization, in the revised part C of title IV of the Social Security Act, for provision of child care services for persons undergoing training or employment—which would be effective on enactment of the bill.

NIT: Welfare-Oriented
Negative Rates Plan
and Negative Rates Plan
for the Working Poor

Robert J. Lampman is a Professor of Economics at the University of Wisconsin and a staff member of the Institute for Research on Poverty. For several years he has been exploring the possibilities and problems in using the federal individual income tax to increase the incomes of those persons classified as poor. This proposal is adapted from an earlier version, "Adding Guaranteed Income to the American System of Transfers," which appeared in Social Action, *November 1967. Mr. Lampman, along with Milton Friedman, James Tobin, and others, has been one of the principal advocates of negative income taxes. The Lampman proposals presented here are best understood as welfare reforms, the expansion of welfare coverage to the working poor. This incrementalism sharply distinguishes Lampman's negative tax scheme from the anti-poverty negative tax plans of chapters 9 and 10.*

In the postwar period, and in the last few years in particular, we have made considerable progress against poverty. Broad economic growth, full employment policies, selective labor market programs, and income maintenance efforts have reduced the number of poor persons, as defined by

Robert J. Lampman, "Expanding the American System of Transfers to do More for the Poor," Wisconsin Law Review, Volume 1969, Number 2, pp. 541–549. Copyright © 1969 by the University of Wisconsin.

the Social Security Administration,[1] from 39 million in 1959 to 30 million in 1966, or from 22 to 15 per cent of the population.[2] The poverty-income gap, that is, the difference between the money income of all poor households and what their money income would be if they were just over the poverty threshhold, was $13.7 billion in 1959 and $11 billion in 1965. By projecting these trends, we can estimate that at the end of 1969 about 24 million people (12 per cent of all people) will be poor. The poverty-income gap will be about $10 million, or 1.2 per cent of the expected gross national product.

This progress is due in part to vigorous development of the American system of transfers. Transfers refer to all public and private means for providing money income or goods and services to persons on a basis other than their current productive activity. The grand total of such transfers in 1964 was $97 billion, $57 billion of which was in the form of health, education and other services. The pre-transfer poor, who were 28 per cent of the total population, received an estimated $38 billion worth of transfers, over half of which came in the form of social insurance and public assistance. In return they pay $8 billion in taxes and private contributions. Hence, they gained $30 billion.[3] This is a good measure of the size (though not necessarily the effectiveness)' of our antipoverty effort in 1964.[4]

In 1964, money transfers of $40 billion lifted 8.5 per cent of all families out of poverty and reduced the poverty-income gap by $10 billion. These transfers were divided about equally between the poor and nonpoor. However, while they amounted to only four per cent of the income of the nonpoor, they were about half the income of the poor even though only about half of the after-transfer poor families received a transfer. The several types of transfer payments differ widely as to their distribution. Most unemployment insurance and veterans benefits went to the pre-transfer nonpoor, while public assistance went chiefly to those who remained poor

1. *See* Orshansky, *The Shape of Poverty in 1966,* SOCIAL SECURITY BULLETIN 3 (March 1968).

2. REPORT OF THE COUNCIL OF ECONOMIC ADVISERS, ECONOMIC REPORT OF THE PRESIDENT 130 (1968).

3. *See* the author's chapter, *How Much Does the American System of Transfers Benefit the Poor?* in ECONOMIC PROGRESS AND SOCIAL WELFARE (L. Goodman ed. 1966); *cf.* M. March, *Federal Programs for Human Resource Development,* FEDERAL PROGRAMS FOR THE DEVELOPMENT OF HUMAN RESOURCES, 90th Cong., 2nd Sess. 111–54 (1968). *See also* R. Lampman, Transfer and Redistribution as Social Progress (Discussion Paper No. 25, Institute for Poverty Research, University of Wisconsin 1968).

4. Note that this was before the passage of Medicare, the new federal aid to education provisions, the Economic Opportunity Act, and the 1967 amendments to the Social Security Act.

after transfer. The benefits of the largest program, Old-Age, Survivors and Disability Insurance reached many who became nonpoor by receiving transfers.

Money transfers do much more for small families than for large families. Persons in families of four or more persons are 55 per cent of all pre-transfer poor and 62 per cent of those poor after transfers. They comprise only 36 per cent of those taken out of poverty by transfers. Although such persons account for 51 per cent of the poverty-income gap, they get only one-third of all transfers received by the pre-transfer poor. Under this money-transfer system the average payments, net of taxes to pay for transfers, are systematically related to pre-transfer income yet biased against larger families. For families with under $1,000 of pre-transfer income, the average net transfer was $810 for one-person families, $1,280 for two-person families, $1,650 for four-person families, and $1,935 for six-or-more-person families. The average net transfer fell off to zero at $4,000 for one person families and $5,500 for four-person families. Meaningful reform of our transfer system should correct the bias in the present system against the larger family. A carefully designed guaranteed income plan can achieve this and other desired objectives.

The guaranteed income is one name for a family of plans that includes such members as the reverse or negative income tax, the income-conditioned family allowance, the income supplement, and the social dividend.[5] The central idea of all these plans is that net benefits are payable on the basis of family size (or number of eligible family members) and the level of income. This is in contrast with both public assistance and social insurance.

A number of considerations are important in designing a guaranteed income plan. Planners should be conscious of (1) preserving incentives to seek pre-allowance income, (2) maintaining horizontal and vertical equity, (3) paying money out only or mainly to the poor, (4) avoiding incentives to family disorganization, and (5) integrating the plan with the existing tax and transfer system.

An examination of one guaranteed income plan, which we will refer to as "The Welfare-Oriented Negative Rates Plan," reveals the advantages and possible pitfalls involved in designing such a plan. Under the plan a family would receive 50 per cent of the difference between its actual income and the poverty-line income for its family size. Allowances would be paid as shown in Table 5–1.

A family coming under the plan would be confronted by a new set of

---

5. *See* Green & Lampman, *Schemes for Transferring Income to the Poor*, 6 INDUSTRIAL RELATIONS 121 (1967).

Table 5–1.   Net Allowance for Families of Three Different Sizes under Welfare-Oriented Negative Rates Plan

Family Income before Allowance	Net Allowance Based on 50 Per Cent of Poverty-Income Gap		
	One-Person Family, Poverty Line of $1500	Four-Person Family, Poverty Line of $3000	Six-Person Family, Poverty Line of $4000
$ 0	$750	$1500	$2000
500	500	1250	1750
1000	250	1000	1500
1500	0	750	1250
2000	0	500	1000
2500	0	250	750
3000	0	0	500
3500	0	0	250
4000	0	0	0

choices. Consider a four-person family earning $2,000. After the plan is in effect that family would receive a net allowance of $500. If it continued to earn $2,000, it would have an after-allowance income of $2,500. On the other hand, if its income target were $2,000, it could attain that by working less and earning only $1,000. Or, if it decided to earn $2,500, the after-allowance income would raise to $2,750. It is implicit in the table that the family would pay a 50 per cent marginal rate of tax on earnings up to $3,000. This can be seen in the way the net allowances change in response to changes in income before allowance. For example, if their income before allowance rises from $2,000 to $2,500, then their post-allowance income would rise from $2,500 to $2,750.

For purposes of calculating costs, let us assume that the typical family in this situation would do neither more nor less work because of the introduction of the 50 per cent negative rates plan. It should be noted that there is a lively controversy among economists about what would actually happen, some maintaining that people would take more leisure, some that they would take less.[6] There is little controversy about the effect of a plan that would fill 100 per cent of each family's poverty-income gap. Such a plan would take away all monetary incentive for a low-income

6. An experiment involving one-thousand families and designed to test for three years is now proceeding to investigate how people respond to different levels of guarantee and different tax rates. This experiment is financd by the Office of Economic Opportunity and managed by the Institute for Research on Poverty and Mathematica Corporation. For a description of it, see H. Watts, Graduated Work Incentives: Progress toward an Experiment in Negative Taxation (Unpublished Paper, Institute for Research on Poverty, University of Wisconsin 1969).

family to earn or receive income. This would make the pre-allowance poverty-income gap much larger than it now is and result in a greater than proportional increase in the cost of the plan. A 50 per cent rates plan would cost an estimated $7.5 billion in 1969 without any correction for savings on public assistance.[7] Doubling the rate to 100 per cent of the poverty-income gap would more than triple the cost in the opinion of this writer. It seems desirable therefore to avoid allowances that amount to more than half the difference between pre-allowance income and the income level at which allowances are to fall to zero.

Another benefit of the scheme shown in Table 1 concerns horizontal and vertical equity. Incomes after allowance would rise with family size. For example, one-member families earning $2,000 would have $2,000 post-allowance earnings, four-member families would have $2,500, and six-member families $3,000. Incomes would rise with earnings. In no case among families of the same size would a family that had a lower pre-allowance income end up with a higher post-allowance income.

We began this discussion by indicating that the goal was to close a substantial part of the remaining poverty-income gap, which is now on the order of $10 billion. In line with that, we may assert that the most efficient plan is the one that does the most to close the gap per dollar of expenditure. It is necessary to note that there is no plan that would close the $10 billion gap with $10 billion of expenditure. A 100 per cent plan would close the gap, but would cost, as we have indicated, in the neighborhood of $25 billion. A plan that sets the minimum allowance at the poverty line and taxes all pre-allowance income at a tax rate of 33⅓ per cent would close the gap completely, but at a cost of $50 billion, and would pay most of its benefits to people who are not poor. The break-even income for this plan would be three times the poverty line. All persons with income below that break-even level would receive an allowance equal to the poverty line but would pay back one-third of their other income. By contrast, the 50 per cent negative rates plan would cost $7.5 billion, less about $2.5 billion reduction in public assistance (or a net cost of $5 billion), would pay all of its benefits to those who are poor, and would close half of the poverty-income gap.

To make certain that all of the benefits go to the poor, we need to be careful in defining the benefit-receiving unit and the income to be counted in determining the size of benefit. Spouses should be required to file jointly. Unmarried persons under 19 years of age and students under 22 years of age should be prohibited from filing separately. A person who

---

7. For estimates of the costs of various guaranteed income programs see Green & Lampman, *supra* note 5.

iles under this plan could not be claimed as a dependent on any other person's positive income tax return. Income to be counted in reducing the allowance should be broadly defined to include the total money income of all members of the recipient unit. It should include not only earnings and property income, but also public and private transfers (but excluding public assistance), and imputed income from noncash-yielding assets. One could exclude from eligibility families with a gross business or farm income of more than a certain amount, and perhaps families with very large assets or very high incomes in the previous year. This would preclude a certain number of "horror cases," in which benefits would go to rich people who, in some cases, presently pay no income tax.

We need to be alert to the possibility that even a carefully designed plan might encourage husbands to desert their families and might discourage widows from remarrying. For example, a father with a wife and three children, who earns $3,000, presently pays no income tax and would get no allowance. If he deserted he would pay $394 in income tax, but, under the 50 per cent rates plan, his wife might claim $1,500. Or if a widow with two children who had no income but receives an allowance of $1,250 marries a man earning $3,000, which is $2,606 after taxes, she would lose $1,250 while he would save $394. The penalty is $856. While we do not know how much effect these incentives and penalties might have, they do deter us from considering rates higher than 50 per cent, and urge us to recommend reducing the size of the guarantee for persons filing alone.

The final pertinent concern is to integrate the plan with the existing tax-transfer system. Consider how a negative rates plan would tie in with the income tax. In those instances in which the poverty lines are higher than the combined exemptions and deductions under the income tax, a family might have to pay a marginal tax rate of 50 per cent, in the form of a reduction in allowance, plus a marginal rate of 14 per cent on earnings. This is an argument for raising exemptions and deductions or for lowering the break-even income levels for negative rates purposes.

By the following arrangement, the administration of the guaranteed income plan could be integrated with that of the income tax. A family would declare what it thought its next quarter's income was likely to be. If the expected income were so low with reference to family size as to justify an allowance, the Internal Revenue System would do two things: (1) it would mail out allowance checks to the family each month, and (2) it would withhold tax at the source at a rate of 50 per cent. At the end of the quarter the family would make a new declaration, and either the allowance or the withholding rate could be changed to adjust for over- or under-payment in the previous quarter. A final settlement could be reached at the end of the year, at which time account would be taken of the fact that some people who started the year on one side of the poverty line ended up on the other and, hence, experienced both positive and negative rates under the income tax.[8]

One of the most troublesome problems is integrating a guaranteed income plan with public assistance. At the present time, only about 8 million of the 30 million poor persons receive public assistance payments. Most of the 8 million persons on assistance are in families without a worker. Most of the 22 million not on assistance, of whom 9 million are children, are in families with a worker. These 22 million are mostly outside the traditional assistance categories of the old-aged, the broken families, and the disabled. They are poor despite working because of one or more of the following factors: low-wage-rates, irregular employment, or large family size.

The Welfare-Oriented Negative Rates Plan would reach the working poor and at the same time supersede public assistance in low-benefit states. It would assure all families of four persons a minimum income of $1,500 and offer net allowances that diminish to zero at $3,000 of other income. The $1,500 minimum would be an increase for those people on assistance in a substantial number of low-income states, but would merely replace part of the assistance benefits for some in higher-income states.

An alternative proposal is two-stage. The first stage is a federal setting of standards to raise assistance benefits for those four-person families in the traditional welfare categories and with no income to $1,500 in all states. The second stage is to introduce a variant of the negative rates plan called the Negative Rates Plan for the Working Poor. The plan would be aimed at those categorically excluded from assistance.[9] The

---

8. There are other ways to administer such a plan. For a valuable discussion of choices that are open see Tobin, Pechman & Mieszkowski, *Is Negative Income Tax Practical?*, 77 YALE LAW JOURNAL 1 (1967). *See also* Klein, *Some Basic Problems of Negative Income Taxation*, 1966 WIS. LAW REVIEW 776.

9. This distinction between the working poor and the nonworking poor is emphasized by the Kerner Commission. At page 466 of their report, they call for providing

for those who can work or who do work, any necessary supplements in such a way as to develop incentives for fuller employment; (and) to provide for those who cannot work and for mothers who decide to remain with their children, a system that provides a minimum standard of decent living and to aid in saving children from the prison of poverty that has held their parents.

This distinction is also discussed by the Council of Economic Advisers in their 1968 report. They point to the need for income supplements for poor families headed by men of working age and refer to the possibility of a "children's minimum income allowance." They note that "[E]specially difficult problems are involved in any program designed to eliminate poverty for those who can do some useful work but whose earning capacity is limited by their abilities or family responsibilities." REPORT, *supra* note 2, at 147–48.

level of allowance in the event of no earnings would not have to be high, since the working poor ordinarily have earnings. Setting the maximum size of the allowance far below a subsistence level would make it clear that they are expected to work and are not being offered an attractive alternative of subsistence income at no work.

The key features of the Negative Rates Plan for the Working Poor are reflected in Table 5–2's schedule of allowances for a family of four persons. Parallel tables would be established for each family size.

Table 5–2.   Net Allowances for 4-Person Families under Negative Rates Plan for the Working Poor

Family Income before Allowance	Net Allowance	Income after Allowance
$ 0	$750	$ 750
500	750	1250
1000	750	1750
1500	750	2250
2000	500	2500
2500	250	2750
3000	0	3000

Under this plan, the allowance is unchanged as pre-allowance income rises from zero to $1,500. In that range, in other words, the marginal tax rate is zero. From $1,500 to $3,000 of income, the marginal tax rate is 50 per cent.

Most of the poor four-person families are not on assistance and most of them have incomes from work in the $1,500 to $3,000 range[10] If a family is literally able to gain no income in the form of earnings, property income, or social insurance, then it would, just as is true under present laws, be left to the vagaries of public assistance. In other words, this plan would not govern for those in the very lowest income brackets, except for those now on assistance in a few states. However, it would supplement earnings of most poor four-person families by up to $750 per year. It would pay lesser amounts to smaller families and unrelated individuals and larger amounts to larger families. Hence, it could be called an income conditioned family allowance. While it would not take any family out of poverty, it would fill one-half the poverty-income gap for the 22 million poor persons not presently on public assistance. It would do this at a cost

10. A small percentage of the total number of poor persons are in "the categories" and not on assistance. In 1966, only 3.3 million aged poor and 2.1 million persons in broken families were not on assistance.

of $6 billion, less about $2 billion reduction in public assistance, or a net cost of $4 billion.

It would not do violence to the main purpose of this plan to restrict eligibility to those who are not receiving public assistance. Such a move would dramatize the need for a package of reforms, including a raising of public assistance benefits in some states. In Mississippi, the average Aid to Families with Dependent Children benefit for a family of four is $450 per year, while in New York it is $2,990. The nation-wide average is $1,728. The 1967 amendments to the Social Security Act included changes in public assistance benefit formulas which give assistance some of the characteristics of negative taxation. The first $360 of earnings ($30 per month) are not to diminish the benefits. Beyond that, benefits are diminished 66⅔ cents for every dollar of earnings. This means that in a state with a maximum benefit of $1,500, the income level at which benefits are reduced to zero is $2,632.

The alternative plan would cost on the order of $5 billion. The federal underwriting of a minimum assistance program would do a great deal for the poorest poor. The introduction of the negative rates plan for the working poor would be of moderate help to those not now helped by assistance. Differences would still remain between the treatment accorded equally poor families in the several states and, especially in states like New York, between the categorical and the noncategorical poor. However, the differences would be reduced in all cases. Further, there is no reason why this two-part package could not be combined with other changes, including improved minimum benefits for OASDI and unemployment compensation, retraining and on-the-job training programs, creation of new public jobs, and subsidized private employment opportunities for the poor.

This article offers two proposals in answer to the question: What should we do next in developing the American system of transfers? Both proposals are aimed at adding to the incomes of those in poverty and are made in recognition of the fact that 22 million of the 30 million poor persons are not now receiving public assistance. Either the Welfare-Oriented Negative Rates Plan or the Negative Rates Plan for the Working Poor, together with a federal minimum for the categorical assistance programs, would accomplish almost the same things. Either proposal would cost about $5 billion of new tax money in 1969. Either would channel help to those among the poor who most need it and who are least helped by the existing American system of transfers.

A Family Allowance Program
for Preschool Children

Alvin L. Schorr is the Dean of Social Work at New York University. The selection which appears in this compendium is taken from his book Poor Kids *(1966), which focuses on children in poverty and evaluates proposed remedies such as the negative income tax, fatherless child insurance, and family allowances. Many of the ideas presented in the book were developed while Schorr was working for the Social Security Administration and the Office of Economic Opportunity, where he was the Deputy Director of Research. Mr. Schorr's proposal is a partial welfare reform plan in the form of a family allowance for preschool children, not a remedy for financial poverty in the United States. It is best understood as a means to replace the widely criticized AFDC program with a less stigmatized, though financially insufficient program.*

Of the two family characteristics that lead to childhood poverty but are in no way relieved by social insurance, fatherless child insurance would deal with one. The other family characteristic that makes children vulnerable to poverty is size. If one selects at random a family with six or more children, the chances are even that they are poor. To put it another way, three out of five poor children are members of families with four or more children. The problem for children is not simply that more children re-

Reprinted by permission from Alvin L. Schorr, *Poor Kids* (New York: Basic Books, Inc., 1966), pp. 146–165. Other proposals dealt with in the book are "fatherless child insurance" and a negative income tax for children. © 1966 by Alvin L. Schorr.

quire more family income. Life is harder than that, for larger families have not the same incomes as small families but even lower incomes. In 1963 families consisting of a mother and two children had a median income of $2,910 but mothers with five children had $1,660. Similarly, married couples with two children had $7,180, but couples with five children had $6,380.[1] We have dwelt on the double trouble at the heart of these figures: large families may mean not only higher costs but a competitive disadvantage in improving income. One means of avoiding this disadvantage while doing something for all children is a program of family allowances.

Family allowances may be defined as regular payments for children made without regard to family income or other eligibility conditions. The definition thus does not include public assistance or survivors' insurance. In the operation of these programs, payments may be adjusted to the number of children but a major criterion other than childhood (need, loss of a parent) is involved. The term "family allowance" is occasionally used to include programs that operate within the limits of an income test. Such programs more or less resemble a negative income tax; but, as we have already considered the negative income tax, we shall omit this meaning from the definition of family allowance used here.

The concept of family allowances has antecedents that reach back nearly two hundred years. The British "Speenhamland system," though it is suggestive of the negative income tax, is usually regarded as an ancestor of family allowances. Opposing a minimum wage in 1796, the Prime Minister offered to "make relief, in cases where there are a number of children, a matter of right and an honor instead of a ground for opprobrium and contempt."[2] There followed a short-lived experiment in subsidizing incomes up to varying amounts, depending on the number of children in the family.

On the continent at the end of the nineteenth century, a number of French firms were adjusting wages to employees' family size. This practice spread widely after World War I—clearly as a strategy for meeting family needs without raising wages generally. After World War II family allowances expanded more widely, by this time under government auspices. A majority of the countries of the world and all of the industrialized West, except the United States, now have such programs. The postwar expansion of family allowances represented a new sense of national responsibility for children and for the avoidance of want. In Europe the wish to raise

1. Orshansky, Mollie. "Who's Who Among the Poor: A Demographic View of Poverty." *Social Security Bulletin.* Vol. 28, No. 7 (July 1965).

2. Vadakin, James C. *Family Allowances.* Oxford, Ohio: University of Miami Press, 1958, p. 21.

the birth rate was at least a subsidiary motive. The wish to place a ceiling on wages was now either absent[3] or, as in France, explicitly rejected.[4]

Neighboring Canada has a twenty-year-old program of family allowances. An allowance is paid for all children who are under sixteen and in school. For children under ten, the benefit is $6 a month; for older children, $8. The benefit is normally paid to the mother. The national government bears the total cost. To find a program with substantial payments one must look to France. The payment there varies according to region, the number of children in a family, and their ages. In Paris in 1964, for example, a family with four children received between 380 and 545 francs ($77 to $111) a month, exceeding the legal minimum wage at that time. In addition, various special payments may be made: during pregnancy, at birth, for improved housing. Eligibility depends upon a parent's employment, but exceptions are made and coverage is thought to be virtually universal. The cost is met by a tax on wages paid by employers only. In 1964 the tax rate was 13.5 per cent of wages up to $2,130 a year.

In the United States interest in family allowances has been sporadic. In the mid-1920's Senator Paul Douglas put forward a proposal with which he had taken some pains, attempting to resolve "this dilemma in which our whole wage policy finds itself."[5] The dilemma lay in trying to set a minimum wage that would meet the needs of large families without unduly burdening the economy. The way out appeared to lie in fixing a minimum wage for single men that would be supplemented by allowances for dependents. During the depression there were scattered discussions of family allowances.[6] Following World War II, apparently in response to developments in other countries, several proposals and analyses appeared.[7] In 1955 a number of prominent Senators proposed a study that might have led to the enactment of a program, but the Senate did not pass the resolution.[8]

There are probably two major reasons why sentiment in the United

3. Beveridge, Sir William. *Social Insurance and Allied Services.* New York: Macmillan Co., 1942, p. 134.

4. Schorr, Alvin L. *Social Security and Social Services in France.* Social Security Administration. Research Report No. 7, Washington, D.C.: Government Printing Office, 1965.

5. Douglas, Paul H. *Wages and the Family.* Chicago: University of Chicago Press, 1927, pp. 253 and ix.

6. Epstein, Abraham. *Insecurity—A Challenge to America.* New York: Random House, 1938.

7. Callaghan, Hubert Curtis. *The Family Allowance Procedure.* A Ph.D. dissertation submitted to the School of Social Science; Corley, Francis J. *Family Allowances.* St. Louis: Institute of Social Order, 1947; Vadakin, *op. cit.*

8. S. Resolution 109, submitted June 14, 1955, by Senators Neuberger, Morse, Douglas, Humphrey, Kefauver, Lehman, Kennedy, and McNamara.

States has remained cool to the idea of family allowances. In their statement on the proposed Senate resolution, the Executive Council of the AFL-CIO gave one reason.

> Family allowances [the AFL-CIO said] would represent a considerable departure from the traditional American concept of the living wage. Labor in this country has preferred other approaches to the same objective, through such methods as tax exemptions for dependents, minimum wages, public assistance, social security, etc.[9]

The Executive Council nevertheless recognized that many children were needy and recommended further study of family allowances. The other major reason why family allowances have not received substantial consideration may lie in public attitudes about the national birth rate and religion. As we have noted, interest in raising the birth rate has been a prominent reason why some countries have enacted programs. Americans have not typically been eager to increase the overall birth rate. It has widely been assumed that family allowances would be a Catholic measure; and the relationship of church and government being what it is in twentieth-century America, it has been difficult to enact any national measure that became defined as sectarian.

Although no program of family allowances has ever neared adoption in this country, the principle that income should be adjusted to number of children has been incorporated in a variety of government activities. The income tax offers credit worth upwards of $84 per child (that is, a $600 exemption at a minimum tax rate of 14 per cent) to families with sufficient income to profit from it. During the war the government paid a serviceman's family monthly, in addition to his own contribution, $40 for his wife and one child and $10 for each additional child. The rationale—explicitly rejected by Congress in setting peacetime compensation—was to assist in the support of larger families. In the development of the social security system, benefits have been related to the number of dependents in a family. In administering workmen's compensation and unemployment insurance, a minority of the states provide allowances for dependents in addition to the basic benefit. Some public school systems have paid teachers in accordance with their family responsibilities. The practice persists in a few small school districts, despite formal opposition from the National Education Association.

Nonproposal

A straightforward proposal for family allowances (which we will state only to abandon) might be made as follows: For the first child in a family,

---

9. AFL-CIO Executive Council. Miami, February 1956.

while he is under eighteen and in school, an allowance of $10 a month would be paid. For all subsequent children the benefit would be $40 a month. The cost would be borne out of general revenue. The present income tax exemption for children would be eliminated and the allowance would be taxable. Family benefits in social security would be adjusted downward and in other programs eliminated.

The amount of $40 is selected because it slightly exceeds the average per child expenditure in AFDC. It would at least affect childhood poverty to the degree that AFDC now does. The benefit for the first child is nominal, so as to help limit the cost of the program and to concentrate on relieving family cycle squeeze. As families would receive directly the value of exemptions for children, those exemptions for tax purposes would be eliminated. For similar reasons, social security and other programs would not need to provide as high benefits for dependents as they do now. The changes in the tax and social security structures would assist in reducing the net cost of the family allowance program.

Even so, the net cost would amount to about $14 billion, allowing for savings in taxes, social security, and public assistance. We have noted that the aggregate deficit of all poor families in the United States, including those without children, is only $11 to $12 billion. Furthermore, calculations make clear that the payment envisioned would not eradicate poverty even among children. For example, of poor families with three children (families large enough to benefit), fewer than half would be brought over the poverty level. For an amount of money greater than the combined deficit all poor people suffer, we expect a larger return. It does not therefore seem reasonable to analyze this straightforward proposal in further detail. Instead we present for consideration a more modest proposal for family allowances.

A Modest Proposal

A benefit of $50 a month would be payable for each child under six years of age. The cost would be borne out of general revenue. Present income tax exemptions for all children would be eliminated, and the benefit itself would be taxable. To distinguish this proposal from one of family allowances for all children up to eighteen years of age, we shall call it a preschool allowance.

A preschool allowance provides more money for each eligible child but reduces the total cost through several devices. First, the program concentrates on one of the two periods we have called crucial. Second, the benefit is itself taxable. Although it may seem unjust that the poorest families may have to pay taxes, they will be paying at the lowest rate. A tax-free allowance would support a lower level of benefits; poor families would lose more in accepting a lower level of benefits than by paying taxes on somewhat higher benefits. Third, the overall cost is reduced by wiping out the income tax exemption for all children, regardless of age. Families with an adequate income would not lose money in the long run, a point to which we will return.

We do not without concern preclude children six and over from the benefits of the proposal. In doing so, we will fail to deal with the poverty of many children and we will not deal with it effectively in the case of the large families who are usually regarded as the major beneficiaries of family allowances. Two steps should be taken on behalf of the children left out. First, money released to public assistance by preschool allowances should be redirected to assuring older children more nearly adequate assistance. (In calculating the cost of preschool allowances, therefore, we will not estimate net savings in public assistance.)

Second, we have noted that assistance given in the form of public services is tending to be directed through the schools. Health services, diet supplements, vocational aids, and cultural opportunities are almost naturally distributed in connection with school. Moreover, the concentration of public services where geographically they appear to be needed may avoid the cost of universal service programs without creating the potential problems of an income test (onus and incentive). We assume, therefore, that a program of preschool allowances would be accompanied by a vastly expanded program of public services for children who are in school. Not all these services need actually be administered by schools. Like recreation services, they may also be administered by other agencies for children old enough to take advantage of them. With the passage of the Economic Opportunity Act and the 1965 Education Act the nation has already moved toward expanded public services.

Reach of the Proposal

The program described would reach all children below the age of six and, as we shall see, some older children. It would cost $5.9 billion a year.[10]

The data required to calculate the impact of such a program accurately —classifying income simultaneously by size of family and age of children —are not available. We do know that, of poor families with children, almost two thirds have children under six and they average two preschool

---

10. In 1964 there were 24,836,000 children under six in the United States. At $600 for each, the gross cost would amount to $14.9 billion. Tax collected on this income may be estimated at $2 billion and collections resulting from wiping out the income tax exemption for all children may be estimated at $7 billion. Of the gross cost of $14.9 billion, $9 billion would be recaptured—leaving a net cost of $5.9 billion.

children per family. In 1964 these families had an average income of $2,307.[11] The preschool allowance would raise their average income to about $3,300, which is about $14 a month above the poverty level for a family of four. A substantial minority of these families were families of three. Rather more of them included older children and other family members and were therefore families of five, six, or more. In other words, half or perhaps somewhat fewer families with children under six would be brought out of poverty by a program of preschool allowances. For the rest, poverty would be substantially ameliorated.

We may approach the question of impact differently by reasoning from the effect of a $600 payment for *all* children in the country. Of 15.6 million children in 4.7 million poor families, four million children in 1.8 million families would remain poor.[12] About three out of four of the children who concern us would find themselves in families no longer poor. Of the 4 million children who remained poor, the majority would have received three fourths or more of their deficit. Though still poor, they would have been brought within hailing distance of the line. Obviously a program of payments to all children exaggerates the impact of a preschool program on preschool children—apparently by about 50 per cent. However, we may assume that these proportions would apply to the first years of family life, when all children in a particular family are under six. Of ten poor families in this first stage, we may thus anticipate that the program defined would avert poverty for seven or eight, and come close to averting it for one. One family out of ten in the first stage would not even come close to escaping poverty.

After several years the impact on each family would begin to decline. As each child reached school age, the family allowance would be reduced and the family might conceivably be poor as a result. As income is pooled for family spending, younger children would probably suffer as well as older children, even though they were still receiving an allowance. The corollary of this statement is that older children in poor families would benefit from the program as long as they had younger brothers and sisters.

The impact of a family allowance program has been described so far

11. Putnam, Israel. *Dimensions of Poverty in 1964.* Office of Economic Opportunity, October 1965, p. 15.

12. Allowing for the lowest tax rate (14 per cent) on the $600 allowance, the net value of the allowance to poor families is calculated at $514. Since this assumption exaggerates the total tax that poor families would pay, the initial calculation (4,324,000 children in 1,906,000 families) is rounded down.

The data on which this estimate is based [Orshansky, *op. cit.*] show the current income of poor families, including public assistance. The estimate would be accurate only if public assistance were not reduced as a consequence of the allowance payments. This effect could be achieved by exempting the allowance from consideration as income for purposes of public assistance or by raising public assistance standards.

in terms of whether families would be freed from poverty. We have said, however, that optimum conditions for take-off include some surplus of income over the barest minimum needs. In order to estimate how well the proposal would achieve a surplus, we must again make an inference from data dealing with all poor children. (Details of the data used are provided in the first table in [Alvin L. Schorr, *Poor Kids*] Appendix III.) The major effect would be felt during the first six years in which a family received an allowance. In these years, half the children we have said would not be poor might find themselves in families with at least $650 over the poverty level we have defined. The greatest impact would be felt in the largest families. After the initial six years, the program would tend less and less to provide a surplus.

In sum, the proposed program of allowances would reach all preschool children. Those in young families would be reached with substantial effectiveness. The effectiveness of the program in averting poverty would decline as one child after another in a family reached school age.

But Would It Alter Fate?

In that the payment is assured and substantial, the effects of preschool allowances would resemble the effects of fatherless child insurance. The two proposals differ in that one selects for aid all young children and the other children of any age who are socially orphaned. In cases of premarital pregnancy preschool allowances would exert a more neutral influence than FCI. Though FCI would provide an incentive for marriage, the family allowance would be available for the child whether or not his parents were married. The preschool allowance provides no incentive for marriage; in fact it assures an income to illegitimate children—who may need it most.

In any event, the large majority of families begin with marriage. Once a family was started, the preschool allowance would provide a poverty-free period of at least six years for most. Half of the children who would otherwise have been poor would find themselves in families with a substantial surplus of income over minimum requirements—substantial in any terms they might have known. As we have seen, the beginning of the family is the crucial period in which family and vocational patterns are established. Under a program of preschool allowances a family would have an income it could depend on at this critical time. It would be able to plan a move, a job change, or training with comparative certainty about its resources. The arrival of a child should not be an immediate financial blow for a family, one that precipitates the father to flight or abandonment of plans for self-advancement. Food, shelter, and clothing should be adequate, providing biological permission for optimism, pride, and ambition.

As their first children reached school age, families would experience the family cycle squeeze—but with modified force. Mothers and fathers would be in their mid-twenties or older, and family income would have advanced beyond its initial low point. Moreover, the family would be losing the preschool allowance in stages. The mother presumably would have chosen to stay home while her children were of preschool age. The children's entrance into school would provide her with the incentive and opportunity to work. Her income would help take up the deficit left by the termination of the preschool allowance.[13] Finally, school-centered programs and somewhat more adequate public assistance might meet the continuing needs of older children.

Preschool allowances might be expected to help promote intact families. For one thing, mothers would be encouraged to remarry. Children for whom there was some financial provision would be somewhat less likely to be regarded as financial liabilities by potential stepfathers. On the other hand, probably some married couples stay together only because their income is insufficient to support separate households. Some small number of such marriages might dissolve with increased income; whether such dissolutions would be regrettable is another question. But these are short-range effects. In the long run, decent income might be expected to lead to more nearly middle-class views of marriage and therefore greater stability.

The proposal does not have any direct bearing on the second crucial period of a poor family's development—when children in their young teens are formulating the choices that will set their own family and income patterns. In terms of the family-income cycle, this is the major limitation of the proposal: it spends all its force on children in the preschool years. The early impact should be substantial, but if the program fails to achieve its objectives, a family may experience chronic low income during the time when their children are in school. In that event, the program does not have any renewed effect until a new family has started.

Just as one inevitably is led to wonder whether fatherless child insurance would encourage family breakdown, it seems natural to ask whether preschool allowances would encourage a higher birth rate. We have already dealt with this issue in some detail. It might be anticipated that some poor families would go ahead and have more children because preschool allowances held out a means of supporting them. (Such families must, of course, expect to assume support after the children are six years

---

13. ". . . the proportions of all families found in poverty diminishes as age removes the hindrance of such children [under six] to increased family earnings . . ." Putnam, *op. cit.*

old.) But the weight of evidence is that large poor families result from an inability to control family size rather than from an express wish. It must be supposed that at least as many couples would find in decent income the resources and reason for limiting their families as for having more children. We have concluded that the net birth rate is more likely to respond to other forces (economic conditions, style) than to a new income maintenance program. In the long run, if people are indeed helped to move up, their child-bearing patterns might be expected to converge with those of other middle-class families—that is, they would have no more than three or four children.

Those Who Are Not Poor

General improvement of the quality of child care, whether or not children are poor, is not our objective here. Yet three fourths of the children who would be reached by a new income maintenance program are not poor. If the effects of the program on them were merely neutral, then that money would be wasted. Children who are not poor obviously do not need such a program to the extent that poor children do; yet it may be anticipated that they will benefit to some degree. The early child-bearing years put pressure on middle-income families as well as poor ones. Their income is then at its lowest, and they are making the sacrifices in the interests of self-advancement that we wish poor people to make.

There is, in fact, evidence that large families with incomes a good deal higher than the poverty level suffer compared with smaller families. A series of English studies established that larger families *in every income bracket* have a higher rate of infant mortality, poor nutrition, and poor educational attainment.[14] No American studies are available either to confirm or to contradict this finding, but is it reasonable to assume that middle-class families in the United States fare better than high-income families in England? Large families with adequate incomes may have a special family pattern; infant mortality in large families may indeed have biological causes. However, as Tony Lynes writes:

> . . . the crucial question is not whether the handicaps of the child in a large family are caused solely by the inadequacy of the family income, but rather whether an increase in the family income can help to counteract these handicaps.[15]

14. Lynes, Tony. "A Policy for Family Incomes." *The Listener.* Vol. LXXIII, No. 1878, March 25, 1965, pp. 436–37. Citations offered in evidence on this point are: Neville R. Butler and Dennis G. Bonham, *Perinatal Mortality,* 1963; Royston Lambert, *Nutrition in Britain, 1950–1960,* 1964; London County Council, *Report on the Heights and Weights (and Other Measurements) of School Pupils in the County of London in 1959,* 1961; J. W. B. Douglas, *The Home and School,* 1964.
15. *Ibid.*

Those who have a satisfactory income—and several children—would benefit by a program of preschool allowances as well as poor families. Such a program would in effect bring forward a portion of their decent life incomes to the time when their income was least adequate to their needs. The quality of care for middle-income children should therefore improve.

Fair Shares?

We should be more exact about the effects of preschool allowances on the distribution of income. A family that pays a tax of 25 per cent on its highest income (net taxable income of about $12,000) would find that the preschool allowance provided as much income in six years as would otherwise have been saved in taxes in eighteen years. That is, of each $600 a year the family received in allowances, it would retain $450—for six years. Under 1966 tax laws, the same family would save $150 a year in taxes for eighteen years.[16] Families with higher incomes would register a net loss under the proposal compared with what they would otherwise receive for a child. Families with taxable incomes of $4,000 to $10,000 would register a small net gain for each child, as extra income would be taxed at a rate of about 20 per cent. Poor families should show the largest gain, $514 a year or more for each child. Thus, in the framework of the income tax provisions for children, the effect of preschool allowances would be: (1) to bring the benefit forward to an earlier point in the family cycle, and (2) to reapportion the current federal subsidy in order to favor poor children. These two reallocations would account for more than half the money actually paid out. The remaining $5.9 billion, representing the net cost of the program, would come from general revenue. That portion of the cost would be borne rather more by those with middle and higher incomes than by low-income families.

It is implicit in what has already been said that the problem of incentive to work does not arise under a program of preschool allowances; the program permits families to do, without penalty, what they consider to be to their benefit. Nor would any group be stigmatized for receiving support. Young children would receive allowances as older children receive free schooling—as a matter of right.

As family allowances were, in origin at least, intended as a device to limit wages, we should take note of this issue. A program of preschool allowances might affect wage levels in two ways, through influencing the

---

16. Actually few families have a stable income for eighteen years; most start with a lower income and slowly acquire a higher income. Families that rise from a lower income to a net taxable income of $12,000 after several years of marriage would, under the proposal, register a small net gain compared with their experience under 1966 tax laws.

number of people available for work and through the collective bargaining process. With a program of preschool allowances the make-up of the labor force might change in the following ways. In 1960, 2.4 million women with children under six were working;[17] if those women had an assured income, the number of them in the working force might somewhat decline. As the problem of incentive does not arise, the number of men at work would be unaffected. The program indirectly ameliorates the situation of some older children who are poor; conceivably a few of them would delay beginning work. In sum, the effect of the program on the number who want to work would not be large. The demand for goods would be un-affected—not to say higher—and the labor force, if affected at all, some-what smaller. If salaries and wages responded at all to these conditions, they could only rise.

Earlier it was thought that a program of family allowances would weaken the position of the worker or trade union in collective bargaining. An employer might take the position that allowances meet the needs of the employees' children; therefore salaries need meet only the needs of adults. However, collective bargaining has not for many years been conducted in the United States in order to secure a "living wage." At issue, rather, has been what increases are necessary in order to meet rising costs and to provide employees with a share of rising productivity. The determination of neither issue would be greatly altered by a program of allowances. Apart from costs and productivity, the results of collective bargaining are also affected by economic conditions which may for the moment strengthen employers or employees vis-à-vis each other. Allow-ances would not have much impact on these conditions. In short, it is difficult to conceive how a family allowance program reaching all children might, in modern American circumstances, reduce wages. It is even more difficult to imagine how preschool allowances might reduce wages. During two thirds of a child's life, the wage earner would be supporting him without any allowance.[18]

A few words should be said about the administration of the program. The conditions of eligibility are simple—name, birth date, parent's or guardian's name and address. The program would be essentially a book-

17. U.S. Department of Commerce. Bureau of the Census, 1960 census. *Employment Status and Work Experience.* PC(2)–6A, Table 6 (Chapter IV); Table 8 (Chapter IX).

18. In proposing a family allowance program for all children, one would consider reducing or at least not further increasing current allowances for dependent children in various social security programs. For example, with a family allowance program, unemployment insurance benefits would not be so inadequate for families with several children as they are now. As the proposal we are considering is limited to young children, however, we cannot consider that it disposes of the need for family benefits in social security.

keeping and clerical operation. Provision may need to be made for cases in which there is a question as to whether funds have been used properly. The question whether funds would actually be used for children arises in relation to family allowances more frequently than with other programs. Perhaps other programs are envisaged as having a supervisory staff and family allowances imagined in the simplest possible terms. At any rate, in the carrying out of none of the programs developed abroad has neglect of children or misuse of funds been found to be a serious problem—not in the family allowance programs of Canada or France,[19] not in the father- less, child insurance program of New Zealand,[20] and not in the negative income tax program of Denmark. Such problems as arise seem likely to involve a very small percentage of families.

In the United States the protection of children is assumed basically by local and state governments. Whether an agency administering benefits for children should specifically safeguard the payment in relation to the child depends upon the philosophy of the program. The income tax pro- vides a benefit for children, but no one suggests that the Internal Revenue Service investigate whether particular children benefit. The Social Security Act provides for a payment to be made to a relative or other person if it appears that a beneficiary's best interests would be served. A similar pro- vision might be written into a new program, particularly if the sums in- volved were substantial. The provision could be administered through the agency's own field staff or through an arrangement with local child pro- tective agencies.

One other administrative question arises: Should the father or mother receive the payment? In the case of fatherless child insurance, the pay- ment is received by the parent who has the children—usually the mother. In a program of NEGIT,[21] the person who files for the family would automatically receive the payment. As the choice is left to the family, pre- sumably the payee would usually be the father. As for family allowances, many countries make the payment to the mother; this practice emphasizes the special intent of the family allowance and where necessary safeguards the money for children. It might be argued that payment to the mother interferes with the father's conception of himself as the family head and wage earner.[22] However, the special purpose of the allowance and the

---

19. Schorr. *Social Security and Social Services in France.*

20. Watson, W. L. Social Security Commission of New Zealand. Personal communi- cation, August 23, 1961.

21. [NEGIT refers to the Negative Income Tax. Schorr presents a more detailed discussion of the NEGIT and Fatherless Child Insurance (FCI) in *Poor Kids,* chap- ters 7 and 8.]

22. Schorr, Alvin L. "Problems in the ADC Program." *Social Work.* Vol. 5, No. 2 (April 1960).

special responsibility of mothers for it would probably by widely understood, even by men whose self-regard was vulnerable.

Alternative Line of Program Development

Preschool allowance payments may be in such amounts as to encourage poor families to take off. But this can happen only if two kinds of calculated costs are accepted, both of which arise from wiping out income tax exemptions for all children. In the first place, families with comparatively high incomes would show a net loss compared to their current situation. Although it may be practical to try to favor poor children in distributing the *additional* wealth that the nation accrues from year to year, it may be impractical to try to accomplish this out of what the nation has at any given moment. In other words, it may be impractical to try to give poor children more by giving rich children less. In the second place, even though families with moderate or middle incomes would show a net gain over a period of eighteen years, it might seem unfair to expect them to forego both family allowances and income tax exemptions while they are supporting school-age and still dependent children. The situation is particularly unfair for poor families with school-age children. They will pay little in taxes, but that little will seem much.

Both objections may be met by provision of a family allowance that pays $25 a month for each child up to six years of age and $10 a month for each child between six and eighteen. In effect, families would receive —in exchange for yielding the income tax exemption—at least the equivalent of a $600 exemption at a 20 per cent rate of tax. The net cost of this proposal would be smaller, about $4 billion. Poor children would receive a fairer share of the national income, as they would under a program of preschool allowances.[23] However, the alternative proposal does not contain the most attractive feature of a preschool allowance program—a payment large enough to assure poor families surplus income at a critical point in the family-income cycle. At $25 a month, only one out of four preschool children would be brought out of poverty. Only a handful of

23. The gross cost of the proposal would be $12.7 billion. Seven billion dollars would be recaptured by wiping out the exemption for children under eighteen and an additional $1.7 billion would be collected from taxing the allowance itself.

Of the gross outlay, poor families would receive $2.8 billion. Assuming that loss of the income tax exemption and the tax collected on the family allowance would together represent $300 million, poor families would be receiving a $2.5 billion net increase in income at a net cost of $4 billion. As poor families have 20 per cent of the children, obviously the proposal favors them.

The way the advantage falls is represented in the second table of [Schorr. *Poor Kids*] Appendix III.

children would be members of families with surplus as large as $650 a year.

One may nevertheless regard the "$25 and $10" family allowance as a conservative start toward a more substantial program.

Conclusion

The cost of a universal but modest program of family allowances approximates $14 billion. We judge this to be more expensive than is reasonable in terms of its probable impact on childhood poverty. Therefore we have formulated a more substantial program that would benefit directly only children under six years of age—but all children at those ages would be reached. For a highly significant half dozen years, poverty would be averted for three children out of four. The median child for whom poverty was averted in those early years would live in a family with a surplus of $50 a month over its barest needs. For the remaining children in those first half dozen years and for many school children later on, poverty would be alleviated but not averted.

The program would provide a powerful push toward the achievement of a decent income and family stability in the first years of marriage. From a variety of points of view—when the mother is encouraged to work, when it provides surplus income, when encouraging intact families—it promotes exactly the patterns that may lead to take-off. The program would not represent as significant a force in the early careers of *middle*-income families but nevertheless would tend to add to the quality of their children's care. When children arrive at school age, the program would end. This is its major drawback. This drawback might be compensated for its preschool allowances are seen in tandem with the development of public services delivered through schools and community centers. Finally, the proposal as formulated would tend to give to children now poor a larger share in the nation's resources.

In comparing the merits of preschool allowances with the first two proposals, it is important to bear in mind that preschool allowances carry the largest cost figure, one almost twice that for a negative income tax. A cost limitation is imposed upon NEGIT by the incentive problem and upon fatherless child insurance by the program's definition. NEGIT has a limitation on benefit levels that cannot be circumvented and FCI a built-in limitation on coverage. According to point of view, one reads these limitations as advantages or disadvantages.

PART THREE

Major Antipoverty Proposals

These proposals aim to reduce American poverty substantially and thus require expenditures far greater than those estimated for the welfare reforms presented in Part II.

The Schwartz plan (Chapter 7) emphasizes the goal of providing an "adequate and equitable income" for all citizens, and argues for a guarantee level set at the poverty line. Schwartz assumes that work incentive provisions would be added on that base, but does not calculate the increased costs they entail. Hence, the $11 billion cost estimate understates expenditure requirements; it applies only to a program where a dollar of earnings results in a dollar reduction in the income guarantee.

Both the *Yale Law Journal* and Heineman Commission proposals attempt to combine relatively adequate benefits with strong work incentives. The stipulation of universal eligibility, national administration, and 50 per cent marginal tax rates characterize both plans; these features suggest the wide agreement among professional economists about the proper structure of an income maintenance system. The Yale plan guarantees an income at approximately the poverty line; the Heineman proposal begins with a $2400 guarantee, but suggests moving towards the poverty standard. The result is that first year cost estimates of the two programs exaggerate the difference between them. The Heineman plan may be thought of as an initial, less costly version of the class of plans in which the Yale scheme falls: antipoverty negative income taxes administered nationally and relatively impersonally without invidious categorization of groups among the poor.

133

The Brazer child allowance plan (Chapter 8) combines tax reform and antipoverty objectives. But it is the poverty of American families with children that commands Brazer's attention. He suggests, on the benefit side, $50 per month payments to *all* children. To concentrate net benefits on lower income families, Brazer offers three instruments: the withdrawal of tax exemptions for children, the inclusion of child allowances as taxable income, and a special recoupment device by which taxpayers add to their "tax liability as ordinarily computed (after including children's allowances received in income) an amount equal to an increasing proportion of children's allowances received as income rises." These devices have the effect of producing a net program cost of some $15 billion in a scheme with gross costs of over $40 billion. Similarly, these devices turn the Brazer plan into the equivalent of a moderate negative income tax for families with children.

The differences among these antipoverty proposals may be understood as expressing conflicting views of the political acceptability of various target populations, cost levels, or administrative devices.

A Demogrant Approach:
The Family Security Program

Edward E. Schwartz is the George Herbert Jones Professor, School of Social Service Administration, University of Chicago. He was one of the early advocates of a family allowance and participated in the National Association of Social Workers' Round table discussions (early 1960s) on cross-national studies of family allowances. His family security plan, which appeared in 1964, provides benefits that are applicable to all families, not only those with children. It represents an early effort to reduce poverty directly through a universal cash transfer program guaranteeing incomes at or close to the official poverty line.

The Kennedy-Johnson war on poverty is avowedly aimed at the abolition of poverty. The grand strategy as revealed thus far is *prevention* through increased provision of gainful employment.

The social work profession has long been committed to the objectives of this war and to the strategy of prevention. Social workers strongly support measures for increasing the demand for employment and for preparing young persons and displaced workers better to meet the demands of the labor market through improved educational, health, and other community services. Yet at any given time not all persons and families

Edward E. Schwartz, "A Way to End the Means Test," *Social Work*, IX, No. 3 (July 1964), pp. 3–12. Copyright 1964 by the National Association of Social Workers.

will—or necessarily should—be related to a payroll. To insure victory the attack on unemployment must be supported by a system of defense that will assure the maintenance of income for all families. The treatment of poverty, like the treatment of other ills, through alleviation, reduction, and control, is in itself a necessary form of prevention against the spread and perpetuation of the problem. This may seem obvious to social workers, but it is also obvious that this fact has to be repeated frequently.

The current chief defense against poverty is, of course, the social security system; the last line of this defense is public assistance. A most notable aspect of the public assistance programs in the United States today is the dissatisfaction expressed toward them by all parties concerned—the applicants for and the recipients of assistance, the rank-and-file of public assistance staff, legislators, and the public at large—and it is hardly possible to exaggerate the extent and depth of this dissatisfaction. The *treatment* aspect of the war on poverty will require a more effective operation than can be provided through our battered, tired public assistance programs. The public assistance programs will not be good enough even though they be pasted together with surplus-food stamps, glossed over with pseudo-service amendments, or even braced up with Kerr-Mills old age medical payments.

Like many other groups in the population, social workers have become increasingly critical of the public assistance programs, but for their own reasons. They have shown their skepticism of the possibilities of providing high-standard professional services within the framework of public assistance agencies clearly, but chiefly silently, by staying away in droves from employment in these programs. More recently a few lonely academics, crying in the wastelands, have publicly raised important questions and given vent to righteous indignation about the vagaries and inequities of the treatment of the poor.[1]

The recent social work literature of this country appears to offer no specific proposals that would be better suited to contemporary society than is public assistance for maintaining the income of the millions of impoverished families who are untouchable (not covered) by the "social insurances." Recently Walter C. Bentrup inveighed, feelingly and effectively, against the archaic public assistance means test approach and challenged the social work profession ". . . to visualize the characteristics of a better one."[2] The purpose of this article is to propose an income

1. *See* Eveline M. Burns, "What's Wrong With Public Welfare?" *Social Service Review*, Vol. 36, No. 2 (June 1962), pp. 111–122; and Alan D. Wade, "Social Work and Political Action," *Social Work*, Vol. 8, No. 4 (October 1963), pp. 3–10.
2. "The Profession and the Means Test," *Social Work*, Vol. 9, No. 2 (April 1964), pp. 10–17.

maintenance program that would involve neither a means test nor contributions to an earmarked insurance fund and to discuss some of the salient features of this plan.

Family Security Program

The proper treatment of poverty in the United States today is for the federal government to guarantee to every family and person in this country, as a right, income sufficient to maintain a level of living consonant with American standards for the growth and development of children and youth and for the physical and mental health and social well-being of all persons. The right to a livelihood must be recognized and guaranteed as a constitutional civil right. The most satisfactory way to implement such a guarantee is through a modification and expansion of the present mechanism for the collection of the federal income tax.

Every person who is either the head of a family or is not a member of any family would file each year a financial statement of his anticipated income for the coming year, as well as a statement of his income for the past year, and information on the number of his dependents. If his anticipated income for the coming year is below his Federally Guaranteed Minimum Income (FGMI) he may then file a claim for a Family Security Benefit (FSB) in the amount of the difference. If his anticipated income is above his FGMI he will pay an income tax as under present tax law and procedures. After the first year of operation of the Family Security Program, reports of a family's income for the past year and any changes in the number and kinds of dependents will be used to revise prior statements of anticipated income and to make adjustments of Family Security Benefits received for the past year.

Reports of income on which benefits are based will be made in the same style used for individual income tax returns. Methods of checking and auditing of claims for FSB will be developed as expansions of present methods for processing individual income tax returns. This includes field investigation of a sample of cases and of all cases that are highly complex, questionable, or involve large sums. Procedures for checking and auditing will include those recently instituted by the Internal Revenue Service for charging to the individual account of each taxpayer all payments to him of wages, salaries, and other income now subject to identification by a social security number. The kind of automatic data processing equipment now installed at Morgantown, West Virginia, for checking income tax returns against collated information on income payments to individuals can be used as well for checking the validity and accuracy of claims for FSB.

The level of the FGMI for families of different size will be established by a presidential commission. Provision will be made in the legislation for annual automatic adjustments of dollar amounts on the basis of changes in an appropriate cost-of-living index and for decennial adjustments to reflect changes in standards of living as indicated by appropriate research.

To what extent should FGMI be adjusted to differences in family maintenance costs related to characteristics of members of the family such as age and sex, or to place of residence, regional or urban-rural? Although the use of computers and automatic data processing makes possible increased flexibility in the design of a plan, it should also be recognized that each elaboration increases the complexity of administration and should be adopted only after the net advantages are clearly established.

A problem likely to generate popular interest is involved in the making of FSB payments to families with limited current income but substantial non-income or low-income producing assets. Should FSB payments be made to an aged couple, for example, whose income is below their FGMI but who have $60,000 invested in tax-free municipal bonds yielding 3 per cent per annum? Or the widow who lives in her own home in which she has an equity of $30,000? A solution to this problem is suggested by the finding that the median net worth of the fifth of all spending units (roughly equivalent to the total of families and unrelated individuals) having the lowest incomes in 1962 was only $1,000, mostly in the form of equity in dwellings.[3] Persons claiming FSB could be required to include in their annual reports of income a statement of their net worth. Families having a net worth of, perhaps, not over $13,000 of equity in their own dwellings or $2,000 exclusive of sole equity would then not be eligible for benefits.

Can the Nation Afford This?

In discussing the problem of poverty in America the President's Council of Economic Advisers selected the figure of $3,000 (before taxes and expressed in 1962 prices) as the minimum income for a decent life for a non-farm family of four.[4] The council noted a study made by the Social Security Administration that defines a "low-cost" budget for a non-farm family of four and finds its cost in 1962 to have been $3,955. The Bureau of Labor Statistics City Workers' Budget, also designed for a family of

3. *Economic Report of the President* (Washington, D.C.: U.S. Government Printing Office, 1964), p. 67.
4. *Ibid.*, p. 58.

four, but described as neither "minimum maintenance" nor "luxury" but rather as "modest but adequate" when last priced (1959), exclusive of allowances for the payment of taxes and insurance ranged from $4,622 for Houston to $5,607 in Chicago.[5] For the country as a whole, $5,000 is taken here to represent the cost of a "modest but adequate" annual budget for a family of four.

Using these standards as rough guides the following equally rough estimates may be made of the general order of magnitude of total national payments of FSB as the following levels: minimum maintenance level, $3,000 = $11 billion per annum; economy level, $4,000 = $23 billion per annum; modest-but-adequate level, $5,000 = $38 billion per annum.

The economic feasibility of a proposal for a Family Security Program at the minimum maintenance level is specifically attested to by the Council of Economic Advisers in the following terms:

> Conquest of poverty is well within our power. About $11 billion a year would bring all poor families up to the $3,000 income level we have taken to be the minimum for a decent life. The majority of the Nation could simply tax themselves enough to provide the necessary income supplement to their less fortunate citizens. The burden—one fifth of the annual defense budget, less than 2 per cent of GNP—would certainly not be intolerable.[6]

The council's report goes on to express a preference for a solution to the problem of poverty that would permit Americans "to *earn* the American Standard of Living." However, the report further states:

> We can surely afford greater generosity in relief of distress, but the major thrust of our campaign must be against causes rather than symptoms. We can afford the cost of that campaign too.[7]

The gross national product of the United States is now about $600 billion per annum. If the Federally Guaranteed Minimum Income for a family of four were set at the $5,000 per annum modest-but-adequate level the *gross cost* would be less than 7 per cent of the gross national product—still quite tolerable. At whatever level the FSB is set the *net cost* of benefit payments would of course depend on the extent to which these were offset through reductions in expenditures of existing welfare programs.

All public welfare payments under present federal, state, and local programs including public assistance, veterans' benefits, unemployment

5. Helen H. Lamale and Margaret S. Strotz, "The Interim City Worker's Family Budget," *Monthly Labor Review*, Vol. 83, No. 8 (August 1960); pp. 785–808.
6. *Economic Report of the President, op. cit.*, p. 77.
7. *Ibid.*

compensation, and old age and survivors insurance benefits, but excluding health and education, now total about $33 billion. Public assistance payments alone are close to $5 billion and almost the entire amount could be taken immediately as an offset against payments of Family Security Benefits. Savings from other welfare programs would be dependent on the extent and rate at which they could be phased out. Appreciable savings would also be effected through the substitution of modern accounting and auditing techniques and the use of automatic data processing for the present costly, slow, and labor-consuming procedures for determining initial and continuing eligibility of each family through office interviews, home visits, investigation of each family's income and resources, and computation of individual budgets and budget deficits on a case-by-case basis.

A fresh and useful perspective on how much this country can afford to spend for welfare measures may be gained by a look abroad. Data gathered by Gordon show public welfare expenditures in various nations as a per cent of national income in 1950, 1953, and 1957.[8] In each year the United States ranked lower than any of the sixteen western and eastern European countries reported, and lower than Canada, Chile, Australia, New Zealand, and Israel. The only nations reported that are out-ranked by the United States in this "measure of welfare effort" are Guatemala, four Asian, and three African and Middle Eastern countries.

In a recent analysis of the share of industrial production allocated to the beneficiaries of governmental welfare programs, Colm selected for comparison Sweden as the western European country most advanced toward the welfare state and Germany as that which is often considered the nearest approximation to a free enterprise country. He found that the relative size of social welfare expenditures was about the same in both countries and considerably higher than in the United States. He declares that there is a great deal of unfinished business in the development of our social welfare programs and concludes:

> With the technical knowledge of our age we will have the material means available for eliminating poverty as a mass phenomena [sic]. We can only hope that we will also develop the attitudes necessary to use these resources for the benefit of those who will not automatically benefit from economic growth and rising incomes *and from the conventional security and welfare programs*. [Author's italics.][9]

8. Margaret S. Gordon, *The Economics of Welfare Policies* (New York: Columbia University Press, 1963), pp. 15–16.

9. Gerhard Colm, "The Economic Base and Limits of Social Welfare," *Monthly Labor Review*, Vol. 86, No. 6 (June 1963), pp. 695–700.

Now that our war on poverty blows hot we should be able to find the wherewithal to wage it.

Origins of the Proposal

Schemes for a redistribution of income have a long and interesting history and in fact and in fancy constitute a substantial portion of Utopian literature.[10] Utopian ideas represent leaps—sometimes highly creative and fruitful leaps—into the future. Proposals for social policy, such as this modest one, are more likely to be simply a drawing together and reformulation of existing ideas about a state of affairs deemed more desirable than the existing situation and one that may be achieved by a series of specified actions, that is, through a plan. An examination of the origins of the essential ideas brought together in this proposal for a Family Security Program will serve to point up some of the issues that will have to be faced in considering a plan of action.

The present proposal derives somewhat from the literature and history of family allowances, but more directly from the writings of Lady Rhys Williams. Her proposal is for a new social contract

> . . . whereby the State would acknowledge the duty to maintain the individual and his children at all times and to assure for them all of the necessities of a healthy life. The individual in his turn would acknowledge it to be his duty to divert his best efforts to the production of the wealth whereby alone the welfare of the community can be maintained.[11]

Under this contract a benefit would be paid to every person who is employed or unemployable, or, if unemployed, is willing to accept suitable employment. Benefits would be paid in addition to earnings and income from other sources. Financing would be through a flat rate income tax that, when combined with per capita benefit payments, would produce the net effect of a progressive income tax.

The social contract is designed to solve the following problems: (1) the distribution of wealth, (2) the freeing of the unemployed to undertake

10. *See,* for example, Lewis Mumford, *The Story of Utopias* (New York: Boni and Liveright, 1922). In the present atomic-space age it is easy to forget that the earliest form of science fiction was social-science fiction and that this genre too had its uses. Shall we also think on why latter-day social-science fiction (e.g., Huxley's *Brave New World*, Orwell's *1984*) is not Utopian but "Dystopian"?

11. Lady Juliet Rhys Williams, *Something to Look Forward to* (London, England: MacDonald and Company, 1943), p. 145. This book is, unfortunately, out of print, but a short selection from it appears in William D. Grampp and Emanuel T. Weiler, *Economic Policy, Readings in Political Economy* (Homewood, Ill.: Richard D. Irwin, 1953), pp. 284–292.

part-time work for profit, (3) the maintenance of a stable price level, (4) the ending of opposition between taxpayers and state beneficiaries, (5) the complete abolition of the means test, without involving state bankruptcy, (6) the maintenance of full employment, without resort to compulsory labor. Considering the number and magnitude of its objectives, the social contract idea seems disarmingly simple, but when subjected to analysis turns out to be amazingly powerful. The Beveridge plan, which relies heavily on the social insurance principle and was developed contemporaneously with *Something to Look Forward to*, won immediate political interest and support. Subsequent critiques by competent British economists point to distinct advantages in the new social contract.[12]

In this country, Friedman and Theobald recently proposed ways of treating poverty that are reminiscent of Lady Rhys Williams' writings.[13] The similarity of Friedman's and Theobald's proposals is noteworthy in view of the marked variations in their general stance and economic philosophies.

Friedman identifies himself as a liberal, in the nineteenth-century meaning of that term. He is committed to political decentralization and to economic reliance on private voluntary arrangements arrived at in the marketplace. He believes that the most desirable way of alleviating poverty is through private charity, but recognizes that government action is necessary, at least in large impersonal communities. Friedman's proposal, which he terms "a negative income tax," is that if an individual's income is less than the sums of his exemptions and his deductions he would receive from the government as an income subsidy a percentage of the difference. The levels at which subsidies would be set would be determined by how much taxpayers are willing to tax themselves.[14]

If Friedman's philosophy is characterized as the liberalism of the nineteenth century, then Theobald's can safely be placed in the twentieth century—if not later. Theobald's proposal for basic economic security is as follows:

> One of the fundamental principles of the present United States tax system is the "exemption" of a part of an individual's income from taxation. At its inception, this exemption insured that taxes would not be paid on that portion

12. Alan T. Peacock, *The Economics of National Insurance* (London, England: William Hodge & Company, 1952), p. 94 *ff*. *See also* Denstone Berry, "Modern Welfare Analysis and the Forms of Income Distribution," in Alan T. Peacock, ed., *Income Redistribution and Social Policy* (London, England: Jonathan Cape, 1954), pp. 41–51.

13. Milton Friedman, *Capitalism and Freedom* (Chicago: University of Chicago Press, 1962); Robert Theobald, *Free Men and Free Markets* (New York: Clarkson and Tatten, 1953).

14. Friedman, *ibid.*, pp. 190–192.

of income required to provide a reasonable standard of living. However, the Government lost sight of this aim when increasing the tax load to pay for World War II, and the value of this exemption has been further reduced since the end of World War II by the effects of inflation. The original aim of the federal tax exemption should be raised immediately to a level which would guarantee an un-taxed income adequate for minimum subsistence. Those whose incomes from earnings or from capital did not reach this level would then be entitled to receive further government payments sufficient to raise the incomes to this level and assure their basic economic support.[15]

Theobald points out that the provision of medical care as well as education as a community responsibility would simplify the establishment of appropriate levels of basic economic security. A consulting economist, he is primarily concerned with the effects of technology, especially cybernetics, the combination of automation and computers, on the distribution of income and on the labor market. He believes that because of the increased productive capacity of our economy it is not only unnecessary but impractical to attempt to make everyone's livelihood dependent upon his working. He accepts the position that Galbraith developed in *The Affluent Society* that we are in an economy of abundance rather than in an economy of scarcity and asserts that an absolute constitutional right to a "due income" is not only possible but essential for the future of the economy.[16]

The Incentive to Work

Arguments against the treatment of poverty through the use of taxes represent a curious congeries of theories, ideas, and biases. Some are of historic interest only, some persist over time, and still others may be of more recent coinage.[17] For example, the early attacks against the Elizabethan Poor Laws launched by Malthusian enthusiasts: in its current form this movement has, of course, been diverted from criticisms concerning support by the state of the "spawning poor" to the support of birth control programs. The banner of Social Darwinism has long been raised against the puny forces of poor relief in this country, and garnished by the symbols of racial prejudice it is still flaunted in the benighted backwoods around certain state capitals.

Some of the disadvantages of the direct treatment of poverty cited by some contemporary economists are (1) it must be done over and over

15. Theobald, *op. cit.*, pp. 192–193.
16. John Kenneth Galbraith, *The Affluent Society* (Boston: Houghton-Mifflin Co., 1958).
17. Samuel Mencher, "The Changing Balance of Status and Contract in Assistance Policy," *Social Service Review*, Vol. 35, No. 1 (March 1961), pp. 17–32.

again and (2) productivity may be inhibited by (a) diverting money from capital formation and from investment in the nation's industrial plant to taxes and (b) reducing the incentive to work, and especially to work as much as possible.[18]

The only comment that will be made here about the criticism listed first is that, although true, it can also be leveled against eating. The current curious and unique phenomenon of universally bullish economic indicators together with the recent tax reduction should help to mute although not inhibit continued expressions of anxiety about the tax burden.

The chief argument against the present proposal and in favor of the retention of the means test is also one that can be expected to persist over time and that is based on the theory that by insuring everyone a livelihood and removing the whiplash of hunger "most folk won't work"—and that this will be not only demoralizing for the general populace but ruinous of the economy. Social workers and others familiar with modern dynamic psychology may contend that this fear and the argument as a whole derive from an outmoded, simplistic view of human behavior. We can also oppose our professional ethic of ameliorism against what may appear to us to be an unduly pessimistic view of human nature and we can, if need be, produce a considerable amount of clinical evidence to show that mature individuals strive to be productive. However, perhaps the best that can be hoped for here is a verdict of "not proved," for there appears to be an absence of the kind of data needed for policy formulation.

Lady Rhys Williams posits the necessity of providing economic incentives for work as one of the basic tenets of the social contract. Her proposal, like state unemployment compensation laws, provides for payment only if persons accept suitable employment. At the other extreme, Theobald's basic economic security plan is focused on the problem of too few jobs rather than on the problem of too few takers, and it seems likely that increasing numbers of people will agree with his contention that it is unjust to insist that a person work or starve if no one will give him a job.

Friedman says of his proposal:

> Like any other measures to alleviate poverty it reduces the incentive of those helped to help themselves but it does not eliminate that incentive entirely as a system of supplementing incomes up to some fixed minimum worth. An extra dollar earned always means more money available for expenditure.[19]

18. Allen G. B. Fisher, "Alternative Techniques for Promoting Equality in a Capitalist Society," in Grampp and Weiler, *op. cit.*, pp. 277–278.
19. *Op. cit.*, p. 192.

This effect is gained under Friedman's proposal because the subsidies granted are a fraction of the sum of personal exemption and deductions, which in turn may or may not equal the required income. Friedman's built-in incentive feature is therefore obtainable only at the expense of sacrificing the assurance that all families will receive the income they need.

A work incentive feature can be incorporated into the present proposal for a Family Security Program without sacrificing the guarantee of a minimum income merely by reducing Family Security Benefits by a percentage of earnings. Assuming a family of four and a Federally Guaranteed Minimum Income of $3,000 the effects of reducing FSB by a percentage that would increase with each earnings bracket is demonstrated in Table 7-1.

Table 7–1

Earned Income	FSB/Taxes	Total Income
$ 0–$ 999	$3,000–$2,400	$3,000–$3,399
1,000– 1,999	2,399– 1,700	3,399– 3,699
2,000– 2,999	1,699– 900	3,699– 3,899
3,000– 3,999	899– 0	3,899– 3,999
4,000– 4,499	0	4,000– 4,499
4,500 and above	Tax on amounts above $4,500	4,500+

The net effect in this illustration would be that in addition to receiving a $3,000 FSB, families earning up to $1,000 would retain up to 40 per cent of such earnings. If family earnings were between $1,000 and $1,999 the family would retain between 35 and 40 per cent of this income in addition to their FSB, and so on. An extension of the work incentive feature is gained by fixing an income bracket within which a family could not claim FSB but would be tax exempt. Families earning from $4,000 to $4,500 would receive no FSB and would pay no taxes. Families earning above $4,500 would receive no FSB and would pay taxes only on income above $4,500.

Total national expenditures for FSB payments including incentive allowances for earnings if the FGMI were set at $3,000 for a family of four would of course fall between previous estimates of $11 and $23 billion. Substantial additional costs, however, would arise from narrowing the present tax base as a result of exempting family income up to $4,500, in the form of reduced revenues from the income tax.

The Law of Parsimony, the dictates of administrative simplicity, and the social work ethic would all argue against including the incentive feature in the FSB plan, unless and until experience indicates the need for it. However, this is the kind of issue that, if properly structured, may provide reasonable men with grounds for agreement. And those who feel strongly about the necessity of a work incentive should have the opportunity of considering the payment of the additional cost.

FSB and Social Welfare Manpower

Of the 105,000 social welfare workers in the United States, 35,000 or one-third are employed in state and local public assistance agencies.[20] The overwhelming proportion of the time of public assistance staffs goes into the mechanics of eligibility determination and the handling of details of financial assistance and precious little into the provision of restorative, rehabilitative, therapeutic, integrative, socializing services. Suggestions have been made from time to time that one way of achieving a better balance in public assistance programs between the provision of financial service and other welfare services would be to establish functionally specialized staff units for each type of service in the same agency or possibly in two separate agencies.[21] The weakness of this type of proposal is that it does not go far enough. As long as the two functions—the administration of financial service and of other welfare services—appear to require the same kind of activity (for example, interviewing, traveling, home visiting) by the same kind of staff and with the same clientele it seems highly unlikely that many administrative takers will be found. Contrast with this the evident and substantial gains in the efficient utilization of manpower that would be made available by the adoption of the policies and procedures possible under the federal Family Security Program.

The establishment of a federal Family Security Program would enable state and local public welfare agencies to change the focus and emphasis of their programs in the direction so presciently indicated by the change in the name of the federal Bureau of Public Assistance to the Bureau of Family Services. Poverty is, of course, sometimes preceded by psychological, emotional, health, and other problems of the individual. However, social workers will testify that of far greater import is the effect chronic, hopeless, and grinding poverty, produced by massive external social and

20. *Salaries and Working Conditions of Social Welfare Manpower in 1960* (New York: National Social Welfare Assembly, undated), p. 20. Figures given are exclusive of recreation workers.
21. *See* Editor's Page, *Social Work,* Vol. 7, No. 1 (January 1962), p. 128; and Eveline M. Burns, *op. cit.*, p. 122.

economic forces, has on the appearance and exacerbation of problems in the individual and his family. These effects may persist even after financial support is provided and are likely to be of an order that require and respond to social work treatment, fortified by a strong battery of community welfare services.

An important part of a plan to transfer the income maintenance function of the public assistance programs to a federal Family Security Program would be to extend and expand the extremely limited range of state and local welfare services now provided through public assistance agencies, and to fashion them into a comprehensive flexible program of public services for families. Together with our developing public child welfare service programs we would then have an organizational base for a well-rounded public welfare service available to all the people. Freed of the incubus of the means test and properly selected and equipped and well related to the community and to the social work and other professions, state and local public welfare staffs would have a fair and rare opportunity of making a great contribution to the war against poverty.

Political Realities

Politicians as well as caseworkers know how to "partialize," and among the kinds of questions that will be asked about the present proposal sooner or later will be, "Do you have to have all of this?" and "What part of this is most important?" One possible ploy will be, "Let's start with children or better yet the aged—they vote."

Almost two decades ago the writer suggested that the unfolding of the Canadian experience with family allowances could be observed with benefit by those in the United States who are concerned with social security and child welfare.[22] Over the years social workers, when overwhelmed by public assistance bureaupathology, are wont to murmur rather wistfully that perhaps they ought to start thinking about family allowances. It is, of course, possible that the present proposal to abolish the means test may not seem to be overly modest to some people and we may be forced to settle at this time for a family allowances program. But this should be resisted even by those of us who think children are the most important people but who would also like to prevent further "hardening of the categories" and increased complexity in the intricate mosaic or crazy-quilt pattern that characterizes our present social security and welfare nonsystem. The case for starting a noncontributory Family Secur-

22. Edward E. Schwartz, "Some Observations on the Canadian Family Allowance Program," *Social Service Review*, Vol. 20, No. 4 (December 1946), pp. 451–473.

ity Program for the aged might have political appeal, but the fact is that parents of children vote too.

Temporizing is another technique of practical politics and, in a form that social workers themselves have been known to use, includes the appeal to "demonstration and research." We must have research and we must also be clear about the function of research and how it differs from careful planning, detailing, documentation, and justification of proposals for social policy.

Nevertheless, consideration may well be given to the desirability of a geographically limited demonstration of some aspects of the proposal for an FSB plan. For example, through use of federally available research and demonstration funds a state welfare agency might develop a procedure for checking the feasibility of a central mechanical check of eligibility through the use of data processing equipment after the necessary arrangements were made for social security or other numerical identification of all salary, wages, and other types of income payments within the state.

This kind of jurisdiction-limited demonstration would appear to be feasible in a state having a small daily commuting population and an effective state income tax law. Financing of assistance payments in this kind of demonstration would not require new federal legislation inasmuch as nothing in the present public assistance titles of the Social Security Act requires the kind of means test currently used and states are free to submit their own plans for determining need. One of the points of administrative interest in such a demonstration would be a check on possible differences in the completeness of social security identification of income in low- as compared with middle- and upper-income brackets. Other administrative problems such as the frequency of FSB payments and methods of adjusting reports of anticipated income to subsequent experience could also be tested in practice on a restricted demonstration basis. Necessary research on an FSB program would of course be expedited if there is clear evidence of interest in abolishing the means test.

If a Family Security Program can be administered on a state basis, why go to a centralized federal program? The answer to this, in part, is that not all states meet the conditions necessary for a demonstration and that in a population as mobile as ours, national administration would appear to be an administrative prerequisite. A more fundamental reason is simply that the experience of the past three decades clearly points to the greater probability of meeting the most essential elements of a Family Security Program—*the right to an adequate and equitable income—* through a federally administered program than through a federal-state grant-in-aid scheme. Some of the disadvantages of the public assistance approach have been documented as follows:

> In theory, public assistance should take care of all current need, coming into play when all other sources of income fall short of socially acceptable minimum levels and underpinning all other income-maintenance programs. How far short of this standard the existing public assistance programs fall can be measured in several ways.
>
> One recent study used as a standard of need twice the amount of a low-cost food budget as calculated, with regional variations, by the Department of Agriculture.[23] A standard under which 50 per cent of total income must go for food is minimal indeed. Yet in 1958, to meet this standard, assistance payments for families receiving aid to families with dependent children would have needed to be increased for the country as a whole by 72 per cent. . . . In the West a 27-per cent increase would have brought actual expenditures to the level where they would meet the standard, and in the South a 149-per cent increase would have been required.
>
> . . . It was estimated that to provide an income of twice the cost of a low-cost food budget to all persons on the public assistance rolls in 1958 would have required expenditure of $1 billion more than the $3 billion actually spent for public assistance by all levels of government in that year. . . .
>
> The Michigan study referred to earlier found that less than one-fourth of the families living in poverty in 1959 were receiving public assistance.[24]
>
> Public assistance is a Federal-State program, with levels of assistance and conditions of eligibility determined by the individual States. For this reason the raising of standards for public assistance is a far more complex and difficult problem than it is for a national insurance program. It must be noted, also, that Federal financial aid is available only for selected categories; general assistance is financed entirely by State and local funds and in many places entirely by local funds. It is important to keep in mind these structural barriers to the transfer of resources released by disarmament.[25]

The possibility of obtaining equitable and adequate support for families in all the states through the federal-state public assistance program may well be more remote—and in that sense more Utopian—than through a conversion to the proposed federal Family Security Program.

23. Ellen J. Perkins, "Unmet Need in Public Assistance," *Social Security Bulletin,* Vol. 23, No. 4 (April 1960), pp. 3–11.

24. James M. Morgan *et al., Income and Welfare in the United States* (New York: McGraw-Hill Book Co., 1962).

25. Ida C. Merriam, "Social Welfare Opportunities and Necessities Attendant on Disarmament," *Social Security Bulletin,* Vol. 26, No. 10 (October 1963), pp. 10–14.

Tax Policy and
Children's Allowances

Harvey E. Brazer is a Professor of Economics at the University of Michigan. The first draft of this selection was written for a conference on children's allowances, sponsored by the Citizens' Committee for Children in October, 1967. Brazer put forth the idea of a "vanishing allowance" to meet some of the major objections to children's allowances: the claims that equal children benefits would be inadequate and inefficient for sharply reducing American poverty. His plan combines tax reform and antipoverty objectives through the mechanism of an income-conditioned child allowance that adjusts grants to family income indirectly through the tax system.

To many of us the awareness that something less than $15 billion per year would suffice to eliminate poverty in the United States is a source of both impatience and challenge. The impatience arises because the sum involved looks so small—less than 2 per cent of the Gross National Product, about 6 per cent of total government spending, and about half the annual cost of pursuing the war in Vietnam—relative to the gains to be realized. And the challenge is found in the recognition that some means must be devised for effecting the required transfers.

Harvey E. Brazer, "Tax Policy and Children's Allowances," *Children's Allowances and the Economic Welfare of Children,* Eveline M. Burns, ed. (New York: Citizens' Committee for Children of New York, Inc., 1968), pp. 140–149. Copyright © 1968 By Citizens' Committee for Children of New York, Inc.

Given this impatience, a reading of the recent literature on schemes to alleviate or eliminate poverty leads to a sense of frustration, for it seems that no one plan is capable of achieving the objective at a cost that is not substantially greater than the so-called poverty gap.[1] Rather, it appears that the poverty problem must be approached from several directions by means of an integrated set of schemes, each of which can be expected to do no more than a part of the job. The difficulties involved arise, in part, from the fact that poverty stems from a wide range of causes, including prolonged unemployment; incapacity, when employed, to earn enough to bring income above the poverty line; absence of a male head of family; and incapacity owing to age or physical or mental infirmity.

But irrespective of why people are poor, their poverty tends to be transmitted from generation to generation through their children. Thus, for at least a substantial proportion of the poor, the best hope for breaking the poverty cycle appears to lie in a program specifically aimed at those who suffer the misfortune of having been born into a family whose income is inadequate to provide the basic necessities of life. Without these necessities—decent shelter, adequate nutrition, and clothing—provided in an atmosphere and in a manner that encourages aspirations and rewards effort and initiative, supportive programs in education and training are likely to be least helpful to those among the poor and near-poor who are most in need of help.

The needs of many of the poor may be met by expanding and improving existing programs under social security and categorical assistance. But the position of poor families with children, especially when there is an employed adult breadwinner present who is incapable of earning an adequate income, requires a new program. In the American economic system employers are not expected to adjust workers' compensation to take into account the number of children dependent on them. Nor should they be obliged to do so, for the obvious reason that the larger his family, the more difficult it would be for the individual to find and keep a job. And yet, when earnings of the family head are low, the children, unless these earnings are supplemented, are likely to be caught in the poverty trap.

It is not difficult, therefore, to make a formidable case for children's allowances and alternative programs designed to achieve the same objectives. Before examining the tax and broader fiscal policy issues associated with such programs, however, it should be noted that any one scheme that is designed to serve all or part of the needs of a segment of the poor

---

1. For a fine summary of the literature *see* Christopher Green, *Negative Taxes and the Poverty Problem* (Washington, D.C.: Brookings Institution, 1967).

population should meet several criteria: (1) It should not carry the stigma associated with a "dole" and its accompanying means test. (2) It should not discourage efforts to earn income. (3) It should be efficient, in the sense that the portion of the cost attributable to benefits realized by the nonpoor is zero or as near to zero as is compatible with the first two criteria. (4) It should be susceptible of being administered in a manner that involves neither continued or frequently repeated questioning of the right of recipients to benefits nor excessive costs.

These criteria—and the list is by no means meant to be exhaustive—impose conditions or constraints that should provide some guidance in the effort to narrow the choices among alternatives. In this examination of the alternatives the writer will examine children's allowances and look briefly into a tax credit for dependent children and the negative income tax.

Children's Allowances

The United States is the only major Western nation that does not have a children's allowance program. In some countries, such as Belgium, France, Germany, and Italy, the program is tied to social insurance and financed through payroll taxes imposed on the employer, whereas in Canada, Sweden, and the United Kingdom it is unrelated to social security and financed out of general funds. At current exchange rates monthly benefits per child range from about $6 to $10. Eligibility generally extends to all children, irrespective of family income.

COST OF THE PLAN

Adoption in the United States of a similar program would suggest a monthly allowance per child under age 18 of about $15, a figure that reflects our higher level of personal income. This would cost some $12.5 billion per year, of which almost 80 per cent would go to children in non-poor families. Its net cost, if benefits were to be subject to federal income tax, would be about $10.5 billion. Financing this cost would entail such alternatives as additions of 1.8 percentage points to employer and employee social security tax rates or a 3.3 per cent increase in all personal income tax rates.

It seems patently clear that a program with these dimensions has little appeal, irrespective of whether it is financed out of income or social security taxes. It would not go nearly far enough toward alleviating poverty among families with children, it is inefficient in the sense in which that term is used in the criteria, and its cost is excessively high when viewed against its limited accomplishments.

But rejection of a children's allowance plan more or less patterned after those of Canada and the major nations of Western Europe does not imply rejection of any or all such plans. A children's allowance of $50 per month would remove an appreciable proportion of presently poor families from the ranks of the poor and, on this score, is appealing. But if it were to be paid to all families its gross cost would be, at about $42 billion, unacceptably high. And, as in the case of the $15 allowance, some four-fifths of this cost would be attributable to allowances paid to nonpoor families. The problem, then, is to attach to it provisions that will serve to concentrate benefits primarily on the poor and near-poor and bring the net cost down to a feasible level, certainly below $15 billion, while at the same time not imposing excessively high effective marginal tax rates on earnings of low-income families.

INCLUSION IN TAXABLE INCOME

One means of reducing both the net cost of the plan and the benefits accruing to middle- and high-income families is the inclusion of family allowances received in taxable income. Although other forms of public transfer payments, whether or not they are income conditioned, are now generally tax exempt, this appears to be the result of a lack of overt policy rather than a part of an overall plan designed to achieve horizontal and vertical equity under the personal income tax. Exemption of children's allowances would be inconsistent with horizontal equity, for it would favor this source of income relative to others. Vertical equity, or equity among people receiving different amounts of income, is, at best, a murky concept, but whatever it may mean it is hardly likely to be advanced by exemption of this form of income. Thus, taxing children's allowances would appear to be consistent with tax policy aimed at greater equity under the personal income tax.

Subjecting a $50 per month children's allowance to income taxation would recoup approximately $7 billion of the gross cost of $42 billion, to bring the net cost to $35 billion. Its further effect would be to increase the proportion of net benefits accruing to poor families from 20 per cent to over 25 per cent.

SUBSTITUTION FOR DEPENDENTS' EXEMPTIONS

Under present income tax law the taxpayer is permitted an exemption of $600 for himself and a like amount for his spouse (plus an additional $600 if either is over 65 and/or blind) and each of his dependents. These exemptions serve several purposes. They add a major element of progression to the income tax, avoid the administrative and compliance costs that would otherwise attach to taxing those with very low incomes, recognize that the first $600 per capita of family income represents little or no capacity to contribute to the support of government, and permit recognition of the fact that family size, at all levels of income, is an element in the determination of taxpaying capacity. What, if anything, is suggested by the introduction of a children's allowance for the role of the presently allowed income tax exemptions?

With respect to the exemption for the taxpayer and his spouse, as well as for dependents other than children who would qualify for the children's allowance, it seems that no change is called for. But the children's allowance should be viewed as a substitute for the exemption presently allowed for dependent children. The effect of this substitution would be to introduce an important element of the negative income tax at low levels of income, increase after-tax income of families and heads of households with taxable incomes of less than $4,000 and $3,600 respectively, and reduce it for those with higher taxable incomes. The effect of the suggested change is illustrated in Table 8–1 for married taxpayers with two children at selected income levels.

As is indicated in the table, the increase in after-tax income effected by the substitution of the children's allowance of $50 per month per child

Table 8–1. Effects of Children's Allowance Subject to Tax and Elimination of Exemptions for Dependent Children, Married Taxpayer, Two Children

Adjusted Gross Income	Present Law		With Children's Allowance		Increase in After-Tax Income
	Tax[a]	After-tax income	Tax[a]	After-tax income	
$ 0	$ 0	$ 0	$ 0	$ 1,200	$1,200
1,000	0	1,000	56	2,144	1,144
2,000	0	2,000	200	3,000	1,000
3,000	0	3,000	354	3,846	846
5,000	290	4,710	692	5,508	798
7,000	603	6,397	1,034	7,166	769
10,000	1,114	8,886	1,574	9,626	740
20,000	2,910	17,090	3,490	17,910	620
30,000	5,372	24,628	6,135	25,065	437
50,000	12,188	37,812	13,254	37,946	134
100,000	34,848	65,152	36,136	65,064	— 88
200,000	88,748	111,252	90,258	110,942	— 310
400,000	207,300	192,700	208,854	192,346	— 354

[a] For simplicity it is assumed that the standard deduction or minimum standard deduction is taken at incomes up to $10,000 and that itemized deductions equal to 15 per cent of adjusted gross income are taken at higher levels of income. It is further assumed that all the taxpayer's adjusted gross income is in the form of wages or salary.

for the dependents' exemptions begins at $1,200 when income is zero, is $1,144 when income is $1,000 and $1,000 when income is $2,000, declines to $740 at an income level of $10,000, and assumes negative values at the top of the income range. But the fact remains that elimination of the income tax exemption for children eligible to receive a children's allowance reduces the net cost of the allowance only to about $28 billion and the proportion of net benefits accruing to the poor is increased only from one-quarter to approximately one-third.

As it has been outlined thus far, therefore, the children's allowance plan meets three of the criteria but fails to meet the fourth: benefits would not carry any stigma, it offers simplicity in administration, and the increase in marginal tax rates on earnings is small. However, the cost of the plan is twice as high as would seem feasible and approximately two-thirds of the benefits accrue to the nonpoor.

If the criterion that is not met is accepted as an overriding constraint, it is clear that something more is needed if the very poor are to receive children's allowances of as much as $50 per month per child. It is also clear that this "something more" must involve impinging on full compliance with the other criteria.

"VANISHING ALLOWANCE"

It is desirable to retain the distribution of the allowance to all families. Otherwise it would be necessary to define and identify the poor at least at yearly intervals, thus admitting a means test and all that it implies into the scheme. The task, then, is to devise a method for recouping the allowance from those it is not intended to benefit. In effect this suggests a "vanishing allowance," one that declines in value to the recipient at a substantially more rapid rate than can be accomplished simply by substituting the allowance for the dependents' exemption and subjecting it to ordinary income tax rates. If, however, some differentiation for size of family is to be retained in tax liabilities, the allowance should not be permitted to decline to zero.

One way in which this feature can be built into the children's allowance plan is by requiring that the taxpayer add to his tax liability as ordinarily computed (after including children's allowances received in income) an amount equal to an increasing proportion of children's allowances received as income rises. In developing the rate schedule to be used for this purpose, two objectives conflict. The more steeply progressive it is made, the smaller will be the proportion of net benefits accruing to the nonpoor and the lower the total net cost. On the other hand, the steeper the progression, the higher are the implied marginal tax rates on earned income. Clearly, any suggested schedule must reflect the author's judgment and his own subjective terms of trade between minimizing disincentive effects and maximizing the share of benefits going to the poor while keeping costs within tolerable limits.

Before setting up an illustrative schedule and testing its impact on families at various income levels, a decision must be made as to the concept of income to which rates are to relate. The writer's own preference is to relate them to taxable income, including the children's allowance, since this concept presumably reflects the family's welfare more precisely than adjusted gross income, because it offers the advantage of being the concept to which taxpayers are accustomed to applying tax rates and because it would give full effect to the progression effected by the minimum standard deduction and exemptions for taxpayer and spouse. Alternative concepts of income are ruled out because their use would involve the disadvantage of losing the convenient tie-in with the income tax and the gain in administration and compliance ease that it offers.

It is proposed, therefore, that under the individual income tax children's allowances be included in income, exemptions for children eligible for the allowance be disallowed, and taxpayers be required to add to their tax liabilities as otherwise computed an amount equal to a proportion of children's allowances received.

For convenience and simplicity it might seem appropriate to adopt the taxable income brackets to which the regular income tax rates apply for purposes of the schedule of children's allowance recoupment rates. But these brackets are too wide to permit avoidance of large increments in these rates. Preferable brackets would be steps of $500 up to $4,000, $1,000 steps up to $8,000, and use of the regular income tax brackets thereafter. A suggested rate schedule is presented in Table 8–2.

Under this schedule the value of the children's allowance would range from $600 per year for each eligible child to $60 at levels of taxable income in excess of $12,000. At least one obvious difficulty appears, however. It enters in the form of extremely high marginal "notch-rates" that apply when taxable income moves from near the top of one taxable income bracket to the next higher bracket. To illustrate, suppose that a taxpayer with two children for whom he receives allowances has taxable income of $2,499. His children's allowance recoupment rate (CARR) would be 20 per cent and he would add $240 to his tax liability. If his taxable income rose to $2,501 his CARR would rise to 25 per cent and his net income would actually fall by $58 ($300 − $240 − $2) plus any ordinary tax payable on his additional $2 of income. This implies a marginal tax rate of more than 2,900 per cent! This problem might be solved in a number of ways. One of these is to apply a rate equal to that applicable to the next lower income bracket plus the increment in rate multiplied by the ratio of the taxpayer's taxable income falling within his bracket to the width of that bracket. Thus, in the case at hand the CARR applicable to a taxpayer with taxable income of $2,501 would be 20 per cent plus 1/500 of 5 per cent, or 20.01 per cent. His effective marginal CARR would be only 6 per cent ($.12 on $2) and his combined marginal tax rate 23 per cent (17 + 6). Thus there is no notch problem.

Table 8–2.   Suggested Children's Allowance
Recoupment Rate Schedule,
Married Taypayers[a]

Taxable Income	Children's Allowance Recoupment Rate
$0–$500	0
500–1,000	0
1,000–1,500	10
1,500–2,000	15
2,000–2,500	20
2,500–3,000	25
3,000–3,500	30
3,500–4,000	35
4,000–5,000	40
5,000–6,000	45
6,000–7,000	50
7,000–8,000	55
8,000–12,000	60
12,000–16,000	65
16,000–20,000[b]	90 minus marginal tax rate
Over 20,000[b]	90 minus marginal tax rate

[a] Separate schedules would be required for single taxpayers and taxpayers filing as heads of households.

[b] At these levels of taxable income the children's allowance recoupment rate declines as the individual marginal income tax rate increases, thus avoiding combined marginal rates in excess of 90 per cent.

Assuming again, for illustrative purposes, families with from one to seven children eligible for the children's allowance and selected levels of adjusted gross income, Table 8–3 offers a ready comparison of the effects of the children's allowance on the family's net income position. The table clearly illustrates the fact that the net contribution of the children's allowance to family income declines both with income and the number of eligible children in the family. Thus, for example, with two children the benefits decline from $1,200 when income is zero to just over $600 at an income level of $3,000, to $355 when income reaches $5,000, and to only $39 at the $10,000 level. Similarly, when income is, say, $3,000, the net gain begins at $339 for the first child and decreases to less than $200 for the sixth and seventh children.

That additional children bring declining net benefits may comfort those who are concerned with avoiding pecuniary incentives for bringing large numbers of children into the world. More important, in the writer's view, is the fact that the plan reflects the reasonable assumption that rearing children is an enterprise with declining marginal costs.

The writer does not have a precise estimate of the net cost of the children's allowance scheme as it has been developed here. A rough estimate would place the cost at about $12 billion, perhaps one-third higher than would be desirable. But the plan seems to offer a reasonable way to achieve the desired objectives while meeting all the criteria set forth earlier, not perfectly, but at least in large measure. Obviously, modification is possible and perhaps even desirable. One might wish, for example, to reduce the allowance from $50 per month to, say, $40 per month and to provide a larger allowance for the first than for second and subsequent children. Both these modifications are capable of substantially reducing the plan's cost.

Table 8–3.   Net Change in Income after Tax Owing to Substitution of Children's Allowance for Exemptions, Taxing Allowances, and Applying the CARR, Selected Incomes and Number of Dependent Children[a]

Number of Dependent Children	Adjusted Gross Income							
	$0	$1,000	$3,000	$5,000	$7,000	$10,000	$15,000	$30,000
One	$ 600	$ 600	$ 339	$209	$124	$ 27	$ 13	$−112
Two	1,200	1,144	618	355	218	39	− 45	−211
Three	1,800	1,674	934	483	289	42	− 81	−311
Four	2,344	2,008	1,186	590	315	36	−124	−410
Five	2,874	2,305	1,377	684	313	21	−129	−510
Six	3,112	2,562	1,572	832	304	− 3	−226	−610
Seven	3,280	2,700	1,710	910	322	−45	−305	−709

[a] Computed according to assumptions stipulated in footnote to Table 8–1.

In the general form presented here the children's allowance would not appear to offer major administrative difficulties. Its basic features, to the extent that they relate to the income tax, could be built into the income tax withholding system, including, when appropriate, even withholding on children's allowance payments alone.

The Tax Credit

An alternative means of achieving the same results as are obtainable under a children's allowance may be found in a vanishing tax credit, one that would be allowed irrespective of tax liability as otherwise calculated, including cases in which net tax liability would be negative. The credit would replace the exemption presently allowed for eligible dependents and could be made to decline with income within a range of, say, $600–$60 per dependent. In these respects it would be similar to the children's allowance plan outlined earlier. It would, however, present some difficult administrative problems.

Among these problems is the task of finding a means of providing for distribution of net benefits on a regular monthly basis without requiring people to declare their expected incomes at the beginning of each year. Underestimates would give rise to the need to collect appreciable amounts in tax from taxpayers with low incomes, a task that would involve heavy administrative costs and, undoubtedly, severe hardship in compliance in many cases. Perhaps these are not insuperable difficulties, but on balance the writer is inclined to the view that the merits of this approach relative to the children's allowance are unlikely to be found to be sufficiently attractive to warrant the measures that might be devised to overcome them.

Negative Income Tax

The appeal of the negative income tax lies in its potential capacity to deal with the problem of alleviating poverty irrespective of the presence of dependent children in the family. Those plans that have thus far been presented, however, fail to come to grips adequately with many of the problems involved.[2] These include devising a means of providing regular monthly payments to the poor and of avoiding excessively high effective marginal tax rates while at the same time providing a meaningful level of benefits, keeping the net cost down to a feasible level, and confining the benefits primarily to the poor and near-poor.

It would appear to be more than worthwhile to adopt a limited negative income tax or "negative rates" taxation, especially if it is regarded as a supplement to a children's allowance plan. But as a substitute for or alternative to that plan it is less than attractive. In fact, of course, the children's allowance as outlined earlier could readily be modified to make

2. *Ibid.*, esp. chaps. 4–8 and the references cited therein.

it a "people's allowance." As so modified it becomes a general form of negative income tax; without the modification it is essentially a negative income tax confined to families with children.

Financing Children's Allowances

There is little to be said for financing the net cost of the kind of children's allowance plan set forth here by any means other than the individual income tax. The alternative of financing through the social security payroll taxes is unappealing in terms of equity, since the base is limited to the first $6,600 of wages and salaries, thus excluding property income and part of the wage and salary income of higher income taxpayers. It is, therefore, regressive as well as horizontally inequitable. Nor can this means of financing be justified in terms of any alleged or actual "insurance principle."

For the calender year 1965, reported taxable income under the federal individual income tax amounted to $254.3 billion.[3] Adding to this sum the amount of the children's allowances that would be received by taxpayers and the disallowed exemptions for dependents would raise the total tax base to about $320 billion. Growth at the rate of 6 per cent per year would raise it further to approximately $400 billion by 1969. On this base, financing the net cost of the children's allowance plan would require an average increase in tax rates of 3 per cent. If applied across the board it would mean raising taxes to a range of from 17 to 73 per cent. Alternatively, 3 percentage points is slightly less than one-sixth of the average rate of 19 per cent applicable to taxable income in 1965. Thus, another way of attaining the desired revenue objective would be by raising all rates by about 16 per cent, to a range of 16.2 to 81.2 per cent. Clearly, the latter approach is to be preferred if more rather than less progression is desired.

But if one is to view the prospects for authorization and financing of children's allowances realistically, one must take into account existing demands and pressures on the budget of the federal government. And these are such at present as to suggest that the best that can be hoped for is that cessation of hostilities in Southeast Asia will release funds and resources in sufficient amounts, not only to make it possible to finance the plan, but to make it necessary to find means of sustaining an adequate level of demand in the economy. At this point in time children's allowances, hopefully, will stand high among such alternatives as massive tax

3. U.S. Treasury Department, Internal Revenue Service, *Statistics of Income, 1965, Individual Income Tax Returns* (Washington: U.S. Government Printing Office, 1967), p. 8.

cuts and sharp increases in other kinds of public expenditure. Clearly, it will be far easier to obtain financing out of potentially large and unwanted federal "full-employment" surpluses than through enactment of increases in income tax rates. It is essential, however, that those who favor a meaningful children's allowance plan develop in full the details and appeal of that plan, so that they may be ready to offer it for public and congressional approval as soon as the budgetary position of the federal government and the mood of the Congress become receptive to it.

A Model Negative
Income Tax Statute

James G. Speth, Jr., Richard Cotton, Joseph C. Bell, and Howard V. Mindus were student editors of the Yale Law Journal *(1969). Their proposals incorporated suggestions by Professors Edward Sparer and Boris I. Bittker of the Yale Law School and Professors James Tobin and Peter Mieszkowski of the Yale Economics Department. The model statute presented was originally intended to follow closely the plan presented by James Tobin, James A. Pechman, and Peter Miezkowski in "Is a Negative Income Tax Practical?"* Yale Law Journal, *Vol. 77, No. 1 (November 1967), but has diverged substantially from those earlier proposals. The plan is a major antipoverty effort in the form of a negative income tax.*

After four years, the War on Poverty has produced little more than a series of inconclusive skirmishes, despite the clear need for a far-reaching, comprehensive attack on the problems of the poor.[1] Meager efforts to

1. For the recent emergence of poverty as a public issue, see S. LEVITAN, THE DE-SIGN OF FEDERAL ANTIPOVERTY STRATEGY (1967). Several public and private study groups have advocated a thorough overhaul of our antipoverty efforts. U.S. ADVISORY COUNCIL ON PUBLIC WELFARE, HAVING THE POWER, WE HAVE THE DUTY (1966); NATIONAL ADVISORY COMMISSION ON CIVIL DISORDERS, REPORT 410–82 (1968); STEER-ING COMMITTEE OF THE ARDEN HOUSE CONFERENCE ON PUBLIC WELFARE, REPORT (1968), in *Hearings on Income Maintenance Programs Before the Subcomm. on Fiscal Policy of the Joint Economic Committee*, 90th Cong., 2d Sess. (1968) [hereinafter cited as *Income Maintenance Hearings*]. See generally *Income Maintenance Hearings*.

provide the underprivileged with in-kind assistance or with special educa-tion and job training have had but little effect,[2] while the traditional means of public assistance[3] have failed to raise out of poverty even the few families they reach.[4] In the face of such difficulties, public support for such programs has faltered; at the same time, the deficiences of present welfare measures have turned attention to bolder ideas[5]—the boldest and most seriously considered being the negative income tax (NIT).[6]

2. See the excellent summary of present deficiencies and future needs in the areas of housing, job training, and education in NATIONAL ADVISORY COMMISSION ON CIVIL DISORDERS, REPORT 410–56, 467–82 (1968). On food programs, see generally CITI-ZENS' BOARD OF INQUIRY INTO HUNGER AND MALNUTRITION IN THE UNITED STATES, HUNGER, U.S.A. (1968).

3. Public assistance is the generic name for several programs under the Social Se-curity Act which give financial aid, part federal and part local, to certain categories of persons upon a showing of need. The programs include Aid to the Blind, Social Security Act of 1935, §§ 1001–06, 42 U.S.C. §§ 1201–06 (1965); Aid to Families with Dependent Children, Social Security Act of 1935, §§ 401–09, 42 U.S.C. §§ 601–09 (1965); Aid to the Permanently and Totally Disabled, Social Security Act of 1935, §§ 1401–05, 42 U.S.C. §§ 1351–55 (1965); Old Age Assistance, Social Security Act of 1935, §§ 1–6, 42 U.S.C. §§ 301–06 (1965); Medical Assistance (Medicaid), Social Security Act of 1935, §§ 1901–08, 42 U.S.C. §§ 1396a–96d (Supp. II, 1965–66); Aid to the Aged, Blind, or Disabled, or for Such Aid and Medical Assistance for the Aged, Social Security Act of 1935, §§ 1601–05, 42 U.S.C. 1381–85 (1965).

4. Public assistance is deficient in two critical respects. First, it does not reach 83 per cent of the poverty-stricken families, and, of those who do receive benefits, almost all (five out of six households) are still below poverty lines after the benefits are counted. Second, it imposes restrictions and conditions that encourage continued de-pendency on welfare and undermine self-respect and family stability. *See* Orshansky, *The Shape of Poverty in 1966*, 31 SOC. SEC. BULL., March, 1968, at 3, 28–29; *Income Maintenance Hearings* 108–09; R. ELMAN, THE POORHOUSE STATE (1968); W. BELL, AID TO DEPENDENT CHILDREN (1965); Reich, *Individual Rights and Social Welfare: The Emerging Legal Issues*, 74 YALE L.J. 1245 (1965); ten Broek, *California's Dual System of Family Law: Its Origin, Development and Present Status* (pts. I–III). 16 STAN. L. REV. 257, 900 (1964), 17 *id.* 614 (1965).

See also HUNGER, U.S.A., *supra* note 2, at 70–76; SOUTHERN REGIONAL COUNCIL, PUBLIC ASSISTANCE IN THE SOUTH (1966).

5. Recent income maintenance proposals are surveyed briefly in Nicol, *Guaranteed Income Maintenance: Another Look at the Debate*, WELFARE IN REVIEW, June-July 1967, at 1, and in Schorr, *Alternatives in Income Maintenance*, 11 SOCIAL WORK 22 (1966). Many income transfer schemes are presented and discussed in C. GREEN, NEGATIVE TAXES AND THE POVERTY PROBLEM 14–81 (1967). These studies contain extensive bibliographies.

6. The development of the NIT idea is traced in C. GREEN, *supra* note 5, at 51–61. "Negative income tax" has no precise meaning. When we refer to *the* negative income tax, we mean our own proposal. Of the better-known income maintenance proposals, our plan is closest to Tobin, Pechman & Mieszkowski, *Is a Negative Income Tax Prac-tical?* 77 YALE L.J. 1 (1967). The similarities among most guaranteed income schemes is emphasized in C. GREEN, *supra* note 5, at 62–67.

The widespread interest in the NIT is indicated by President Johnson's reference to it in the ECONOMIC REPORT OF THE PRESIDENT, 1967, at 17 and by his appointment in January 1968 of a Commission on Income Maintenance to study the NIT and related ideas. More than 1228 economists at 143 institutions of higher learning have

Any national income maintenance program should not only assure everyone a minimum standard of living but should also attempt to integrate the poor into society.[7] In light of the distasteful experiences with public assistance and other anti-poverty efforts, the NIT with its direct cash payments scaled to need alone seems the simplest and quickest way to welfare objectives. Whether the NIT can succeed in alleviating and eventually eliminating poverty, however, may depend upon the proper solutions to a number of complex problems of policy and administration. The model statute set forth here attempts to deal directly with these problems, to suggest what the proper solutions may be, and to indicate what an effective negative income tax would entail.

A Simple Sketch of the Model Act

The basic notions incorporated into the proposed statute are easily stated. Each family (including single-member households) may claim as a matter of right an income supplement whose amount generally varies only with the family's size. Supplement payments are paid in cash—twice a month or at the end of a year—from the general tax revenues of the federal treasury; the right to start receiving semi-monthly payments may be asserted any time during the year. There are no restrictions on how recipients can spend the money and no circumstances under which a family can

---

endorsed the NIT approach to income maintenance, and the Arden House Conference gave its tentative endorsement also. *Income Maintenance Hearings* 452, 676. The NIT has its critics, however. *See, e.g.,* Statement of the National Association of Manufacturers, *Income Maintenance Hearings* 658; Vadakin, *A Critique of the Guaranteed Annual Income,* THE PUBLIC INTEREST, Spring 1968, at 53; Moynihan, *The Crises in Welfare, id.,* Winter 1968, at 3; Schorr, *supra* note 5; Statement of Sar A. Levitan, *Income Maintenance Hearings* 212.

7. The NIT seeks to integrate the poor into society by encouraging the employable poor to seek and retain employment. For the unemployable poor, the NIT seeks to provide them, without injuring their dignity, with sufficient money income to enable them to live adequately. Any NIT program hopes that the guaranty of a minimum adequate standard of living will strengthen family ties, foster self-reliance and self-respect, and generally enable people to function as productive members of society. The present public assistance programs thwarts the development of self-reliance by conditioning grants on accepting service and counselling. These conditions often become devices for controlling recipient behavior. *See* pp. 234–235 *infra.* Nonetheless, these restrictive provisions are couched in language that declares it a purpose of the public assistance program "to promote the well-being of the Nation by . . . helping to strengthen family life and helping needy families and individuals attain the maximum economic and personal independence of which they are capable." Social Security Amendments of 1956, § 300(b), 70 Stat. 846, 42 U.S.C. § 301n (1958). INST'NS CODE § 10000 (West 1966): "With regard for the preservation of family life . . . and . . . to encourage self-respect, self-reliance, and the desire to be a good citizen, useful to society."

lose its right to the payments. Once a family elects to receive income supplements, its other available income, comprehensively defined, becomes subject to a special tax at a rate substantially higher than corresponding income tax rates. Although members of the family must still pay the federal income tax, these payments are deductible in such a manner that the combined effect of the two taxes never exceeds the special tax rate.

The "special tax" is no real tax at all—it simply operates to reduce the actual government transfer to a family as its income from other sources increases. Otherwise the NIT benefit would be the same for the well-enough-off as for the truly poor. Under the proposed statute, the annual income supplement for a family of four is $3200—a figure which closely approximates the Social Security Administration's poverty index[8]—, and the special tax rate applicable to the family's other available income is 50 per cent. When the family's unsupplemented income is twice its supplement, or $6400 a year for a family of four, the family will "break even" in terms of obligations to and from the federal government under the positive and negative tax programs. Just above the break-even point, the family will still benefit under the NIT programs, but the benefits will only partially offset positive income tax liability. As unsupplemented income increases further, it will reach a point at which the family's special tax liability alone equals the amount of the income supplement. Beyond this "tax break-even point"[9]—$7916 for a family of four[10]—there is no advantage in being under the NIT program [See Table 9–1].

Because of the NIT's tax-like features and also because of the need to make a clear break with past welfare administration, the proposed statute entrusts the program to a newly created agency within the Treasury Department, the Bureau of Income Maintenance.[11]

8. For a discussion of how these guarantee levels were selected. *See* ["Income Supplement Act" of "A Model Negative Income Tax Statute," *Yale Law Journal*, LXXVIII, No. 2 (December, 1968), p. 298. Hereafter referred to as Income Supplement Act.].

9. The term was originated in Tobin, Pechman & Mieszkowski, *supra* note 6.

10. This income figure and the accompanying table are calculated by assuming that adjusted gross income (AGI) is equal to the sum of the comprehensively defined "available income" of the statute, plus twice the federal income tax on the AGI (an amount deducted in computing "available income.") *See* Income Supplement Act §§ 10, 11, p. 315. Since available income will almost always be larger than AGI (although it is difficult to estimate by how much), the figure of $7916 should really be viewed as a maximum tax-break-even-income for families of four. If the available income of a family of four exceeded AGI by $1000, for example, the tax-break-even point measured in terms of AGI would be only about $6700. If we assume that on the average available income will exceed AGI by 10 per cent, then the average tax-break-even point measured in terms of AGI will be roughly $6900.

11. *See* Income Supplement Act § 20 and accompanying comments. . . .

Table 9–1. Effects of Proposed NIT for Family of Four

a. Before Tax Family Income	b. Positive Tax Liability	c. Negative Tax Liability $(.50)(a-2b)$	d. Total Tax Liability $(b+c)$	e. Basic Income Supplement	f. Net Government Transfer $(e-d)$	g. Net NIT Transfer $(e-c)$	h. After Tax Family Income $(a+f)$
0	0	0	0	3200	3200	3200	3200
1000	0	500	500	3200	2700	2700	3700
3000	4	1496	1500	3200	1700	1704	4700
6000	450	2550	3000	3200	200	650	6200
6400	511	2689	3200	3200	0	511	6400
7000	603	2897	3500	3200	-300	303	6700
7916	758	3200	3958	3200	-758	0	7158

Problems of Drafting: Policy Conflicts and Choices

On its face, the proposed statute may appear to operate smoothly, but most provisions represent uneasy compromises between inconsistent policies. The goal of the model statute is to guarantee an adequate income to everyone while at the same time preserving the incentive to work among recipients, protecting their rights and dignity, treating equal needs equally, and guarding against abuse and fraud—and to do all this at a reasonable cost and without impossible burdens on administration. Yet it is difficult to protect the dignity of the recipients and at the same time police for abuses, to respond equally to equal needs and also avoid an administrative morass, or to remove financial incentives to family splitting without departing from standards of need. It is especially difficult to establish a realistic supplement level and a tax rate that will not destroy work incentives without exceeding reasonable bounds of cost.[12] A brief discussion of work incentives, the overall cost of the program, and the NIT's impact on family structure will demonstrate the severity of the conflicts involved in drafting the statute.

WORK INCENTIVES, INCOME GUARANTEES, AND PROGRAM COST

What effect the model statute would have on work incentives is unknown; the problems can only be raised.[13] The work-incentive goal of the statute is two-fold: to minimize labor force drop-outs and to avoid unduly impairing the potency of wage gains as incentives for intraplant advancement and for geographic and interplant mobility of workers.

An income maintenance program which seriously reduced participation in the labor force would be unsatisfactory from several standpoints. Such a program would thwart the goal of integrating the employable poor into the rest of society and would compromise general economic goals of growth and increasing production. Certain sectors of production would particularly suffer from a decline in the supply of unskilled labor, and differential drop-out rates in various occupations would have a disrupting effect on the present wage structure in the economy.

A statutory work requirement would "solve" the drop-out problem,[14]

12. See Vadakin, *supra* note 6, at 53. *See also* C. GREEN, *supra* note 5, at 62–81.
13. See the discussion in C. GREEN, *supra* note 5, at 113–37. The Office of Economic Opportunity is presently funding an experimental NIT project in several New Jersey cities. The project should be the source of valuable data on the incentives question. N.Y. Times, Oct. 27, 1968, at 52, col. 4.
14. *See* 42 U.S.C.A. §§ 602(a)(19)(A) to -(F), 607(b) (Supp. 1968). Such a policy can be carried to extremes. The New York Court of Appeals reversed the criminal conviction of a welfare recipient for refusing to accept a low-paying job. People v. Pickett, 19 N.Y.2d 170, 225 N.E.2d 509, 278 N.Y.S.2d 802 (1967).

but at the cost of the recipients' independence and dignity. The alternative is to rely on financial incentives to keep recipients in the labor force and responsive to labor market economics. How effective these incentives will be depends on both the NIT guarantee levels and the special tax rate. If the guarantee levels are high, a very low special tax rate might not be enough to prevent substantial labor force drop-outs. The supplement levels proposed here are already the minimum incomes set by the Social Security Administration poverty lines, so it would defeat the major objective of the program to reduce them. The problem then becomes one of selecting the appropriate tax rate.

A special tax rate approaching 100 per cent would have a severe drop-out effect. Since there are few non-financial rewards for low-wage employment, almost no one participating in such a program would take a job unless he could earn an after-tax income substantially greater than his family supplement level—perhaps $4000 a year for a family of four. Experience in the public assistance program with reducing benefits dollar-for-dollar as earned income increases has indicated the anti-employment consequences of this system.

A very high tax rate would also severely interfere with the labor market's efficient allocation of those NIT recipients who continued to work. If workers retained only a small fraction of the increased wages they would gain through promotion or by moving to a new plant or geographic region, their sensitivity to wage differentials would probably decrease sharply. Moreover, a high special tax rate might pressure workers (and unions) to demand higher wage increases to offset the high rate, thus increasing the cost-push inflationary pressures in the economy.

Any lowering of the special tax rate, of course, reduces the incentive to drop out of the labor force by increasing the portion of earned income a family may retain. A lower tax also increases workers' willingness to move or to seek advancement in order to obtain higher wages. These effects on work incentives are likely to be disproportional to the financial gains to the individuals involved, since the retained earnings will represent the family's first really discretionary income,[15] and the family will be able to plan its consumption against the background of a secure income. Thus at the other extreme from the 100 per cent rate, a special tax rate approaching zero, with the supplement levels proposed here, would probably cause very few people to leave the labor force and have only minimal effects on the operation of labor markets. As the special tax rate is lowered, however, two complications arise. First, the location of the

15. *Cf.* Ayres, *Guaranteed Income: An Institutional View*, in THE GUARANTEED INCOME 173–74, 176–77 (R. Theobald ed. 1967); *Income Maintenance Hearings* 324.

tax break-even point is inversely related to the tax rate, so that participation in the program increases sharply as the rate is lowered. Second, as participation increases, so does the cost. A program with a near-zero tax rate, for example, would cost over $150 billion a year if—as is likely—almost every family in the country elected to receive supplements.

The 50 per cent tax rate proposed in the model statute represents an attempt at compromise between the labor market and budgetary effects, although the result of the compromise may be that neither incentive nor cost goals are fully attained.[16] From the standpoint of the work incentive alone, the 50 per cent rate may still be too high. Over the lower ranges of earned income, it is a higher tax rate than the 1967 Social Security amendments impose on present public assistance recipients.[17] Even assuming no serious drop-out problem at this rate, however, the impact on the labor market of this NIT program may be substantial. Combined with the poverty-line supplement levels, the 50 per cent rate produces a tax break-even point of almost $8000 a year for a family of four.[18] Consequently, at least half the labor force would benefit from the NIT and be brought under the special tax.[19] This high marginal tax rate (relative to present positive tax rates) on such a large portion of the labor market could severely affect the financial incentives of a great number of workers, neither poor nor near-poor.

Finally, the 50 per cent tax rate means that the cost of the program will be substantial—very roughly, $27 billion, after account is taken of the savings that would result from the elimination of state and federal public assistance payments.[20] Because of the relatively high tax break-

16. A 50 per cent rate has been discussed by several prominent economists. *See, e.g.,* Tobin, Pechman & Mieszkowski, *supra* note 6, at 4. Also, officials operating the New Jersey experiment, see note 13 *supra,* believe that the 50 per cent rate has the best chance of success. Lecture by Harold Watts, Director, Institute for Research on Poverty of the University of Wisconsin and Consultant to the New Jersey experiment, at Yale University, November 14, 1968.

17. 42 U.S.C.A. § 602(a)(7)(A) (Supp. 1968) (exempting the first $30 per month of earned income plus one third of the remainder).

18. *See* Table 9–1, p. 242 & note 10 *supra.*

19. *See* Orshansky, *The Shape of Poverty in 1966, supra* note 4, at 3, 19.

20. This calculation is based upon family income statistics to be found in BUREAU OF THE CENSUS, CURRENT POPULATION REPORTS, INCOME IN 1966 OF FAMILIES AND PERSONS IN THE UNITED STATES, Series X P-60, No. 53 (1967). Unlike income statistics from income tax returns, these data include government transfers in income.

The NIT's potential for lowering administrative costs has probably been exaggerated. First, although the NIT statute has been designed to replace public assistance, some functions that public assistance presently performs would have to be continued, and perhaps they should be administered by a residual public assistance bureaucracy. *See* pp. 281–82 *infra.* Second, the cost of administering the NIT itself could be substantial. *See, e.g.,* Income Supplement Act § 20(e) *infra* (authorizing the establishment of local offices of the Bureau of Income Maintenance).

even point, much of this money will be distributed to the non-poor. The wide coverage also increases administrative costs, both because the number of beneficiaries is greater and because the difficulties in determining "available income" increase with greater wealth. The $27 billion estimate may well be exaggerated, because the 1966 data on which it is based make use of a definition of income less comprehensive than available income as defined in the model statute and because personal income per capita has risen since 1966. But even after these corrections are made, the NIT as proposed may be too expensive for many Congressmen. The cost could be reduced substantially by certain minor changes in the NIT program which can be justified in terms of policies (aside from economy) discussed below.[21] But larger savings would require either a higher special tax rate (with the resulting labor market effects), guarantee levels generally below the poverty lines, or both.

THE FAMILY UNIT AND GUARANTEE LEVELS

The second major confrontation of conflicting policies takes place over the determination of what should be the unit to receive NIT benefits. Like most income maintenance plans, the model NIT uses family units, instead of individuals, as the bases for calculating need and disbursing benefits.[22] Given the assumption that the NIT should guarantee only a minimum standard of living to every family, using the family as the basic unit makes very good sense. When a person belongs to a family group which pools its resources and shares expenses, his standard of living depends on the total income available to that group and not merely on his own.[23] Moreover, the larger the family, the less per capita income it apparently needs to maintain a particular standard of living.[24] If an NIT program is going to take family economies into account, it vastly simplifies administration to deal with families as a unit.

The decision to focus on the family and to adjust supplement benefits according to family size, however, reflects popular moral notions and the

21. For example, if the supplemental level for an unrelated individual was lowered from $1200 to $1000 per year and certain economies of scale for families with several dependents were recognized, perhaps $5 billion could be shaved off the present estimate, Tobin, Pechman & Mieszkowski, *supra* note 6, at 8–9; Tobin, *Raising the Incomes of the Poor*, in AGENDA FOR THE NATION (K. Gordon ed. 1969).

22. *See generally* Tobin, Pechman & Mieszkowski, *supra* note 6, at 8–10 (1967); C. GREEN, *supra* note 5, at 99–105 (1967). In Canada, the Royal Commission on Taxation has recommended a shift from the historic focus on the individual to the family as the proper taxpaying unit. 3 ROYAL COMMISSION ON TAXATION, REPORT (1966).

23. H. GROVES, FEDERAL TAX TREATMENT OF THE FAMILY 4–5 (1963); C. GREEN, *supra* note 5, at 100.

24. Orshansky, *Who's Who Among the Poor: A Demographic View of Poverty*, SOC. SEC. BULL., July 1965, at 8.

need to contain the cost of the NIT as well as more technical economic, administrative, and welfare considerations. Providing all recipients with a basic grant adequate for the needs of a single individual and then letting them enjoy any savings realized by marriage or living together would be far less troublesome to administer; but the statute rejects this alternative— partly because it would greatly increase the cost of the NIT and partly because few people agree that the government should give the poor more than they absolutely need.[25] The positive income tax, reflecting not so much a different public morality as a different class of beneficiaries, takes the opposite tack. It not only ignores family economies, it contributes to them through such devices as joint filing.[26]

The basic income guarantee provisions of the model statute are generally based upon the poverty levels determined by the Social Security Administration.[27] The family unit is entitled to receive $1200 for the first claimant, $800 for the second claimant, and $600 for each dependent.[28] More than two claimants in a family unit are not allowed. Dependent allowances do not taper off because of the harsh effect this would have on large families. The Social Security Administration index suggests that for each minor dependent, a family requires $600 a year to maintain its standard of living.[29] The absence of a limit may encourage child-bearing or at least fail to discourage it, but consigning large families to a subminimum standard of living is an inappropriate means for implementing birth control.[30]

The supplement guarantees deviate deliberately from the poverty line in one respect. Studies indicate that a single individual, living alone, needs about 70 per cent as much for a minimum adequate income as two people living together.[31] Thus, if $2000 a year is a minimum income for a couple, a single claimant should receive $1400, and the second member

---

25. C. Green, *supra* note 5, at 71; Tobin, Pechman & Mieszkowski, *supra* note 6, at 8.

26. Int. Rev. Code of 1954, §§ 2, 6013; *see Income Maintenance Hearings* 281–82.

27. *See* Orshansky, *Counting the Poor: Another Look at the Poverty Profile*, Soc. Sec. Bull., Jan. 1965, at 3, 9.

28. Income Supplement Act § 5(a) *infra*.

29. *See* Orshansky, *The Shape of Poverty in 1966, supra* note 4, at 4.

30. There are sound arguments that the setting of a maximum grant per family, thereby discriminating against large families, would be unconstitutional. *See* Collins v. State Bd. of Social Welfare, 248 Iowa 369, 81 N.W.2d 4 (1957); Metcalf v. Swank, 37 U.S.L.W. 2276 (N.D. Ill. Nov. 12, 1968).

31. Estimates of the income required by a single individual living alone relative to a married couple range from an empirically observed 60 per cent for middle-income families to an estimated 80 per cent for low-income families. *See* Revised Equivalence Scale for Urban Families of Different Size, Age and Composition, to be published as U.S. Dep't of Labor, Bureau of Labor Statistics, Bull. No. 1570–2; Orshansky, *Who's Who Among the Poor, supra* note 24, at 9. Seventy per cent has been chosen as a reasonably safe estimate.

of the family unit, whether a claimant or dependent, should increase the family's supplement just $600. Setting up the guarantees in this way, however, would create an $800 incentive for a family to break up—either in fact or in form. Paying a family unit only $1200 for the first claimant and $800 for the second is an attempt to minimize this effect.[32] Furthermore, more than half of the single member family units are old people,[33] who frequently receive benefits from both Social Security and Medicare, have a special priority in admission to public housing, and otherwise need less income. Payments of $1000 for every claimant would remove any incentive for the family unit to split,[34] but this solution seems too great a deviation from the poverty line for single individuals.

Since they can receive more money under the model statute if members file separately, families are not likely to appreciate the reasons for unit filing enough to do it voluntarily. Also, in many families most of the income is attributable to only one member: by filing separately, the rest of the family could receive income supplements while the wage earner evaded the offsetting special tax obligation. The statute must therefore make a certain amount of unit filing legally unavoidable.[35] First, minors—unless they are married, or over eighteen and no longer in school or supported by their parents—cannot claim an income supplement under the program: they may receive benefits only indirectly, as someone else's dependent.[36] Second, married couples, as well as unmarried couples who live together and are the common parents of at least one child, must file as a single family unit.[37]

The logic behind the mandatory family unit requirement, of course, extends to all groups sharing the same dwelling unit. Economically, there is no difference between a married and an unmarried couple living together, and even roommates of the same sex can live substantially more

---

32. *See also* note 46, *infra*.

33. Orshansky, *The Shape of Poverty in 1966, supra* note 4, at 4.

34. Some writers have urged this solution. Tobin, Pechman & Mieszkowski, *supra* note 6, at 8–9. Instead of setting equal benefit levels for the two adults in a family to avoid the incentive to split, the single individual's benefit level could be left at a higher level, individual filing retained, and a provision added to restrict each married couple to only one "head of household" allowance between them whether they filed separately or jointly. *See* H.R. 17331, 90th Cong., 1st Sess. (1968). Thus, while husband and wife could file separately, they would not obtain an increased benefit level. This approach only transfers the point of tension; there would still be an incentive to be unmarried because then the man and woman would be entitled to two "head-of-household" allowances. Secondly, this approach permits the wage-earner to file separately from his family, thereby multiplying administrative and calculation problems in taxing transfers from the wage-earner to his family.

35. *See* Tobin, Pechman & Mieszkowski, *supra* note 6, at 9.

36. Income Supplement Act § 9(b).

37. *Id.* § 9(d).

cheaply than a single person. Yet, however necessary, the requirement is a serious troublemaker, and extending its scope would only multiply problems of enforcement and administration.[38] Unlike marriage and parenthood, more informal relationships leave little documentary evidence of their existence and are generally transitory. Finally, adding to the number of situations in which a group had to file together would imply a much broader duty among recipients to share their income with others than that imposed by state support laws.[39] Since the statute has no provisions to enforce the duties of support it assumes, nothing would prevent a claimant in such a case from withholding benefits from dependents, or from the other claimant. More important, imposing any extra duty of support on a recipient violates the statute's clear policy against placing special burdens on the poor as a condition of their receiving benefits.[40] Consequently, the statute specifically limits the duty of support imposed on adults in required family units to that imposed by state law.

Although the mandatory family unit provision is generally consistent with the duties of support defined by state laws,[41] it still cannot ensure that income earned by one member of the family is available for the support of other members. The statute plainly intends that claimants support dependents out of their own income as well as out of supplement payments;[42] if one claimant refuses, however, the other's inability to file separately severely undercuts the NIT's antipoverty objectives. Parents of a minor who refuses to pool his earnings[43] can at least avoid reporting the money as family income by not claiming him as a dependent. Where a wife or child is not getting a share of a husband's income, the mandatory filing provision leaves them only what comfort they can find in state support and neglect statutes.

Even when all members of a family are willing to pool their resources, the mandatory unit filing rule, coupled with graduated supplement levels, encourages them to feign separation and non-support. Policing for such

38. *See, e.g.,* Reich, *Midnight Welfare Searches and the Social Security Act,* 72 YALE L.J. 1347 (1963); *cf.* King v. Smith, 392 U.S. 309 (1968).

39. ten Broek, *California's Dual System of Family Law: Its Origin, Development, and Present Status,* 17 STAN. L. REV. 614, 650–58 (1965); *see, e.g.,* CAL. CIVIL CODE § 209 (1954).

40. *Id.* But *see* Lewis & Levy, *Family Law and Welfare Policies: The Case for "Dual Systems,"* 54 CALIF. L. REV. 748, 759 (1966).

41. *See* Income Supplement Act § 9(f) *infra. See also* King & Smith, 392 U.S. 309 (1968).

42. Because the NIT imposes a 50 per cent tax rate, a wage earner included in an NIT family unit is actually required to contribute only one half of his earnings to support the rest of the family unit.

43. *Cf.* Bittker, *Income Tax Reform in Canada,* 35 U. CHI. L. REV. 637, 648–49 (1968).

fraud will place another burden on NIT administration and invite the revival of such bureaucratic abuses as midnight searches.[44] Moreover while the provision might not actually break up families, it does create undesirable tensions.[45] An unmarried couple, living together, would be reluctant to legalize their relationship, and, if they had a child, the father might leave rather than relinquish his status under the program as a separate filing unit. Society esteems a stable family unit built around a legitimate marriage:[46] whatever harmful effects the proposed statute would have upon the family structure of recipients weakens its effectiveness as a means to integrate the poor into the rest of society.

By limiting to $400 the difference between income supplements for the first and second claimants in a two-claimant family unit, the statute attempts to relieve the pressures on the required family units, lessening the incentives either to break up or to cheat. This adjustment does not reduce the incentive for a wage earner to evade the special tax; but by not filing with his family unit, he not only loses $800 of income supplement but must also forfeit the benefit of dependency exemptions and joint filing under the positive tax or risk discovery of his fraud. Unless he were receiving approximately $4000 income a year, no claimant would benefit substantially by not filing with his family.

The NIT: Competitors and Allies

While the NIT proposed here should be the core of the national welfare system, it cannot achieve its goals unaided. A comparison with alternative programs—present or proposed—points out the strength and weaknesses of the NIT and suggests complementary strategies for maintaining personal income at decent levels.

PUBLIC AND GENERAL ASSISTANCE

In performing the basic function of securing a minimum standard of living, the NIT should be far superior to public assistance. Public assistance has not been successful in maintaining income levels or in fostering social integration, and the proposed statute, explicitly designed as a re-

---

44. *See* note 38 *supra.*

45. The rewards are probably not great enough to cause actual separation in many cases, though this is a problem with present welfare programs, which withhold all benefits from families with an employable male head. *Cf.* W. BELL, AID TO DEPENDENT CHILDREN 129 (1965).

46. Gibbard, *Poverty and Social Organization,* in POVERTY AMID AFFLUENCE 45 (L. Fishman ed. 1966); C. GREEN, *supra* note 5, at 103–04; see R. TITMUSS, PROBLEMS OF SOCIAL POLICY 171–83 (1950).

placement for public assistance,[47] reflects in large part the criticisms of present welfare operations. For example, the model statute completely rejects categorical assistance and sets only one criterion for assistance—need; it provides uniform national standards of administration and guarantees adequate benefit levels; it places no restraints on the conduct of recipients or on their use of the benefits; it permits recipients to retain a substantial portion of their other income and assets; and it provides effective remedies to recipients deprived of any of these rights.[48]

Yet public assistance does attempt to perform two important functions which the NIT would not: extending financial aid for health problems and other emergencies,[49] and providing counselling and advisory services.[50] Any model welfare system should meet such needs, though the experience with public assistance shows that one program should not try to combine highly personalized services with income grants; the grants tend to become devices for controlling recipient behavior.[51] Thus, while a residual public assistance supervised by HEW[52] might initially provide these two special services, eventually advisory and counselling services should be totally separate from emergency financial aid.

If Congress passed an NIT bill with an income guarantee considerably below the level paid by public assistance in some of the more generous states, these states might wish to continue some form of public aid so their welfare recipients would not be left worse off. Public assistance legislation might be integrated into the NIT, as suggested by H.R. 17331,[53] presently before Congress, though this would result in needless duplication and perpetuate the perversities of public assistance. For a more satis-

---

47. There is no necessity to repeal explicitly the public assistance portions of the Social Security Act. While NIT benefits will pre-empt the major function of local welfare agencies, these agencies could still continue to administer the programs not pre-empted by the NIT. *See* p. 252 *infra.* A preferable solution would be to repeal the public assistance titles and draft new legislation to provide (1) financial aid for medical and other emergencies, and (2) counselling and advisory services. *See id.*

48. *See* HAVING THE POWER, *supra* note 1; Statement of Leslie C. Carter, Jr., *Income Maintenance Hearings* 2; Statement of Mitchell I. Ginsberg, *id.* 8.

49. *See, e.g.,* 42 U.S.C.A. §§ 302–03, 701–14, 606(e)(1) (Supp. 1968).

50. *See* 42 U.S.C.A. §§ 602(a)(13) to -(15) (Supp. 1968); *Income Maintenance Hearings* 274. Suggestions for reform of the welfare system have urged these counselling services be expanded, but be separated from the payment of money. HAVING THE POWER, *supra* note 1, at 47–66.

51. *See* Statement of Leslie C. Carter, Jr., *Income Maintenance Hearings* 2, 5.

52. *See* note 47 *supra.*

53. H.R. 17331, 90th Cong., 2d Sess. (1968), was an NIT proposal introduced in May 1968 by Congressman William F. Ryan (D.-N.Y.) as a bill "to provide for a comprehensive income maintenance program." The bill provides for sub-poverty index NIT benefits and a continuation of public assistance as a supplement to the NIT for certain categories of persons now eligible for public assistance. *See id.* §§ 2–3; Statement of William F. Ryan, *Income Maintenance Hearings* 354, 356.

factory, though more costly solution, each state could raise the annual income supplement due its residents up to the old public assistance levels.[54]

A last question concerns the relation between the NIT proposal and the increasingly urgent demands for a wholesale reform of public assistance. Any modification of public assistance programs that took into account all the serious criticisms of present welfare efforts—as, for example, do the recommendations of the U.S. Advisory Council on Public Welfare[55] —would result in a system of distributing benefits strikingly similar to the one outlined in the model statute. The NIT and public assistance reform are not so much alternative ways of dealing with poverty as they are alternative ways of dealing with Congress, and the choice between them is chiefly one of political strategy. Since the NIT completely escapes the faulty concepts and spotted history of public assistance, it still ranks as the preferable approach.

JOB PROGRAMS AND THE GUARANTEED JOB

Enactment of the NIT should not foreclose continuation and expansion of national job and manpower programs.[56] Adult education, job training, job creation, relocation assistance, and local development programs should serve as important allies of the NIT.[57] Quite apart from the needs of business, these programs are essential to a comprehensive war on poverty in a society that values employment as a source of income, status, and self-respect.[58] Moreover, job programs, by lowering unemployment and raising the wages of NIT recipients, would reduce the cost of the NIT program.

A guaranteed job program, insofar as it would further the policy of

54. *See* Income Supplement Act § 6.

55. HAVING THE POWER, *supra* note 1.

56. These programs and their problems and prospects are described in S. LEVITAN & G. MANGUM, MAKING SENSE OF FEDERAL MANPOWER POLICY (1967); S. LEVITAN, ANTIPOVERTY WORK AND TRAINING EFFORTS: GOALS AND REALITY (1967). *See also* E. GINZBERG, MANPOWER AGENDA FOR AMERICA (1968).

57. A more vigorous pursuit of antipoverty goals through these programs has been widely recommended. NATIONAL ADVISORY COMMISSION ON CIVIL DISORDERS, REPORT 413–24 (1968); STEERING COMMITTEE OF THE ARDEN HOUSE CONFERENCE, *supra* note 2; THE NATIONAL COMMISSION ON TECHNOLOGY, AUTOMATION AND ECONOMIC PROGRESS, TECHNOLOGY AND THE AMERICAN ECONOMY 35 (1966). E. FOLEY, THE ACHIEVING GHETTO (1967); Statement of Mitchell I. Ginsberg, *Income Maintenance Hearings*, 20–21; Statement of Leonard Lesser, *id.* 199. *See also* H.R. 12280, 90th Cong., 1st Sess. (1967); A. PEARL AND F. REISSMAN, NEW CAREERS FOR THE POOR (1965).

58. *See* M. WEBER, THE PROTESTANT ETHIC AND THE SPIRIT OF CAPITALISM (T. Parsons transl. 1958); *Income Maintenance Hearings* 128, 297, 397.

assuring every American decent employment, is certainly not inconsistent with NIT goals.[59] The guaranteed job, however, has occasionally been suggested as an alternative to the negative income tax, usually by those who emphasize the conflict between the NIT and the American work ethic.[60] The most obvious difficulty with this proposal is that at least one-third of all the families classified as poor have no employable members;[61] more and better jobs is no answer for them.[62] Yet problems with the guaranteed job do not end there. The guaranteed job plan can be effective only if the government is made employer of last resort. In other words, the government would have to stand ready to employ or to find employment for anyone unable to find a job in the private sector that would lift his family out of poverty. If the guaranteed job were not to create a gigantic work camp, it would have to offer a range of jobs accommodating a wide variety of skills and interests. Even so, freedom of choice in taking government employment would inevitably be limited, and the program's bureaucracy would have an unhealthy amount of discretion in allocating jobs. Finally, if guaranteed job benefits were substantial enough to keep participants from living in poverty, they would attract many unskilled workers out of low-paying or unattractive jobs in the private sector. Even complicating the administration of the program with a strictly enforced need-for-employment requirement would not significantly reduce the enormous scope and cost of an adequate guaranteed job plan, and the effects on the private sector labor market would be at least as substantial as under the NIT.[63]

PROGRAMS THAT MAKE AN EMPLOYABLE-NONEMPLOYABLE DISTINCTION

Two arguments encountered in the preceding discussion[64] push strongly toward a program that, while still comprehensive, would treat the employable and the unemployable poor differently. The first argument is political: that there is little support in Congress for paying an adequate

59. A guaranteed job program with the government serving as employer of last resort was proposed by the President's Commission on Technology, Automation and Economic Progress in 1966. *See* TECHNOLOGY AND THE AMERICAN ECONOMY, *supra* note 57, at 34. Congressman O'Hara of Michigan introduced a bill in 1967 which called for the underwriting by the federal government of one million jobs, primarily in state and local agencies, H.R. 12280, 90th Cong., 1st Sess. (1967).

60. *See, e.g.,* Statement of Representative Thomas B. Curtis, *Income Maintenance Hearings* 410.

61. Orshansky, *The Shape of Poverty in 1966, supra* note 4, at 11.

62. *See id.*

63. *See* pp. 245–46 *supra.*

64. *See* pp. 246, 253 *supra.*

income to people who will not work.[65] Arguments against such free-handedness range from calling it un-American to a serious concern over the obstacles it would raise to social integration.[66] The second argument lies in the conflict between costs and work incentives in the NIT. Arguably, this conflict stems from trying to deal with both the employable and unemployable poor under the same scheme, which must then have relatively high basic guarantee levels for those with no other source of income as well as a relatively low special tax rate to preserve work incentives.

One plan, proposed by Professor James Tobin of Yale, would meet some of these objections by attributing to every employable recipient a presumed income equal to twice his basic income supplement and reducing his NIT benefit accordingly. A person unemployed for good cause would be exempt from the presumption, and as employable recipients actually earned income, their presumed income would decrease dollar-for-dollar. Any able adult, except women caring for minors, would ordinarily be considered "employable."[67]

Given this presumption supplement checks might go only to an unemployable member of the family unit, thus in form excluding employable persons from NIT benefits altogether. Since most families would still share benefits with the excluded member, the practical effect of the scheme would be to reduce the supplement level for family units with a non-working employable member. Since the reduced supplement payments, as well as the effective zero special tax rate on all earnings of an employable recipient below his presumed income level, would operate to increase work incentives, the Tobin proposal is primarily responsive to the political objections to the NIT. Because it would not lower the tax break-even point for families with employable members, the presumed-income approach does not prevent participation in the program by families who already have adequate incomes, though it is this over-

65. Senator William Proxmire in an interview with CHALLENGE: MAGAZINE OF ECONOMIC AFFAIRS, March-April 1967, at 24. This judgment reflects public opinion at this time. A recent Gallup poll found 62 per cent of the population opposed to a guaranteed income plan, while 79 per cent favored a guaranteed work plan. Not surprisingly, lower income groups had larger percentages in favor of both plans. Seventy-three per cent of nonwhites favored a guaranteed income plan. N.Y. Times, Jan. 5, 1969, at 44, col. 1.

66. *See, e.g.,* Statement of Representative Thomas B. Curtis, *Income Maintenance Hearings* 410.

67. Statement of James Tobin, *Income Maintenance Hearings* 244. Tobin suggests that the employability category might include all able-bodied persons from 18 to 65 years of age except full-time students and females who are caring for one or more children under 18. He also proposes that a local federal manpower officer certify whether a particular individual's unemployment during a period was for "good cause." The absence of available work due to a recession would no doubt be a justification for unemployment.

breadth more than any other feature which drives up the cost of the NIT. In fact, unless the NIT actually had the serious—and unlikely—drop-out effects its opponents fear, Tobin's scheme would save the government almost nothing at all. Except for very low incomes, moreover, the special tax rate would remain the same and create the same disincentives for job advancement.

The proposal for a two-part NIT—one part for families without an employable member and another part for the rest—does meet the objections based on costs and work incentives, though it also embodies a more fundamental departure from the model statute than does Tobin's suggestion. The unemployables' NIT would have supplement levels at the poverty line and a very high special tax, perhaps 75 per cent or higher, while families with employable members would receive substantially lower supplements (about half the poverty level) and face a special tax rate of 33 per cent. A third possibility is to exclude families with an employable member from the NIT entirely, meeting their need through a guaranteed job program instead.[68] Of course, some sort of guaranteed job plan would be a necessary corollary of all of these proposals.[69]

The advantages of the last two modifications of the NIT are obvious: they increase work incentives, reduce participation by the non-needy,[70] and save the program substantial amounts of money. Although the expenses of an expanded job program might offset savings in the NIT, job programs still are more acceptable politically.

Very grave objections, however, lie against any proposal to treat employable recipients less generously. First, there is the difficulty of decid-

---

68. The AFL-CIO has advocated a similar program package. In his testimony at the Income Maintenance Hearings in June, 1968, Leonard Lesser, General Counsel of the AFL-CIO Industrial Union Department, made the following statement:

> At the core of providing jobs for people is the concept of Government as the employer of last resort, the Government insuring employment opportunities to all workers. . . .
>
> [I]ncome assistance, no matter what its form, should not be expected to and must not be shaped to, make up deficiencies in either job opportunities or earning levels. It cannot be a substitute for a decent job at fair wages. It must not be used to subsidize marginal employers, nor should it be expected to bail out a deficient social insurance system. Rather, it should be designed to provide with dignity the basic minimum need of those who cannot or should not participate as active members of the work force.

Statement of Leonard Lesser, *Income Maintenance Hearings* 199, 201–202.

69. Tobin, in particular, is careful to add that his program should be coupled with a federal guarantee of a decent job. Statement of James Tobin, *Income Maintenance Hearings* 245.

70. Although about half the families in the country would benefit financially from the NIT as proposed in the model statute, only a third would find election to their advantage under this two-part NIT program. *See* Orshansky, *The Shape of Poverty in 1966, supra* note 4.

ing who is to be treated as employable. A reasonable definition of employability might include all able-bodied persons from 18 to 65 years of age, except full-time students and women caring for children.[71] While this reflects a natural inclination toward motherhood, it would place a considerable strain on the family structure since only female-headed family units could qualify for the higher benefits. The family splitting problem might be so great as to require limiting the high NIT program to the aged, the disabled, and the widowed, though this would take the NIT a long way from its original objectives. Second, there is the problem of dealing with the employable claimant who is unemployed for good cause. Families with such claimants would presumably be eligible for maximum NIT benefits, but defining the limits of good faith unemployment presents almost insuperable problems.

Third, once such lines are drawn, the task of placing individual recipients on one side or the other creates far too many opportunities for administrative error and abuse.[72] Fourth, the numerous problems with a guaranteed job program must count as a disadvantage of its partial substitution for the NIT. Finally, the two-part NIT would keep in poverty families whose employable members refused to work. Perhaps this program is politically the most feasible, but punishing the children for the sins of the fathers is an unfortunate theme for the attempt to eliminate poverty in America.

FAMILY ALLOWANCE

In family or children allowance plans, the government periodically pays small sums to *all* families, or at least all families with children.[73] The payment depends solely on family size or the number of children. The program resembles an NIT with vastly reduced annual income supplements and no special tax. Since the payments go to all families, they could not be generous without making the program prohibitively expensive. In fact, the small payments would subsidize the middle classes and do little to alleviate poverty. Of course, with a more sharply progressive positive tax

71. This definition is suggested by Tobin in connection with his presumed wages proposal. *See* note 67 *supra.*

72. A guaranteed job program would simplify the determination of a recipient's employability, but this would not eliminate the risk of error and abuse so much as shift its locus. *See* note 67 *supra.*

73. For two articles which reveal something of the flavor of the NIT, family allowance debate as well as describe family allowance proposals, see Tobin, *Do We Want Children's Allowances?* THE NEW REPUBLIC, Nov. 25, 1967, at 16; and Vadakin, *Helping the Children,* THE NEW REPUBLIC, Dec. 23, 1967, at 15. *See also* J. VADAKIN, CHILDREN OF POVERTY AND FAMILY ALLOWANCES (1968); Moynihan, *The Crisis in Welfare,* PUBLIC INTEREST, Spring 1968, at 3.

and a broader definition of taxable income, the family allowance idea would make more sense, but it would then lose its only real strength—political acceptability.

IN-KIND PROGRAMS

The NIT would insure all families an income sufficient to cover their needs for food, clothing, shelter, and other necessities. The government can also meet these needs directly through programs such as public housing,[74] rent subsidies,[75] and food stamps.[76] In-kind assistance assures that public outlays are actually spent on basic consumption items, but it tends to isolate and spotlight the poor and circumscribe their independence and freedom of choice—both to the detriment of social integration.[77] Such programs treat only the physical symptoms of poverty while irritating the underlying social and economic causes. If Congress were to set NIT guarantee levels too low to cover basic necessities, in-kind programs would still be necessary; at the guarantee levels proposed in this statute, however, in-kind programs would continue to have a useful function only in special cases and emergencies.

SOCIAL SECURITY AND UNEMPLOYMENT INSURANCE

Although Unemployment Insurance and Old-Age, Survivors, and Disability Insurance play a definite role in alleviating poverty,[78] their main purpose is to insure against sudden reductions in family income.[79] For the most part, these programs do not duplicate NIT functions and their expansion would be a poor substitute for the NIT.[80]

THE MINIMUM WAGE

Insofar as the minimum wage has actually protected the living standard of the worker, passage of an effective NIT would go far to make it obsolete. Such a fate would delight the already numerous critics of the minimum wage, who claim that it places an unfair burden on employers in

74. 42 U.S.C. § 1409 (1964).
75. 42 U.S.C. § 1701 (1964).
76. 7 U.S.C. §§ 2011–25 (1964).
77. *Cf.* HAVING THE POWER, *supra* note 1, at 72. For criticisms of in-kind assistance, see, *e.g.,* M. FRIEDMAN, CAPITALISM AND FREEDOM 177–95 (1962); Tobin, Pechman & Mieszkowski, *supra* note 6, at 15–16.
78. *See* Orshansky, *The Shape of Poverty in 1966, supra* note 4, at 26–30.
79. Wickenden, *Social Welfare Law: The Concept of Risk and Entitlement,* 43 U. DET. L.J. 517, 527–31, 534–39 (1966). *See also* tenBroek & Wilson, *Public Assistance and Social Insurance - A Normative Evaluation,* 1 U.C.L.A.L. REV. 237 (1954).
80. Tobin, Pechman & Mieszkowski, *supra* note 7, at 15–16. For a discussion of some of the inequities in Social Security taxation, see Deran, *Income Redistributions Under the Social Security System,* 19 NAT. TAX. J. 276 (1966).

the less technologically advanced sectors of the economy and threatens the unskilled worker with unemployment.[81] To the extent that the minimum wage actually raises wages, however, it should shift some of the cost of the NIT from the federal treasury to private employers.

81. For a brisk discussion of this subject, see, *e.g.,* Lester, *Shortcomings of Marginal Analysis for Wage-Employment Problems,* 36 AM. ECON. REV. 63 (1946); Stigler, *The Economics of Minimum Wage Legislation,* 36 AM. ECON. REV. 358 (1946); Machlup, *Marginal Analysis and Empirical Research,* 36 AM. ECON. REV. 519 (1946). *See also* Bork, *Why I am for Nixon,* THE NEW REPUBLIC, June 1, 1968, at 19.

CHAPTER TEN

The Heineman Commission Proposal. Report of the President's Commission on Income Maintenance Programs

The President's Commission on Income Maintenance Programs was appointed by President Johnson early in 1968 to study the income needs of poor Americans, examine all existing government programs designed to meet those needs, and make recommendations for constructive improvements. The Commission's report, issued in November, 1969, was occasioned by both the discrediting of the welfare system and the Johnson Administration's wish to postpone remedial action until after the election of 1968. The report sets forth a universal negative income tax system that, over time, would eradicate financial poverty. Its structure—complete federal administration and financing, impersonal tests of means, payment levels on the basis of family income alone, substantial work incentives— proceeds from a rejection of the existing welfare system, not an effort to tinker with it.

The Recommended Program

This Commission's main recommendation is for the development of a universal income supplement program to be administered by the Federal Government, making payments to all members of the population with income needs.

Poverty Amid Plenty: The American Paradox, The Report of The President's Commission on Income Maintenance Programs (Washington, D.C.: U.S. Government Printing Office, 1969), pp. 57–63, 149–155.

183

It is clear to this Commission that such a program is needed in the United States to assist persons excluded from existing programs and to supplant other programs. *It is time to design public policy to deal with the two basic facts of American poverty: the poor lack money, and most of them cannot increase their incomes themselves. These conditions can be remedied only when the Government provides some minimum income to all in need.* If we wish to eliminate poverty we must meet the basic income needs of the poor.

The only type of program which we believe can deal with the problem is a direct Federal cash transfer program offering payments to all, in proportion to their need. Such a program can be structured to provide increased cash incomes to all of the poor, and to maintain financial incentives to work. The basic payments should vary by family size, and the payment should be reduced by only 50 cents on the dollar as other income increases. Thus, positive incentives exist for work, and the further development of private savings and insurance, and social insurance systems is not discouraged. By making payments to all in need—regardless of demographic characteristics—incentives to modify family structure in order to become eligible for programs are reduced.

Table 10–1.   Impact of Recommended Program on Total Income of a Family of Four

Other Income	Income Supplement	Total Income
$ 0	$2400	$2400
500	2150	2650
1000	1900	2900
1500	1650	3150
2000	1400	3400
3000	900	3900
4000	400	4400
5000	0	5000

We recommend that such a program be enacted promptly at a level that provides an income of $2,400 per year for a family of four with no other income. Benefits should be scaled to pay $750 per adult and $450 per child to families with no other income. This program would supplement all incomes below $4,800 for a family of four. Table 10–1 shows the amount of payments that would be made to a family of four by income level, and the impact on total family income.

ADEQUACY

The choice of level for such a plan is difficult. The lower the basic guarantee level, the less adequate the program. But as program levels are increased, costs rise rapidly, as do possible side effects induced by the program. We have sought to chart a course between extremes.

Since an income of $2,400 for a family of four is below the poverty line, the basic benefit level proposed would not meet the full needs of families with no other source of income. *This level has not been chosen because we believe it to be adequate, but because it is a level which can be implemented promptly. The Commission recommends that once the program is launched, the level of benefits be raised as conditions and experience allow.*

The Commission feels strongly that such a program should be enacted in the near future so as to provide the relief badly needed by Americans living in poverty and receiving little or no help. Even if initial benefit levels are inadequate for persons with no other income, initiation of this program would ameliorate the worst aspects of the poverty problem. And, this is the only type of program which can provide adequate benefits at reasonable costs.

Initially this program would replace Public Assistance completely in States with low payment levels, and partially in States with high payment levels. As benefit levels rise, categorical Public Assistance programs would be replaced fully, so that States and localities eventually would need to provide only short-term emergency aid. Thus, the dominant role in providing continuous cash income support would be shifted from the States to the Federal Government.

CLEARLY DEFINED RIGHTS

Federal administration of a universal income supplement program according to objective eligibility criteria would, to a large extent, replace the discretion now exercised by local administrators and eliminate one of the most pernicious aspects of current welfare programs. Benefit amounts and eligibility would be spelled out clearly by Federal law and regulations. Swift appeals procedures should be developed by the administering agency.

EQUITY

The recommended program can be adopted with no statutory changes in other programs. Benefits of other income-tested programs will decline automatically under current law or practice as the new income transfers are made. This will help eliminate or reduce the wide variations in benefits and administration.

This program would immediately improve the incomes of many of the poor, including the working poor. It would narrow the inequitable differences that now exist between those eligible for categorical programs and those not eligible, and, as the program level is raised, these inequities would be completely eliminated. We are convinced that a noncategorical approach is required in a basic program if adequacy of benefit levels is ever to be achieved while maintaining equity. Attempts to raise the level of existing categorical programs inevitably have exacerbated current inequities.

In the long run the proposed program could lead to a marked reduction in existing variation in living standards of the poor throughout the Nation. Residents of those parts of the country with low wage and assistance levels would receive the greatest immediate benefit from the basic plan; these areas would adapt over time to rising benefit levels. Attempts to reflect different costs of living in different areas would involve many difficulties and so a uniform National supplement is recommended.

In addition to providing equal treatment for persons in equal need, the program would maintain relative income positions. Under the plan, the worker would always receive more income than the nonworker for a fixed household size, and workers who earn more always would receive higher total incomes than workers who earn less. Thus, the plan would not capriciously reverse positions in the income distribution. It would not equalize incomes at the lower end of the distribution; it would narrow differences.

INCENTIVE EFFECTS

Clearly, any program which provides income without work may affect work effort. Empirical evidence for predicting efforts of such a program on labor force participation is sketchy. But, given the level of the basic income support program, we are convinced that the distinctive effect is not likely to be powerful. Some secondary and part-time workers as well as primary workers may withdraw from the labor force or reduce their hours worked, and some persons may not enter the labor force because they are provided with a secure income base. We would expect reduced work effort to be concentrated among secondary family workers, female family heads, and the elderly, rather than among nonaged male family heads. Thus, some reduced work effort may be socially as well as individually desirable for many of those affected. The fact that support levels for those without earnings under the proposed program are low, and that work will always produce increased income, would maintain strong financial inducements to work.

The alternative to relying on financial incentives to work is to impose work requirements on applicants for aid and to deny aid to those who are deemed employable by some official. We believe that such tests cannot be used effectively in determining eligibility for aid, and are undesirable in any case. Employment tests imposed by currrent programs often are based on largely irrelevant criteria such as age, sex, and the like. While these factors are useful for purposes of manpower planning in the aggregate, they do not fit individual cases well. The only meaningful determination of employability for an individual is the outcome of a freely operating labor market; no timeless definitions of employability can be drawn. Inevitably, any simple test designed to withhold aid from the voluntarily unemployed will deal harshly with some of those who cannot find work. Any degree of complexity involved in the test would introduce elements of subjective evaluation to be exercised at the lowest administrative level. We do not think it desirable to put the power of determining whether an individual should work in the hands of a Government agency when it can be left to individual choice and market incentives. Since we do not now have employment for all who want to work, employability tests lose much of their meaning in the aggregate. But they allow abuses in individual cases.

In any case, we do not believe that employment tests are needed. Our observations have convinced us that the poor are not unlike the nonpoor. Most of the poor want to work. They want to improve their potential and to be trained for better jobs. Like most Americans, the poor would like to do something with their lives beyond merely subsisting. By providing them with a basic system of income support, we provide them with an opportunity to do these things.

Exaggerated fears of massive work disincentive effects often have influenced discussions of income maintenance. Though these effects could be important, our fears should not lead us to forget the crippling effects of poverty. Men and women who are poor cannot afford to take risks. They are seriously impeded in making plans. They usually are precluded from accepting opportunities that require the investment of time or money. Most of their time and energies are absorbed in survival on a day-to-day basis. Once the poor are assured a minimum stable income, they will be in a much better position to use other antipoverty programs. Education, job training, and employment counseling can be expected to operate more successfully on persons who have a base of economic stability on which to build. It is unrealistic to expect these programs to be utilized effectively by persons whose basic incomes are inadequate, uncertain, and unstable. And to require people to enter such programs as a prerequisite for income support is unnecessary. We have noted that existing training programs generally are oversubscribed with volunteers. Unless jobs were abundant and the training programs had adequate capacity, any requirement that unemployed recipients of income support accept training would be meaningless. The Commission believes that market incentives and not compulsion should be the basis for accepting both employment and training.

Because the recommended program would make payments to all in proportion to their need, financial incentives to alter family composition would be reduced sharply. With payments available to male-headed families with low income, the strong incentive for family splits inherent in AFDC would be mitigated. Similarly, payments would be available to families and individuals without children, thereby removing inequities between childless couples in need and families with children in need who may currently be eligible for AFDC.

PROGRAM TRANSFERS

The recommended plan would increase net Federal budget costs by an estimated $7 billion in 1971. If States which currently make assistance payments above the recommended initial level of the Federal program made supplementary payments to current recipients up to their current standards, State and local spending would be reduced by one billion dollars. An estimated 28 States would not have to make supplementary payments to recipients of AFDC since their payment levels are below or about equal to the level of the new Federal program.

Thus, the estimated net added cost of the recommended program to all levels of Government would be $6 billion in 1971. This amount is the increase in the disposable income of the 10 million households receiving payments under the plan. Five billion dollars of increased income would be received by the estimated eight million households poor prior to receiving payments, and the remainder by households somewhat above the poverty line. Over one million households would be removed from poverty, while all of the poor would have significantly higher incomes. Half of the poverty income deficit would be eliminated by this program alone.

Over half of the increased income from the program would be received by households not currently receiving public income-conditioned transfers. Approximately one-third of the net payments would go to households where the head works full-time all year.

Thus, enactment of this program would represent a significant step towards eliminating poverty in America. And as benefits are increased in the future, further inroads would be made. Successful pursuit of other programs—as outlined elsewhere in this report—would result in faster achievement of this goal.

Costs of Alternative Plans

Plans that supplement incomes can be set at various levels and have different structures. (As detailed review of specific design considerations is contined in Appendix C of the full report.) This section presents data on the sensitivity of costs and program coverage to changes in levels.

Table 10–2. Breakeven Income Level by Reduction
Rate and Guarantee Level, Family of Four

Guarantee	Breakeven Income by Reduction Rate		
	30 per cent	50 per cent	70 per cent
$2,000	$ 6,667	$4,000	$2,857
2,400	8,000	4,800	3,428
2,800	9,333	5,600	4,000
3,200	10,667	6,400	4,573
3,600	12,000	7,200	5,143
4,000	13,333	8,000	5,714

PROGRAM COSTS

Table 10–2 shows how the basic program structure varies with the two
basic parameters: the income guaranteed to a family with no other income,
and the rate at which payments are reduced as other income rises. The
breakeven income is the level at which supplementation ceases.

For a fixed basic grant level, the higher the reduction rate the lower
the breakeven level and vice versa. The number of eligible persons and
the program cost vary directly with the reduction rate. For a fixed guarantee, costs would appear lower for a high reduction rate. However, the
higher the rate, the greater the potential adverse effects on work incentives. The Commission has chosen a 50 per cent reduction rate for this
reason.

Table 10–3 shows how costs of programs would vary for a fixed reduction rate (50 per cent), as the guarantee level varies. The costs are pro-

Table 10–3. Estimated Net Transfer Cost and Population
Receiving Payments of Universal Supplement Programs by
Guarantee Level, 50 per Cent Reduction Rate, 1971

Guarantee	Breakeven	Net Cost[a] (billions)	Population Coverage (millions)	
			Households	Persons
$2000	$4000	$ 3.5	7.8	26.9
2400	4800	5.9	10.5	36.8
2800	5600	9.3	13.5	48.1
3200	6400	14.0	16.7	60.2
3600	7200	20.0	20.5	74.6
4000	8000	27.5	24.2	88.3

[a]Cost estimates are net of offsetting savings in existing programs to all levels of
government.

jected to 1971. As other income rises due to economic growth, the cost of such programs would decline, so that the cost magnitude of higher level programs for years later than 1971 would be lower than those indicated.

EFFECTS ON POVERTY

Clearly, any program which provides for an income guarantee below the poverty level will not eliminate poverty. But programs tailored closely to family size and income have the effect of channeling the bulk of payments to the poorest, and most of the money will go to the poor. The higher the level of the programs, the greater the reduction in the poverty income deficit of the poor. Table 10–4 shows the effects of introducing the new

Table 10–4.   Estimated Effect of New Income Supplement Plan on Poverty Income Deficit,ᵃ 1971 (in billions)

Poverty Income Deficit	Guarantee Level					
	$2000	$2400	$2800	$3200	$3600	$4000
Before program	$9.2	$9.2	$9.2	$9.2	$9.2	$9.2
After new program	6.1	4.8	3.7	2.8	2.1	1.6
Reduction	3.1	4.4	5.5	6.4	7.1	7.6
Per cent reduction	34%	48%	60%	69%	77%	83%

ᵃPoverty income deficit is the aggregate dollar gap between the actual income of the poor and the poverty line. Estimates are based on a projected growth in the poverty level of 2.7 per cent per year due to price increases.

program, again for 1971. Even the lowest level shown—which lifts very few people from poverty—has a rather large effect on the income gap of the poor.

Table 10–5 shows, as a rough measure of program efficiency, the proportion that the reduction in poverty deficit is of total program net costs.

Table 10–5.   Estimated Reduction in Poverty Income Deficit per Dollar of Net Program Expenditure, 1971 (in billions)

Program Measure	Guarantee					
	$2000	$2400	$2800	$3200	$3600	$4000
Reduction in gap	$3.1	$4.4	$5.5	$ 6.4	$ 7.1	$ 7.6
Total net cost	3.5	5.9	9.3	14.0	20.0	27.5
Reduction/cost	.89	.75	.59	.46	.36	.28

While less than 100 per cent, the efficiency ratios are quite high compared with extension of any existing program.[1]

As would be expected, the proportion of benefits filling the poverty gap declines as the program level rises. Inherent in this type of program is a tapering off of benefits as income rises to preserve financial work incentives rather than an abrupt cutoff at the poverty line. As the guarantee level is set higher, the breakeven income level rises above the poverty line and supplementary benefits go increasingly to the nonpoor (but still to low-income persons). In the case of the program guaranteeing $2,400 to a family of four, supplements are paid to such families up to $4,800—which exceeds the projected poverty line of approximately $3,900 for a family of four in 1971.

ADMINISTRATIVE COSTS

Administrative costs for the recommended program are estimated to be less than 3 per cent of Federal payments to recipients—or approximately $200 million.[2] Under the current Public Assistance programs administrative costs are approximately 15 per cent. The difference reflects the simpler eligibility terms for the recommended program than currently apply to Public Assistance. Administrative costs are directly proportional to the complexity of eligibility determination.

Review of Program Operation

The basic income support program recommended by the Commission, if enacted, would represent only a first step toward assuring an adequate income for all persons. In years to come many modifications will have to be made in the design of the program if it is to be an effective basis for a system of income maintenance.

In order to provide for continuing systematic evaluation of the program as conditions and opportunities change, the Commission recommends that the legislation establishing the program create a permanent review commission.

The review commission should reevaluate program adequacy periodically and make recommendation on changes in both program levels and benefit reduction rates. Since poverty is a relative measure which de-

1. For a discussion of such measures applied to current programs, see U.S. Department of Health, Education, and Welfare, Office of Assistance Secretary (Program Coordination), *Income and Benefit Programs,* October 1966.

2. U.S. Treasury Department, Internal Revenue Service, "Administrative Cost Estimates for an Income Supplement Plan," unpublished paper prepared for Commission, August 8, 1969.

pends on the values and resources of a society, our notion of an adequate income guarantee undoubtedly will change and the review commission continually should seek to define benefit levels relevant to the prevailing standard of living.

The other major function of the review commission would be to determine methods of increasing the program's operational effectiveness. Even with research and careful planning it is impossible to design a new program that will operate perfectly in every respect. Providing every family with the right to a minimum income is a significant innovation which should be undertaken. It may, however, present unforeseen administrative, legal, economic, or behavioral problems. Only experience with the program itself can indicate the changes that will have to be made if benefits are to be increased to adequate levels.

The review commission should report annually to the President and the Congress on the operation of the program, and any needed changes. It should be independent of the agency administering the program and of other Government agencies. Such independence would insure that day-to-day operating considerations of the administering agency would not infringe on the objective evaluation required.

Program Design

The specific operational and definitional features of the income supplement system recommended can affect the program operation significantly. Different benefit structures, definitions of family units, and the like can change the program effect. This Appendix reviews alternative design features, and notes specific operational program features which seem desirable.

Level

The level of the allowance establishes the amount of income provided to families or persons with no other income. The Commission plan proposes an allowance of $750 for each of the first two adults in a family and $450 for additional members. As outlined in the Report, this provides an income of $2,400 per year to a family of four with no other income. While not adequate as a living standard, this program would be a major step towards an adequate income support system. Many of the poor would be removed from poverty, and many others would receive significant income increases.

Since benefits decline by only 50 cents for each dollar of other income, some benefits are provided to families of four with incomes up to $4,800. Tables 10–6 and 10–7 show the amounts of Federal payment that could be

Table 10-6. *Annual Amount of Federal Payment by Household Size and Amount of Other Income, Proposed Program*

Household Size	Amount of Other Income[a] (in dollars)									
	0	500	1000	1500	2000	3000	4000	5000	6000	7000
1	750	500	250	0						
2 (1 parent, 1 child)	1200	950	700	450	200	0				
2 (couple)	1500	1250	1000	750	500	0				
3 (1 parent, 2 children)	1650	1400	1150	900	650	150	0			
3 (2 parents, 1 child)	1950	1700	1450	1200	950	450	0			
4 [b]	2400	2150	1900	1650	1400	900	400	0		
5 [b]	2850	2600	2350	2100	1850	1350	850	350	0	
6 [b]	3300	3050	2800	2550	2300	1800	1300	800	300	0
7 [b]	3750	3500	3250	3000	2750	2250	1750	1250	750	250

[a]Other income includes income from all sources other than income-tested Public Assistance and Veterans Pensions.
[b]Assumed to include two adults. One-adult families of the same size would receive $300 less.

made and total family income by size of family and amount of other income.

Benefit Structure

Two types of benefit structures have been proposed for such programs: those which are related to the poverty line, and thereby take account of economies of scale in family living by having benefits per member decline as family size increases; and those which provide flat payments per family member. The former provide roughly equal standards of living to families of varying size; the latter provide equal money income per family member.

Proponents of structuring the benefit level in relation to the poverty line point out that there are economies of scale in family living, and that the first family member requires more to survive than succeeding family members. Proponents of flat grants point out that if a considerably larger amount is given to the first individual with considerably smaller amounts for succeeding individuals there are financial incentives for single adults to separate from the family to maximize total family transfers. Indeed,

Table 10–7.   Total Annual Income by Household Size and Amount of Other Income, Proposed Program

Household Size	Amount of Other Income[a] (in dollars)									
	0	500	1000	1500	2000	3000	4000	5000	6000	7000
1	750	1000	1250	1500	2000	3000	4000	5000	6000	7000
2 (1 parent, 1 child)	1200	1450	1700	1950	2200	3000	4000	5000	6000	7000
2 (couple)	1500	1750	2000	2250	2500	3000	4000	5000	6000	7000
3 (1 parent, 2 children)	1650	1900	2150	2400	2650	3150	4000	5000	6000	7000
3 (2 parents, 1 child)	1950	2200	2450	2700	2950	3450	4000	5000	6000	7000
4[b]	2400	2650	2900	3150	3400	3900	4400	5000	6000	7000
5[b]	2850	3100	3350	3600	3850	4350	4850	5350	6000	7000
6[b]	3300	3550	3800	4050	4300	4800	5300	5800	6300	7000
7[b]	3750	4000	4250	4500	4750	5250	5750	6250	6750	7250

[a]Other income includes income from all sources other than income-tested Public Assistance and Veterans Pensions.

[b]Assumed to include two adults. One-adult families of the same size would receive $300 less.

there are financial incentives for collusion and fraud, since by reporting income separately two adults in the same household can increase the total grant available to the family.

*Table 10–8. Effect of One Adult Separating
on Total Transfer Income of Family under
Alternative Benefit Structure, Family
with No Other Income*

Family Size	Benefits Scaled to Poverty Index[a]	Flat Grant per Member[b]	Commission Plan[c]
I. Family Intact, Total Household Income			
2	$1530	$1200	$1500
3	1870	1800	1950
4	2400	2400	2400
5	2830	3000	2850
6	3180	3600	3300
II. One Adult Separated: Income of Two Households			
2	$2360	$1200	$1500
3	2710	1800	1950
4	3050	2400	2400
5	3580	3000	2850
6	4010	3600	3300

[a]68 per cent of poverty index for nonfarm family, $1180 for single individual.

[b]$600 per person.

[c]$750 for first two adults, $450 for each additional member.

The Commission proposal represents a compromise between these possibilities. It provides flat benefits, but differentiates in benefit levels between adults and children. The first two adults in a family receive $750 each while succeeding family members receive $450 each. Table 10–8 shows the basic allowance level for a program scaled to the poverty line that pays $2,400 to a family of four with no income, a program paying a flat $600 per family member, and the Commission program. These plans all provide $2,400 to a family of four but pay different amounts to families of different sizes.

The Commission proposal has the effect of not providing any financial gain for adult members of the family with no other income to separate from the family for the purpose of increasing the total transfer income received by the family. But the Commission plan roughly takes account of economies of scale for larger families. Thus it is superior to both of the pure alternatives. For families in which only one adult has earnings there still may be financial gain from separating. This potential gain is lower than under current programs however.

To avoid large payments to very large families, ceilings sometimes are proposed. Recent court rulings have cast doubt on the constitutionality of family maximums on payments in Public Assistance programs. Thus, it would seem undesirable to introduce such features in a new program. One could argue more justifiably on the grounds of economics of scale for reducing the benefit amount per family member for members beyond some number. The Commission has not made recommendations in this area, but presents some data for review. Table 10–9 shows the costs and number of recipients of supplementation for the Commission plan, for a plan which pays no added benefits for the eighth or succeeding family members, and for a plan in which the eighth and succeeding members receive only $225 in basic allowance (half the amount added by the third through seventh members).

As discussed above, attempting to design allowances to provide equal living standards requires that the allowance per family member must decline for successive family members to reflect economies of scale in family living. In addition, the age of family members should be taken into account and allowances should be adjusted to reflect differences in the cost of living in different areas of the country. Making these latter features operational, however, would be very difficult. While it is clear that there are economies of scale in family living, the means of quantifying them are not nearly so obvious. Economies of scale are specific to particular consumption patterns, and consumption patterns vary with income, family size, and age composition. Age and sex adjustments in equivalent incomes are very difficult to quantify.

An additional problem is that we do not now have the necessary data to adjust accurately for specific geographic differences in the cost of living.

Table 10–9.   Estimated Net Cost^a and Coverage of
Commission Program and Two Variants, 1971

Cost and Coverage	Commission Plan	Limited to Seven Members	Reduced Benefits for Eighth and Succeeding Members
Net cost (billions)	$5.9	$5.2	$5.5
Number of households (millions)	10.5	10.3	10.4

^aNet added cost to all levels of government.

The Department of Labor recently completed extensive budget studies for comparable standards of living in urban areas. Using their lowest standard of living as a basis, we find that of the ten highest cost living areas, three are in the West, four in the North Central region, two in the Northeast, and one in the Southeast.[3] Available data indicate that simple and clear-cut regional patterns in living costs do not exist.

Aside from difficulties of developing adequate data sources for accurate measures of regional living cost differences, it is not clear that such variations are desirable. Factors that partially account for gross variations in living costs are regional differences in levels of living standards and income. This program is designed partially to reduce the extreme differences in these patterns across the Country. Regional variations in payments would retard the economic integration of the Nation that might be induced by the recommended program.

Reduction for Other Income

Decisions regarding the appropriate level of the reduction rate of benefits for other income (the "tax rate") basically represent compromises between two opposing forces. Increasing the rate reduces the direct cost of the program and the number of beneficiaries. It reduces the net allowance received at all levels of other income and it reduces the level of income at which supplementation ceases. However, increasing the rate also increases the possibility that some people may be discouraged from working and either work less or withdraw from the labor force entirely. This, in turn, increases the indirect cost of the program. Little is known of the incentive effects of various rates, but the bulk of professional opinion holds that rates in excess of 50 per cent could cause significant labor force withdrawal. Lower rates significantly increase costs by raising the level up to which earnings may be supplemented and, therefore, the number of beneficiaries.

Definition of Income

Since the purpose of the program is to supplement the income of the "poor," the definition of income used should be comprehensive. If special exclusions and exemptions are allowed the program could pay net benefits to quite affluent persons.

3. U.S. Department of Labor, Bureau of Labor Statistics, Bulletin No. 1570–5, *Three Standards of Living for an Urban Family of Four, Spring 1967.*

GROSS INCOME

The most comprehensive economic definition of a household's income is its consumption plus its change in net worth. This would include all forms of money income, income-in-kind, and accrued capital gains. This definition would require an unreasonable amount of sophisticated bookkeeping on the part of the poor. It would also be very costly to administer. The definition of income recommended by the Commission is more comprehensive than the definition used for income taxation, but less comprehensive than the ideal definition. Specifically, we would include money receipts from work, ownership and transfers, wages and salaries, rents, interest, dividends, proprietorship returns, nonmeans-tested public transfers (that is OASDHI, Veterans Compensation, Workmen's Compensation, employee pensions, Unemployment Insurance benefits), and private transfers through gifts and bequests in excess of $100. It also should include an imputed value of income from nonincome-producing assets other than personal effects and furnishings. Since the poor as a group do not have significant amounts of assets other than homes and their personal belongings, this feature is designed to achieve two objectives: to avoid making payments to those with large amounts of assets not producing current income, and to provide for horizontal equity between homeowners and renters. The amount of imputed income is to be calculated as 10 per cent of the value of net assets. Forms of income-in-kind and accrued capital gains are excluded.

NET INCOME

Gross income as outlined above does not recognize the expenses of earning income. Not subtracting these expenses from gross income implies an effective marginal tax rate on the earnings of some households which may be higher than the nominal rate associated with the program. The ideal way of recognizing work expenses is to allow households to itemize them as deductions. This is costly in terms of administration and necessarily involves subjective evaluations of claims. It is not done under the income tax. Alternatively, a flat sum or percentage of earned income could be exempted from the definition of income. That approach, in effect, provides preferential treatment for earned income rather than recognizing actual work expenses. And it adds a great deal to program costs.

In view of these difficulties the Commission recommends the inclusion of all income from sources other than entrepreneurship without subtraction of work expenses in the income subject to the 50 per cent reduction rate. Self-employment income is included net of ordinary business expenses.

RELATIONSHIP OF WEALTH TO THE INCOME BASE

It can be argued that, in addition to the household's income, its stock of capital or some fraction of that stock should be included in "income" subject to the offset tax. The argument for including at least some fraction of wealth is that the household should be forced to liquidate at least part of its wealth in order to be eligible for an income supplement. This approach has been standard under Public Assistance programs, in which typically all assets, sometimes including owner-occupied houses above a minimal value, must be disposed of to establish elegibility. The result is that applicans must become complete paupers before they can receive aid.

Income from wealth—either actual income or imputed income as discussed earlier—should be taken account of in defining income. But there are two basic arguments against the inclusion of the gross value of income-producing assets in income. First, current income comprehensively defined is the appropriate measure of economic well-being. Second, the inclusion of wealth would involve high administrative costs, while the actual effect of making this inclusion would be negligible. In practical terms the exclusion is insignificant; few assets other than homes are owned by the poor.

Vehicles for Differentiation

There are several means of differentiating among various groups in the population: varying tax rates for demographic groups or income sources; varying guarantee levels for different groups; or excluding some forms of income from consideration. The Commission has allowed no variations in its program in any of the basic parameters for different groups.

As an example, one could propose a high tax rate for the aged along with a guarantee level higher than for the nonaged. This would discourage the aged from working. While many of the aged do not work, increasingly the aged can work and want to work. We see no reason to penalize that effort. Nor do we find a good reason for providing a higher guarantee for an aged poor person than for a nonaged poor person.

As an example of differentiation in income definition, "unearned" income—public transfers under social insurance, rent, dividends, private pensions—could be taxed at 100 per cent on the grounds that this treatment would reduce program costs and not discourage work. But in fact, these sources of income generally are viewed as deferred compensation. They are a form of earnings. To tax them at 100 per cent rate would have the undesirable effect of discouraging savings, and the future development of social insurance and private pensions for lower-income workers.

The Commission proposal is universal in coverage and does not make distinctions between population groups. When allowance is made for family size in determining income need, the relevant criterion for making supplementary payments is that of income need and not demographic factors.

Integration with the Positive Income Tax

Integration with the Federal income tax is an issue if the family's break-even level of income is greater than the family's exemptions and deductions defined by the Internal Revenue Code. This is potentially true for all family sizes under the recommended program.

There are basically three ways in which to integrate the two systems. The first way is to have individuals and families continue to pay the positive tax at their present rates; in effect netting their supplement against their Federal tax liability. The advantage of this approach is that there is a smooth transition in terms of disposable income between taxpayer and tax recipient. There are two disadvantages. The major disadvantage is that the marginal tax rate increases from 50 per cent to 65 per cent over the range of income where the individual both pays the 15 per cent positive tax and receives a supplement. For a 4-person family, positive income tax would be paid on income over $3,000 at a 15 per cent rate, and benefits would be reduced at a 50 per cent rate on income up to $4,800. A second disadvantage is that logically it does not seem appropriate for income supplement recipients to pay Federal income taxes if their incomes are below levels that the Government deems in need of supplementation.

A second approach is to have individuals pay no Federal income tax as long as their net allowance is positive, after which they would pay the Federal tax at their present rates. The only possible advantage to this approach is its simplicity. The major disadvantage is that it creates a notch, with confiscatory marginal tax rates occurring at the breakeven level of income. Consider a family of four with an income of $4,800. At $4,800, their net allowance is zero and total income is $4,800. If the family earns another dollar of income, it is subject to the Federal income tax. A family of four has exemptions and deductions of $3,000, giving it a taxable income of $1,801. This results in a Federal tax liability of $260, leaving the family with a disposable income of $4,541. Thus, the additional dollar of income costs the family $260.

A third approach is to forgive part of positive tax payments for some part of the income range above the level of exemptions and deductions to keep the effective marginal tax rate to a maximum of 50 per cent. This is achieved by allowing families either to pay ordinary Federal income tax, or to accept a net allowance based on receiving a gross allowance and paying an "offset tax" of 50 per cent on their other income—including income beyond the nominal breakeven level. It is assumed that they will choose whichever gives them the largest disposable income. Program costs are somewhat higher, since some families, in effect, pay reduced Federal income tax.[4] The Commission has adopted the third alternative in developing its program, and tax losses are reflected in cost estimates.

Administration of the Program

Decisions regarding the administration of a program can have almost as great an effect on the final outcome of a program as decisions regarding the basic design and, like the design decisions, should be made to reflect social policy objectives. The Commission has several suggestions as to how the program should be administered. Whether or not these suggestions can be implemented depends on their operational feasibility. Ultimately, these are decisions which the administrators must make.

COVERAGE AND FILING UNITS

There are three issues of concern: general eligibility, the definition of the filing unit, and the definition of an adult.

The first and third are relatively straightforward. Assuming an income deficit, the eligible population includes resident aliens, legally incompetent persons under wardship arrangements, and all U.S. citizens except for civilians living abroad, institutional inmates, and members of the Armed Forces. The definition of an adult is any person over 18 or any married couple, irrespective of their ages. Whether or not the individual actually receives the higher allowance depends on how many other adults are in the filing unit.

The appropriate definition of the filing unit is considerably more difficult. The ideal unit is clear. Individuals living as a family unit should file together. Individuals who are legally and financially separate from a family unit should file separately. The objective is to provide equitably for families who are separated in fact without providing encouragement for intact families to split or pretend to split. The following rules would accomplish that objective. Married couples and dependents related by blood or marriage and living together must file a joint application, pooling all

4. For a detailed explanation of this plan see James Tobin, Joseph A. Pechman and Peter Mieszkowski, "Is a Negative Income Tax Practical?", *Yale Law Journal*, Nov. 1967, p. 14.

of their income. In addition, individuals who do not live with the family but who receive at least 50 per cent of their support from the family must file with the family unit.

FILING AND PAYMENT

The Commission suggests that payments be made on a monthly basis and that income be reported on a quarterly basis. Payments can be based on the income reported for the preceding four quarters. That is, the accounting period for income determination is a full year.

Having the net allowance based on a four-quarter moving sum of income means that immediate income needs are covered only for those with chronic low incomes. For those with sharp income declines, payments are received with lags. This accounting period would focus benefits on the long-term unemployed, unemployables, those who chronically work at low-level wages, or who work at medium-level wages but with regular periods of unemployment, and so forth. It does not fill immediately the income needs for individuals facing sudden losses in income. As a result the individual has the greatest incentive to find additional work in the first few quarters following a drop in income. Conversely, it discourages individuals from voluntarily not working for short periods of time.

An alternative to this accounting period is to require a declaration of projected income for some period ahead. Such procedures raise serious enforcement problems. Recoupment of overpayments becomes important. The four-quarter moving sum feature requires no recoupment feature, since payments always are made on the basis of past income. Thus, when income rises due to finding employment, the recipient will continue to receive some benefits under this program based on past income inadequacy, with benefits tapering off as earnings enter their current average income. This provides even greater short-term work incentives to individuals because the 50 per cent tax rate does not become effective immediately upon entering employment.

An accounting period based on current estimated income maximizes the responsiveness of payments to current needs at the cost of greater administrative difficulty and recoupment problems. Accounting periods are possible which shorten time lags between income changes and changes in payments. The Commission has recommended a period based on past income to avoid problems of recoupment. Adjustment of the accounting period can be made in the future to shorten time lags between a drop in income and the onset of payments. In the early stages of implementation it is most important, however, to avoid overpayment problems. As experience develops, accounting periods that minimize lags can be developed.

AUDIT STANDARDS

At the initial filing and any time subsequently, income supplement recipients could be required to support the information reported on their returns. Sampling procedures should be used to maintain credibility of enforcement. The Commission suggests that auditing be done by the Internal Revenue Service.

APPLICANT ASSISTANCE

The Commission has proposed a system of Neighborhood Service Centers. In these centers, there could be personnel from the administering agency to assist people in filing their returns. Other persons providing services also could help income supplement recipients with their returns.

PART FOUR

Tax Equity Proposals

Rolph (Chapter 11) and Pechman (Chapter 12) both address the issues of tax reform and poverty reduction, but with different emphases. The Rolph plan constitutes a single attack on both objectives. Its cash benefits (uniform and universal) aim at a "socially desirable level of income for everyone" and are comparable to the major anti-poverty proposals of Part III. It is the tax reform features of Rolph's financing scheme that sets it apart from other cash transfer plans. He suggests a major transformation of the positive income tax, removing all deductions and subjecting all income to a proportional tax (25–30 per cent). Such changes have the effect of both financing the antipoverty scheme and dealing with the range of equity issues that are raised by the special treatment of different forms of income in the present tax system. Rolph's plan represents a combined effort to reform welfare, reduce poverty, and make the tax system more equitable.

Pechman takes up the same set of issues, but deals with them serially. His tax reforms fall into two major groups. Some (including changes in regressive state, local, and social security taxes) would reduce the tax burden on the poor, but not raise them out of poverty. Others would bring into the tax system the "large amounts of income [that] have been allowed to escape taxation by means of various special provisions and deductions" (such as capital gains, interest on state-local bonds, and income-splitting) Pechman separately deals with cash transfers that would directly attack the poverty problem; he recommends a negative income tax plan similar to those suggested in Chapters 9 and 10. Both Rolph and Pechman, it should be noted, link the concern for the circumstances of poor persons and their tax treatment with the broader issue of more equitably taxing the nonpoor.

A Credit Income Tax

*Earl R. Rolph is a Professor of Economics at the University of Califor-
nia, Berkeley. He has worked as a tax economist and consultant for the
U.S. Treasury Department and a Research Associate for the National
Bureau of Economic Research. His main fields of interest are taxation,
economic and fiscal theory and money and finance. Rolph's proposal, published in 1967, is aimed both at alleviating poverty and reforming the tax
structure to make it more equitable and efficient.*

The persistence in the United States of millions of people who are poor
is a basic reason for the interest in what is often called negative income
taxation. In a society which is supposedly the most affluent in the world,
the presence of 30 to 35 million people described as poor, depending on
one's definition of poverty, scarcely accords with the American dream. In
the minds of some, it may raise nagging doubts about both the political
structure and the economic system that generates such results. Strong
supporters of the American system finds it less embarrassing to diagnose
poverty as a consequence of some deficiency in poor people, such as lazi-
ness, and enjoin them to reform their behavior. But such a diagnosis implies that people are poor out of choice, that they happen to have a strong
preference for leisure. Such a diagnosis scarcely fits the evidence.

The reasons why millions of people have low incomes can be enumerated almost indefinitely. People's mental and physical characteristics differ

Earl R. Rolph, "The Case for a Negative Income Tax Device," *Industrial Relations*,
VI, No. 2 (February 1967), pp. 155–165. Copyright, 1967, by the Regents of the
University of California, Berkeley.

in innumerable ways. Individual talents and inclinations for obtaining gain are subject, as well, to a wide dispersion. The main problem in explaining the income distribution observed in a complex society is not how to explain low incomes. Rather, it is how to explain why the distribution does not have normal statistical properties and in particular why the tail of the low end, including the range of negative incomes, does not have properties similar to those of the upper tail.

Welfare programs in the United States, insofar as they have any rationale, have been based on the theory that the "causes" of low income can be enumerated. Specific measures related to those causes can supposedly provide adequate assistance. Thus there are the categorical aid programs, unemployment insurance, and old age and survivors' insurance. Since the causes are not exhaustive, some cases of distress are inevitably left uncovered by public programs.

A welfare system aimed at alleviating poverty should adopt the premise that income dispersion, including negative income and small positive income, is normal and will not disappear next year or the year after. Since human productivity varies widely, as do other abilities, there are always some groups whose productivity will be low judged by some standard appropriate for "normal" people. If people of low productivity are to be employed in the absence of special subsidies, employers, to have an incentive to hire them, must be permitted to pay low wage rates. People's incomes from work will leave some of them and their dependents in poverty. To the extent they are denied the choice of working, by the establishment of minimum wages, their incomes will be even lower.

The income distribution as it naturally arises does not guarantee affluence for everyone in an affluent society. Government policy must be consistent with the fact that there are some able-bodied males who are not capable of earning as much as $3,000 a year or even $2,000 a year. Present welfare programs, geared as they are to various presumed causes of personal financial distress, presuppose that people not subject to special difficulties, such as ill health, old age, unemployment, etc., can earn adequate incomes and can bring up children who will develop into effective members of society. The presupposition is scarcely consistent with the facts. Mollie Orshansky found, for example, that 22.3 million people out of 27.9 million defined as poor were in families headed by a male. In addition: "Of the 15 million children counted poor in March 5.7 million were in the family of a worker who had a regular job in 1963 and was not out of work any time during the year."[1] There are poor people who are unem-

---

1. Mollie Orshansky, "Who's Who Among the Poor: A Demographic View of Poverty," *Social Security Bulletin,* XXVIII (July, 1965), 21, 24.

ployed or unemployable, but there are others who work and do so regularly. A wage structure that eliminates unemployment and underemployment of people with modest skills cannot be expected to end poverty levels of income, although such a pricing arrangement would result in a vast improvement for many presently disadvantaged groups. There is nothing in economic theory nor in the inherent characteristics of human beings that precludes equilibrium wage rates of one dollar an hour or less for some types of labor services.

If, then, the premise is adopted that the dispersion of income, including low income, is a normal feature of economic affairs, what social measures are appropriate to obtain a social acceptable level of income for everyone? Negative income tax devices are techniques to solve this problem.

Poverty Gap Approach to a Negative Income Tax

One approach to the problem is to define poverty as an amount of income less than some standard taken to be reasonably adequate, treat the difference between a person's actual income and the standard as the poverty gap, calculate the number of dollars required to close the gap, and give each person the difference between his actual income and the standard. Poverty is then cured since by definition no one is left below the standard. Only few proponents embrace this position as stated in this bald manner. It is, however, a widely embraced basic premise both in and out of official circles.

Implementation would require legislation to define the standard, to provide for a definition of income as close to a person's total gain as is feasible, and to tax income obtained by the person from his own efforts at a rate of 100 per cent up to the poverty standard. Beyond this point, but not necessarily at it, the federal individual income tax may come into operation. We would then have two individual income taxes, possibly administered by different agencies—one for people with incomes below the standard and another for those above it.

The poverty gap approach to the negative income tax follows the philosophy of public assistance with some important modifications. Public assistance, as administered by states and localities, varies widely in the details of its administration. Common features of public assistance and a pure poverty gap negative income tax are a 100 per cent tax rate and, to a lesser degree, the use of income as the index of a person's or family's economic position. However, in public assistance and relief programs generally, financial aid is given only to those who apply, and then only if the applicants are deemed qualified according to the rules. The amounts of financial support provided typically fall well below the poverty level as defined by the Department of Health, Education, and Welfare.[2]

Thus, a poverty gap negative tax would, if fully implemented at proposed levels, be a complete substitute for public assistance. This type of negative income taxation would differ, however, in the following ways from public assistance: (1) everyone whose income falls below the standard would receive assistance, thereby eliminating the need to make application; (2) reported income of those eligible would presumably be accepted as correct, subject to the same type of checking which now applies to income reported for federal income tax purposes; (3) the amount of assistance paid to an eligible family would be greater, in many cases several thousand dollars a year greater, than that under public assistance; and (4) the effective tax rate would not ordinarily exceed 100 per cent; under public assistance the rate for a person who takes a temporary job may be on occasion 200 per cent or even 1,000 per cent, depending on the rules applied to him, the difficulties he has returning to the relief rolls, and loss of free medical care for children. Rates in excess of 100 per cent mean that a person is punished for taking a job.

There are a number of difficulties with the poverty gap approach. A major one is that it is unfinanced. Billions of dollars would need to be disbursed to people with low incomes, and billions of dollars are not now presently lying around in the federal budget. In the happy event that the Viet Nam war is brought to a satisfactory conclusion, the funds used for it might be shifted to closing the poverty gap. Otherwise a major tax increase would be required. Such a tax increase would have to be over and above that presently needed for anti-inflationary purposes. In the absence of clear evidence of "progress" in the Viet Nam war, the poverty gap program may become financially feasible only some years hence, if at all.

The 100 per cent tax rate feature of the poverty gap approach is, of course, unworkable. Apart from other considerations, a 100 per cent tax rate means that people must work for nothing or else conceal their incomes. To enforce such a rate would probably require a return to the relief approach. Then a person who refuses a job may be disciplined by cutting him and his family off the rolls. Recognizing the unworkability of 100 per cent rates, poverty gap advocates have suggested lower rates, such as 80 per cent; few seem willing to go below 50 per cent.

2. According to one study, a nonfarm family of two adults and two children requires $3,100 a year to reach the poverty line and $3,980 a year to reach the "low-cost level." Relief payments fall well below such figures. See Mollie Orshansky, "Counting the Poor: Another Look at the Poverty Profile," *Social Security Bulletin*, XXVIII (January, 1965), 70.

This compromise of principle with practicality requires that the goal of closing the poverty gap be abandoned in favor of a more modest goal and that the non-poor be subsidized. If an income of $3,000 a year for a family of four is taken as the poverty line, and if for reasons of enforceability the tax rate is placed at 50 per cent, the goal of ending poverty would require an allowance of $3,000 a year to ensure that a family with a zero income would achieve a disposable income of $3,000. This technique would mean, however, that a family with an income of $5,000 would get an allowance of $3,000, pay $2,500 in gross tax, and receive a net sum of $500 a year from the Treasury. Thus, people who are defined as nonpoor would obtain a net subsidy if the allowance is placed at the poverty line with any tax rate below 100 per cent. To poverty gap thinkers, payments to those above the poverty line are viewed as inefficient or wasteful of public funds.

If, on the other hand, the allowance is placed below the poverty line, the goal of eliminating poverty is partially sacrificed. Instead of a disposable income of $3,000 for a family of four, a smaller allowance must be established. Obviously, the lower the credit, the greater will be the poverty gap remaining. The possible combinations of allowance size and tax rate are indefinitely large, but all would leave the poverty gap more or less unfilled.

There are numerous objections to the establishment of two federal income taxes, one for the poor and one for the non-poor. With two laws, means would have to be found to prevent some members of a family from successfully classifying themselves as poor by splitting off from the family for tax purposes. A large financial incentive would exist to divide the family into zero income units, leaving perhaps only the father to report positive income. The precise gain to a family would depend on the size of the allowance, the tax rate for low incomes, the tax rate for high incomes, and the definition of income. Rules might be devised to minimize family splitting for tax purposes. Effective rules have not, however, been devised for the present federal income tax law for families with property income. It remains feasible to give children assets, the income from which is taxed at lower rates than it would be if left in the names of the parents. The incentive to split income within the family arises from rate graduation under present law.

A further difficulty in a poverty gap design of a negative income tax is the treatment of people who, in a particular year, have a low income but are not poor. A person with assets of, say, $1,000,000, may in a particular year have an income of a negative amount or a small positive amount. He would, however, be classified as poor under a poverty gap system. A young engineer just completing his Ph.D. degree may have an income of

$2,000 in one year, and hence be eligible for negative tax treatment, and have an income of $15,000 the following year. Given the fact that the income of some people fluctuates, there are certain to be people who are highly affluent, judged either by their net worth or by their average income over several years, but who have low incomes in particular years.

According to the usually accepted principles of income taxation, there is no objection to paying money to people who normally pay tax, but who, in a given year, happen to have low incomes. Under present law, for example, there are some modest averaging provisions, and persons in business who report negative incomes in a given year may be entitled to take advantage of loss carry-back and carry-forward provisions. In the case of loss carry-backs, people who so qualify are paid by the treasury for the year in which they suffer losses. In this aspect, the present law is negative income tax. Provisions would be necessary to ascertain a person's negative or positive tax liability in the event he attains less than the poverty level income in a given year. To avoid hopeless confusion, the two income tax laws would have to be made consistent in their treatment of people with fluctuating incomes.

The above difficulties are a small sample of the actual difficulties likely to arise from having two federal individual income taxes. Until and unless the details of the laws are actually drafted, it is impossible to know all the problems that would emerge and what rules would be needed to prevent abuses. The one sure result is even greater complexity than now exists in income taxation in the United States.

Credit Tax Approach

There are many ways of designing a single federal individual income tax and a system of allowances. I shall set forth here a plan described as a credit income tax. The goals of this plan are: (1) to redistribute income systematically in the direction of reducing the present inequality, (2) to minimize incentive problems associated with high marginal rates, and (3) to reduce radically the complexity of the present federal income tax law.

The plan would reduce, and reduce substantially, the incidence of genuine poverty in the United States. However, the complete elimination of poverty would be at best a long-run target. As in other areas of economics, the critical issues are in the nature of more-or-less, rather than all-or-none. Poverty can never be totally eliminated unless society places those who are hopelessly incompetent in managing their own affairs in institutions and denies them their freedom.

The credit income tax suggested here has two main features: a system of flat-sum credits to which all residents of the United States would be entitled, and a general proportional income tax with zero exemptions. A person's or a family's net tax liability, plus or minus, is given by the formula, $T = Yr - Cu$, where T is the net tax liability, Y is taxable income, r is the tax rate, C is the size of the credit (assuming uniform per capita credits), and u is the number of credits for the unit (normally the family).

To illustrate, suppose the credit is $500 a person a year, and the tax rate is 30 per cent. Table 1 shows the tax liability for a family of four. This combination of tax rate and credit would provide a net payment by the Treasury ranging from $2,000 for a person or family with an income of zero (ignoring truly negative income) to zero at a level slightly in excess of $6,000 of income.

The higher the credit, given the tax rate, the larger will be the net payments made to people with low incomes. On the other hand, the tax rate depends on the size of the credit. The rate also depends on the desired yield of the tax to the Treasury and the size of the tax base. To calculate the tax rate for the country as a whole, the following formula may be used: $r = (\Sigma C + R)/Y$, *where* ΣC is the sum of the credits, R is the desired yield, and Y is total taxable income. Taking the population in round figures to be 200 million, the credit to be $400 per capita, the desired yield to be $50 billion, and total taxable income to be $500 billion, we get:

$$r = \frac{\$80 \text{ billion} + 50 \text{ billion}}{500 \text{ billion}} = 26 \text{ per cent.}$$

In recent years, the yield of the federal individual income tax has been in the neighborhood of 9 to 10 per cent of personal income. If personal income were the tax base, a credit of $400 per capita would cost about 16 percentage points in the rate. This result does not mean that the average rate of tax would rise from 10 to 26 per cent of personal income. The effective or average rate would remain at 10 per cent. The extra percentage points become the price paid for redistribution, including redistribution to one's self.

To implement the credit income tax plan it would be necessary to redraft large parts of the present federal income tax law. It might seem rather drastic to suggest that the federal income tax should be radically changed in order to increase the incomes of people who presently have low incomes. In fact, however, a great part of this task would consist of simplifying the present law. Many of the complexities of the law as it now exists are a direct consequence of gradual rates. As Blum and Calvin have emphasized in this connection, much of the work of lawyers in the tax field arises from the simple fact that the tax rates vary, depending on how much income is reported for tax purposes in a given year.[3] Among other things, all the complexities arising because of incentives that now exist to split income within the family would disappear. In addition, the inequities and the rules designed to deal with these inequities arising from the definition of the tax-paying unit would also disappear. Under a proportional tax, the problem of averaging, a very serious problem under the present law, is solved automatically.

There are, from the point of view of tax design, large advantages to be gained by eliminating progressive rates. We ordinarily have thought in the past that it was necessary to have increasing rates of tax in order to have progressive taxation. This view turns out to be incorrect. It is possible to have proportional rates and progression by the device of a general credit, as illustrated by Table 11-1.

Table 11–1.   The Credit Income Tax[a]

Income	Net Tax	Disposable Income
0	− 2,000	2,000
1,000	− 1,700	2,700
2,000	− 1,400	3,400
4,000	− 800	4,800
6,000	− 200	6,200
8,000	+ 400	7,600
10,000	+ 1,000	9,000
20,000	+ 4,000	16,000
50,000	+ 13,000	37,000
100,000	+ 28,000	72,000
1,000,000	+298,000	702,000

[a]Assumes a tax rate of 30 per cent and credits of $500 a person for a family of four.

There would be social costs associated with the installation of a general credit income tax. For example, people who presently are not required to file would have to file to be eligible for the credit. This is about 10 per cent of the population. Although the group is relatively small, the compliance task would not be simple. Many of the nonfilers have rather complicated problems. Some are small-scale farmers who are not accustomed to keeping books, some are occasional workers at odd jobs. Hence, an educational task of some magnitude would be in order.

From an economic point of view, however, the social costs of the credit income tax would be negative and would be negative by a large amount.

3. Walter J. Blum and Harry Calvin, *The Uneasy Case for Progressive Taxation* (Chicago: University of Chicago Press, 1953), p. 15.

Under the present system, many children are growing up without the advantages of proper food, shelter, clothing, medical care, and education. By increasing the financial means of parents, we would give offspring, on the average, higher levels of living. Society would gain in real terms in the form of greater productivity of the current generation of poor children when they become adults and of greater productivity of contemporary poor adults. Financial means are instrumental in obtaining work, when finding a job requires relocation away from depressed areas, proper dress to impress employers, and meeting living expenses while training. A credit income tax would not, to be sure, provide jobs for people with little skill; as already indicated, the legal and institutional restrictions on realistic wage rates for such people must be moderated as a necessary condition for achieving substantial progress in this area.

Closely related, and of much greater importance than an increase in the output of goods and services, is the effect of a credit income tax on the problems arising from concentrated pockets of city poverty. Although city poverty has been a feature of American life since the latter part of the nineteenth century, the current-day ghettos differ in two important respects from ethnic ghettos of the past: the hope of significant economic improvement within a generation has all but disappeared, and the city poor are no longer content to be poor.

Systematic redistribution in favor of lower income groups by a technique that carrys no stigma would immediately end the despair of many of the city poor. This change would be a large improvement. It would also improve the finances of cities by removing a substantial portion of the costs of relief from city budgets, permitting cities to finance measures to assist low income groups. Systematic redistribution would also tend to reduce the migration of the rural poor to the cities. These groups, as beneficiaries of a credit income tax, would find their position improved in their own communities and would, presumably, have little or no incentive to migrate. A city slum, however dismal, has held the only hope of improvement for many of the rural poor in the deep South. This is in part due to capricious methods of distributing relief (not limited to the South), including the practice of granting or withholding relief to discipline those whose behavior offends the politically dominant group. A credit income tax by contrast would afford no such power to local officials and would automatically give poor rural people greater economic and political security than they now enjoy.

Socially, the process of preparing people for working and living in metropolitan areas can be achieved at a lower cost in the hamlets of Alabama than in the ghettos of New York or Chicago. The large cities must be given the opportunity to take measures to improve the lot of the city poor without being handicapped by large numbers of newcomers out of the rural South.

Concluding Observations

A credit income tax may appear to some to be a radical measure out of keeping with the American political tradition. Those who are inclined to take this view should weigh against it the large and expensive but inefficient programs that transfer goods and money to some groups at the expense of others. More of the same can be expected in the future in the absence of a program of systematic redistribution. With a credit income tax, any possible excuse for continuing agricultural price supports, for example, is removed. Subsidized public housing can be opposed without seeming to be ungenerous; low income groups, bolstered by the credit, may buy their own housing services in the market. From the point of view of high income groups, a credit income tax, if the credit is made modest in size, may be the less expensive alternative.

Those who like big government may find a credit income tax objectionable. No measure, to my knowledge, is a greater threat to the growth of nonmilitary government programs; the credit income tax undermines the most telling argument for many of these programs, namely, financial or real assistance to some group or groups.

A credit income tax can be installed in the near future without waiting for the end of the Viet Nam war. The Treasury and the Congress would need to redraft the Internal Revenue Code to include within the definition of Adjusted Gross Income many of the large classes of income presently fully or partially exempt from taxation, to reduce those deductions presently allowed for purposes other than to provide a more accurate definition of taxable income, and to simplify the code as a consequence of the adoption of a one-rate system. I do not wish to imply that such a change would be easy to achieve.

In the initial phase, the determination of the size of the credit may be accomplished by an estimation of the size of the tax base and the fixing of a rate deemed to be politically acceptable, perhaps 25 per cent, and then fixing the credit at the amount that would exhaust the difference between the potential yield and the desired yield of the income tax at that rate. If such a calculation permitted a credit of only $200 per capita a year in the first year, the automatic increase in the potential yield as income increased would permit the credit to be raised.

Once a credit income tax is established, the size of the credit and of the tax rate can be expected to become a political issue of some importance, with many people with persistent low incomes favoring a larger credit and many people with high incomes favoring a lower rate of tax. The political question of what the income distribution ought to be would then be clearly posed. Whatever the outcome over the years, at least a fundamental feature of economic life would become an explicit political question.

A credit income tax may be looked upon as a direct competitor with the Social Security program. A credit income tax, provided the size of the credit is not a trivial amount, would raise the level of incomes of those with low incomes; and, to the extent the Social Security program does likewise, as in the case of public assistance, aid to dependent children, and medicare, it is in fact competitive. But Social Security, unless the basic philosophy for its main programs—that it is an insurance program—is abandoned, cannot cope with large-scale poverty. An insurance approach implies that participants are buying insurance through the device called contributions, meaning of course taxation, and only those who pay their way get benefits. No one would seriously hold that the radical income inequality found in the United States will be corrected by persuading everyone to acquire insurance against possible disasters. Social Security cannot, except by abandoning the insurance principle altogether, reach the genuine poor; many of these people are in a continuous state of disaster. Public assistance, one of the most unpopular and, for true believers in Social Security, one of the most embarrassing programs in the country, is direct testimony of the failure of the insurance principle. If a credit income tax eliminates public assistance, few tears need be shed. But if a credit income tax is installed and if, in another decade, the credit is made the equivalent of $1,000 a person a year, the entire Social Security program will need to be restudied to ascertain what features remain justified in a society in which poverty has been effectively eliminated as a social problem.

Tax Policies for the 1970s

James A. Pechman is the Director of Economic Studies at the Brookings Institution. In 1966–67 he was the Irving Fisher Research Professor of Economics, Yale University. He is the author of several works on social security and income maintenance including Social Security: Perspectives for Reform *(1968) and "Is a Negative Income Tax Practical?" (see headnote for Chapter 9). The proposal in this compendium is amied at reducing the tax burden of the poor and closing the loopholes in the present tax structure. It separately discusses negative income taxes as a means to reform welfare and reduce poverty.*

The United States should be able to enjoy high levels of prosperity in the coming decade. After the fighting stops in Vietnam, unemployment will rise somewhat as resources are redirected from production of war goods to peacetime production, but the transition should be brief. The nation managed such a transition successfully twice in this generation—after World War II and after the Korean War—and in both cases the problem was much bigger than the one likely to be faced after Vietnam. Unless we are terribly stupid or hopelessly divided, our gross national product (corrected for price changes) should continue to grow by an average of 4 per cent per year or better.

But despite our affluence, we cannot use our tax resources indiscriminately. The demands for public services at all levels of government are large and growing at a rapid rate. Tax rates are already high; an un-

Joseph A. Pechman, "Tax Policies For the 1970s," *Public Policy,* XVIII, No. 1 (Fall 1969), pp. 75–93. Copyright © by the President and Fellows of Harvard College.

fair distribution of the tax burden makes it all the more difficult to raise the urgently needed revenues. Reform of the national tax system—which involves revision of federal, state, and local taxes, as well as the system of intergovernmental fiscal relations—would make the burden of financing our federal system of government more acceptable to the average citizen. It would also make a major contribution to a better allocation of economic resources, and to the solution of some of our major social problems.

Taxation of the Poor and Income Transfers

One of the dramatic developments in domestic affairs in recent years has been the increasing concern of experts and laymen alike about the economic circumstances of the poor. Full employment and a high rate of economic growth have greatly reduced the number of persons who live in poverty in this country, but today the number is still in the neighborhood of 22 million. It is evident that continued growth will not by itself eradicate the problems associated with poverty. Those of us who are well off have an obligation to help the poor lift themselves out of poverty through their own efforts, or, if that is not possible, by giving them a decent minimum income. Humanitarian considerations should be enough to justify support for an effective antipoverty program, but it is also a matter of self-interest for those of us who are well-to-do—we may not be able to enjoy our affluence unless poverty is removed from our midst.

It is perhaps surprising to raise the issue of poverty in a discussion of tax policy, but I do so for two reasons. In the first place, the federal government extracts $1.5 billion of payroll taxes and $200 million of income taxes from those who are officially classified as poor, and billions more are taken by the states and local governments in sales and property taxes. While new programs are devised to help the poor, they are required to pay taxes that greatly reduce their ability to make ends meet on their meager incomes. The Council of Economic Advisers estimated that in 1965 the average effective rate of taxes paid by those with incomes below $2,000 was over 40 per cent. Subsequent increases in federal payroll taxes and in state-local sales and property taxes have made this burden even heavier.

Second, the nation's welfare system and the income tax system grew up side by side in response to different pressures, but recent discussions of alternative income maintenance plans have drawn attention to the relationship between the two. Direct assistance to low-income persons is an extension of progression into the lowest brackets, with negative rather than positive rates. Once this relationship is understood, it is a natural step to consider "negative" as well as positive income taxation. Without recognizing the relationship at first, those who propose modernization of the public assistance system have turned to income tax principles for guidance in proposing their reforms.

The appeal to tax principles is a direct result of the failure of the public assistance program. It is now widely acknowledged that this program is inadequate, inefficient, and demeaning, and that it discourages welfare recipients from working. The major reforms proposed by experts to make the system workable would, in effect, convert it to a type of negative income tax. For example, everybody now agrees that the 100 per cent tax rate imposed on the income of welfare recipients reduces incentives to earn income. It is not perhaps generally known that the 1967 amendments to the Social Security Act required the states, by mid-1969, to permit welfare recipients to keep $30 per month plus one-third of the excess of any income they receive above $30 (that is, to reduce the marginal tax rate from 100 per cent to 66⅔ per cent). Thus, state welfare administrations and the Internal Revenue Service are both in the business of levying taxes on incomes of the poor. Although the overlap may not be troublesome now, it will become troublesome once welfare payments are raised and the system is universalized to include the working poor.

In addition, there is growing support among welfare administrators to grant eligibility to applicants on the basis of a simple affidavit, which is not very different from the simple income tax forms used by low-income taxpayers. As this practice spreads, claims of welfare recipients will be checked more and more on a sample basis, a practice which has been employed by the Internal Revenue Service from the beginning of the income tax. In fact, a public assistance system or negative income tax requires decisions on the definition of income and of the family unit, the tax rate (or rates), methods of payment, and a reporting system—all of which have been settled in one way or another in the positive income tax. There is no reason why we should not learn from this experience to improve the administration of the welfare system and to protect the dignity of those who are receiving assistance.

But when one begins to think seriously about a negative income tax, many of the inadequacies of the positive income tax become apparent. A less than comprehensive definition of income is apparently tolerable under the positive income tax, but it is surely not tolerable under a negative income tax. For example, I doubt that anybody would agree that a recipient of $10,000 of tax-exempt interest annually should be eligible for a negative income tax payment. Similarly, the unit under the positive income tax is the individual; the appropriate unit for the negative income tax is the family, since the family provides the basic economic support of its members. Finally, negative income tax allowances should be based on the relative budgetary needs of families of different sizes, but these are not even roughly approximated by the exemption structure of the positive income tax.

Such considerations are important not only for the negative income tax, but also for their possible impact on the positive income tax. To mention only one example, it will doubtless be difficult to explain why some people might be required to pay positive income taxes even though they are eligible for negative income tax allowances, and this will inevitably raise questions about the adequacy of the personal exemption and the minimum standard deduction.

Tax experts showed little interest in the welfare system until very recently. But this situation has been changing rapidly. Numerous articles on public assistance and negative income taxation have appeared in the newspapers as well as in the technical journals, and the topic is actively discussed in government circles. This attention by experts has already raised the level of public discussion of these issues. Although it is impossible to predict the ultimate outcome, it is clear that negative income taxation and its relation to the positive income tax will be lively issues in the 1970s.

Financing Social Security

The nation's social security system is one of the outstanding achievements of our times, and anyone who tries to suggest improvements in it must approach the task with some trepidation and a healthy respect for the political, social, and economic wisdom of those who managed to bring the system to its present state of development. Nevertheless, the traditional method of financing benefits through higher payroll taxes is being seriously questioned, and we have arrived at a point where a reevaluation is essential.

In considering social security revision, much depends on one's views regarding the insurance rationale of the system. Some elements are analogous to private insurance, especially the recognition that social security benefits are an earned right and that there should be a relationship (although not one-for-one) between earnings and benefits. But no one has ever actually contributed enough to justify more than a small proportion of the benefits he receives, and this will continue to be the case indefinitely. Even after the system matures, every generation of workers will receive more than its money's worth so long as benefits keep rising as productivity increases.

Once it is recognized that social security is not insurance, two important conclusions follow. First, past earnings—and hence the payroll tax—are only the starting point from which benefits are computed; many other factors, such as marital status, age and number of dependents, and budgetary needs enter into the calculations. Second, the desirability of using the payroll tax for financing purposes should depend on its merits relative to alternative financing sources, not on the need for maintaining some artificial relationship between taxes contributed and benefits. And since the major and best source of federal revenues is the income tax, the appropriate comparison is between the payroll tax and income tax.

Seen in this perspective, the payroll tax is surely inferior. The differences that do exist between the two taxes—the exemptions, the personal deductions, and the broader income concept—argue in favor of the income tax rather than the payroll tax. (This conclusion holds with particular force if the payroll tax is borne by the workers, and most economists believe that this is the case.) With combined employer-employee rates of 10 per cent already on the books, the tax paid by a worker in this country with wages at the officially-defined poverty level of $3,500 for a family of four is $350. In our society, a worker with such meager wages should not be required to pay so much tax, in addition to the many other taxes he bears indirectly. Such oppressive taxation cannot be reconciled with the objectives of the nation's poverty program.

Because we are at the end of the road in reliance on payroll taxation to finance additional benefits, general revenues are needed to finance at least the benefits of workers who have low earnings. Consideration might first be given to the idea of refunding the payroll tax paid on wages of workers with incomes below the poverty level. Six states already refund the equivalent of the sales tax paid by the non-income-tax-paying population; the federal government should have little difficulty in doing the same thing for payroll taxes. The amount involved is relatively small—$800 million if only the employee tax is refunded, $1.5 billion if both the employee and employer taxes are refunded—and the refund procedures are well established. These refunds would, of course, come from general revenues.

In addition, the social security system will need to be integrated with the improved income maintenance system discussed earlier. When such a system is developed, any differences between the minimum social security benefits and the general income maintenance system will have to be removed. My own view would be to continue to use the social security system to take care of all aged persons, whether eligible for social security or for the general transfer payment system, but this change would require the payment of benefits to the noninsured as well as to those who are insured. Progress will be made in this field if we free ourselves from the notion that the social security system is an insurance system, and accept the idea that the nation cannot finance its antipoverty programs—for the aged and others—by taxing the poor.

State and Local Taxes

Few people listened four or five years ago when public finance experts called attention to the financial crisis which was developing at the state-local level. Now, it is common knowledge that our state and local governments are in deep financial trouble. With rising population, continued growth, and higher aspirations, the demand for the services provided by the states and local governments has been rising more rapidly than the growth in their tax receipts. By contrast, federal revenues (at full employment)—which are based to a large extent on the income taxes—go up much more rapidly than federal expenditures, except in times of war. Part of these rising federal receipts have been given to the state and local governments through grants-in-aid. But this assistance has not been enough. These governments have raised their own tax rates to very high levels, yet no relief from further state-local tax rate increases seems to be in sight. The problem is national in scope and therefore requires the attention of the federal government, as well as of the state and local governments.

The magnitude of the problem may be illustrated by the following example. In fiscal year 1967—the latest year for which data are available—state-local expenditures and revenues amounted to almost $94 billion. Gross national product increased 8 per cent per year between fiscal years 1967 and 1969. Suppose GNP should continue to rise by an average of about 6 per cent per year (a reasonable assumption if we maintain full employment and succeed in moderating inflationary pressures), and state-local revenues rise at the same rate. On these assumptions, state-local receipts (including federal aid) would reach $155 billion by 1975. But if needed state-local expenditures grew 2 per cent a year faster—which seems conservative in the light of recent experience—they would reach $180 billion by 1975, leaving a gap of $25 billion.

In the absence of additional federal aid, the states and local governments would have to raise their own tax rates by an average of more than 15 per cent across the board to fill the entire gap. Governors, mayors, and county executives rightfully fear the wrath of the electorate if they should propose such increases. Furthermore, from the standpoint of tax equity and economic policy, governmental services should not be financed almost entirely by property and consumer taxes—the revenue sources on which state and local governments largely depend. Without additional federal help, state-local tax rates will rise, but not enough to solve their financial problems. The poor will be burdened in two ways—by the increased tax burden, and by the continued inadequacy of public programs which are so vitally needed to help lift them out of poverty.

Many people think they have arrived at the solution to this problem, but there is no panacea. Every level of government will have to do its part to help relieve the financial pressure.

At the state level, the trend is for moderate income and sales taxes. Thirty states have both, and the number is rising steadily. There are, of course, long-standing traditions against one tax or the other in the remaining states, but these precedents are breaking down. The credit against the income tax for sales taxes paid overcomes the objection against the sales tax on grounds of equity. There is increasing recognition of the moderating effect on state income tax progression of the deductibility feature of the federal law, and this fact has made the personal income tax more acceptable. Given the urgent needs for revenue, no state can afford to be without effective income and sales taxes.

The states must also take a leading role in helping to improve the tax systems of their local governments. Despite the pioneering efforts by the Advisory Commission on Intergovernmental Relations, property tax administration is still spotty throughout the country. This tax will continue to be the main source of revenue for local governments, and states should take a strong hand in helping to improve its administration. They might also follow the lead of Wisconsin and Minnesota in refunding property taxes paid by their aged citizens in the lowest income classes. In addition, the states should allocate a larger proportion of their own revenues to grants-in-aid so that the local governments will not be forced to enact high income and sales taxes that tend to drive wealthy taxpayers and businesses to the suburbs. The best arrangement would be to have state-wide sales and income taxes topped by moderate "piggyback" local taxes which would be collected by the state government. (At some date in the not-too-distant future, I hope that all income taxes will be collected by the federal government on the basis of a single return to be filed by the individual taxpayer.)

Aside from adding nonproperty taxes to their revenue systems and improving property tax administration, local governments need to reconsider the appropriateness of the general property tax as their basic source of revenue. The property tax encourages real estate operators to let their city properties run down, and to hold on to vacant land in the suburbs in the expectation that it will appreciate substantially. Nowhere are the high land values which are created largely by the action of local governments taxed to the extent that equity and economic considerations warrant. One does not necessarily have to subscribe to all the dogma of the "single tax" to see the merits of heavier taxation of land values or of increases in land values.

Federal Grants to State and Local Governments

The major development in governmental finances during the past several years has been the sharp rise in federal grants-in-aid to the states and local governments. In fiscal year 1958, federal grants amounted to $4.9 billion, or 12 per cent of state-local general revenues; in fiscal 1970 they will reach $25 billion and will account for about 18 per cent of state-local revenues. Two-thirds of the dollar increase in federal grants occurred in the last five years.

In view of this tremendous growth, it is not surprising that the federal grant system is being seriously questioned in many quarters. But most of the criticism comes from those who believe that the grant system is too cumbersome and that the constraints in individual grant programs are excessively detailed. A move to consolidate the grants into a smaller number of categories and to allow state and local authorities more freedom in the expenditure of grant funds is gathering support. In addition, considerable attention is being given to the addition of general-purpose grants to the federal grant system in order to give the states and local governments a permanent share in the rapidly-growing federal revenue system.

Most revenue-sharing plans would set aside a given per cent of the federal individual income tax base (or of actual income tax revenues) for distribution to the states. Details of the allocation to the various states differ, but in general they rely on a per capita distribution (on the assumption that population is a good indicator of need), sometimes modified by an index of relative state tax effort and sometimes by the incidence of poverty or low incomes. State and local officials would be allowed to spend these funds on any state-local program (except perhaps for highways, which are supported by a special trust fund with its own earmarked receipts). Some would limit the expenditures to education, health, welfare, and housing, but this constraint would be a very mild one because these categories already account for well over half of state-local expenditures.

The revenue-sharing controversy has been concerned mainly with the question of assuring a fair share of the grants to the large cities and other urban communities. All states give aid to local units and most give significant amounts. As a matter of fact, the state grant-in-aid system for local governments is much more highly developed than the federal grant system. In the aggregate, transfers from state to local governments account for more than a third of state expenditures and about 30 per cent of local general revenues. As I have already indicated, federal grants amount to only 18 per cent of state-local revenues. Thus, even without any specific requirements, local governments would receive about a third of any general funds the states might receive from the federal government.

Nevertheless, in the light of urgent local needs and the observed tendency of state capitals to shortchange their major central cities, it is virtually unanimously agreed that an explicit "pass-through" rule is desirable to recognize the legitimate claims of local government. It could be framed in any number of ways, and it is impossible to predict what the ultimate compromise will be.

It should be emphasized that the revenue-sharing grants are not good substitutes for categorical grants. Categorical grants are needed because the benefits of many public services "spill over" from the community in which they are performed to other communities. Expenditures for such services would be too low if financed entirely by state-local sources, because each state or community would tend to pay only for the benefits likely to accrue to its own citizens. Unless the federal government steps in to represent the national interest in the benefits derived from state-local services, the latter will be badly undernourished.

General purpose grants are justified on substantially different grounds. In the first place, all states do not have equal capacity to pay for local services. Even though the poorer states make a larger relative revenue effort, they are unable to match the revenue-raising ability of the richest states. Second, federal use of the best tax sources leaves a substantial gap between state-local need and state-local fiscal capacity. Moreover, no state can push its rates much higher than the rates in neighboring states for fear of placing its citizens and business enterprises at a disadvantage. This problem justifies some federal assistance even for purely state-local activities, with the poorer states needing relatively more help because of their low fiscal capacities.

For these reasons, the general purpose grants should supplement the categorical grants, but not replace them. Considering the large, unmet needs throughout the country for public programs with large spill-over effects, the adoption of revenue-sharing should not be the occasion for reducing categorical grants.

Federal Tax Reform

Aside from helping the states and local governments, the federal government must also put its own tax house in order. Some progress was made during the early 1960s in reforming the federal tax system, but the

Revenue Acts of 1962 and 1964 and the Excise Tax Reduction Act of 1965 represented only the first installments. The Vietnam War halted further activity along these lines and we are again beginning to hear complaints about the oppressiveness of federal taxes. The fact of the matter is that, even though we are fighting a costly war, federal personal income tax rates are now 10 per cent below the pre-1964 tax rates on the average, and the general corporation income tax is only 1.5 per cent above the pre-1964 rates. But the need to extend the surtax for still another year again highlights the inequities in the tax system. It is clearly unfair to impose additional taxes on those already taxable, while those who escape taxation on all or most of their income are not required to make a similar contribution.

Income Taxes of the Poor. The first order of business should be to remove the poor entirely from the federal income tax rolls. The revenues involved are small—only about $200 million a year—but the cost would be much more than that because any exemption or deduction for the poor must be given to those immediately above the poverty levels. Otherwise, an additional dollar of income just above the poverty lines would generate more than an additional dollar of tax. For example, the tax on a single person with income of $1,700 (the current poverty line for an unattached individual) up to $1,725 is $117 (without the surtax). If the $1,700 man were exempted from tax while the man with $1,701 were required to pay tax, the additional dollar of income would generate a tax of $117. This "notch" can be handled by giving some tax reduction to those immediately above the cut-off level as well as those below.

The federal individual income tax already contains a device which can be used to accomplish this objective: the minimum standard deduction. Under present law, taxpayers have an exemption of $600 for each person in the family and may elect a minimum standard deduction of $200 for themselves and $100 for each exemption (including their own) in lieu of the regular standard deduction, with a maximum of $1,000. As a result, the minimum taxable level is roughly equal to the current poverty line for a family of eight, but not for smaller families. An increase in the per capita exemption would not correct this situation, because families of all sizes would receive the same relative benefit; moreover, an exemption increase is expensive, the cost being almost $3.5 billion a year for the first $100 of increase.

The Treasury Department of the previous administration recommended that the minimum standard deduction be raised from $200 to $600 for each return ($300 on separate returns), leaving the $100 bonus for each exemption and the $1,000 limit unchanged. This would be a great improvement over present law—it would remove 1.2 million families from the income tax rolls at a cost of $1.1 billion a year, but another million families would remain taxable.

The new administration devised a new low income allowance which raises the minimum taxable income level by a flat $1,100 above the per capita exemption and happens to duplicate almost dollar for dollar the official poverty lines at this year's prices. To limit the revenue loss, the low income allowance is tapered off by 50 cents for each dollar of income above the present minimum taxable levels, so that the allowance disappears rapidly (at $3,300 for a single person, $3,700 for a married couple, and $4,500 for a family of four). This allowance would eliminate virtually all the poor from the income tax rolls at a cost of only $665 million a year.

An even better alternative would be to give an allowance of $1,100 to all persons filing returns, instead of tapering it off by 50 cents for every dollar of income about present minimum taxable levels. This alternative would have the advantage of giving some relief to all taxpayers with incomes below about $11,000, instead of arbitrarily limiting the relief to the bottom of the income scale. Unfortunately, the cost of this revision would be about $2.25 billion a year, an amount which seems to be beyond the revenues deemed available for low-income relief by the present and past administrations.

Structural Reform. The main trouble with the present income tax base is that large amounts of income have been allowed to escape taxation by means of various special provisions and deductions. If the total income reported by taxpayers were subject to the statutory rates, taxes would begin at 14 per cent on the first dollar of income and rise to 70 per cent in the top bracket. But nobody pays these rates. After allowing for all the subtractions permitted by the tax laws—many of them perfectly appropriate, but others nothing less than outright tax handouts—the maximum average rate for even the highest income classes is no more than about 30 per cent on reported income and 20 per cent on total income (that is, income that is not taxed and not reported on tax returns). By any test of equity, the federal income tax leaves much to be desired—although I hasten to add that, despite its faults, this tax is still the best in the nation's revenue system.

A mere listing of the most urgent reforms will be sufficient to indicate how difficult a job it will be:

> The differential between the tax rates on capital gains and on ordinary income should be reduced or eliminated, unrealized capital gains that are transferred at gift or death should be made subject to tax at the time of transfer, and the definition of capital gains should be revised to limit the application of the preferential rate to gains from the transfer of assets.

The capital recovery provisions for the mining and oil industries are excessively generous. In view of the long history of these provisions, it is perhaps too much to expect that Congress will limit the tax deductions for the recovery of capital invested in these industries to the amount of the investment. At the very least, the percentage depletion rates should be reduced.

The tax exemption privilege for interest on state-local bonds costs the federal government twice as much as the value of the exemption in reduced interest. The discrepancy will rise as the volume of state-local bond issues continues to increase. A better arrangement would be to provide a direct federal subsidy on state-local bond interest payments.

The tax provisions for the elderly are excessively complicated and give the largest benefits to those with the highest incomes. Assuming an adequate system of social security benefits, there would be little justification for any special tax provisions for this group in the population. Presidents Kennedy and Johnson recommended revisions which would have concentrated the benefits in the lower part of the income scale.

The personal deductions for such outlays as contributions, interest, etc., are very costly and greatly complicate income tax compliance and administration. Moreover, most of them are hard to justify on the basis of tax theory. The deduction for interest on personal loans and home mortgages should be eliminated, and "floors" should be placed under the deductions for charitable contributions and state and local taxes (as in the case of medical expenses). Alternatively, it would be possible to simplify the tax return for all but a small minority of taxpayers by putting one floor (for example, 10 or 15 per cent) under all personal deductions and eliminating the standard deduction. Allowable deductions should be allocated between taxable and nontaxable income sources to recognize that outlays for these items come from an individual's total income and not from his taxable income alone.

Income-splitting confers a large tax advantage on middle and high income married couples, and single people as a group feel oppressed by such discrimination. Since it is impractical to raise the tax rates of married couples, the rates imposed on the income of single persons should be moderated. This aim can be accomplished without restoring the old inequalities in the taxes of married couples in community and noncommunity property states.

To correct the anomalies in the law that permit wealthy taxpayers to reduce greatly or eliminate their tax, the deduction of farm "losses" should be limited to some specific dollar amount per year, say $15,000; profits from the sale of commercial and residential properties that reflect prior accelerated depreciation deductions should be taxed as ordinary income rather than as capital gains; and the unlimited charitable deduction for those whose taxes and charitable contributions exceed 90 per cent of their taxable incomes in eight out of ten successive years should be eliminated.

This menu of reforms is hardly likely to be acted on overnight, but a start should be made immediately to introduce a comprehensive tax base into the system. This can be done by enacting a *minimum* income tax which would apply to all the income received by an individual above a generous exemption. Such a tax would require at least some contribution from those few who now escape paying even a small share of the income tax burden.

The federal government also levies estate and gift taxes, but the revenue yield is disappointing—only a little over 2 per cent of federal receipts. They can be avoided by distributing gifts at the lower gift tax rates, by setting up trusts, and by other methods. The rates are high enough; what is needed is a complete overhaul to eliminate the avenues of escape and to tax equal amounts of transfers equally.

Consumption taxes are not very popular in the United States, and they are confined almost entirely to the state and local levels. The federal government has relied on selective excise taxes for consumption tax revenues. When these taxes were last reviewed by the Congress in 1965, the decision was made to eliminate all the selective excise taxes except those on gasoline, tobacco products, and alcoholic beverages. (The taxes on automobiles and telephone calls are still on the books, but they are due to expire in 1972.) Given the productivity and greater equity of the income taxes, there is no reason to upset this decision in the foreseeable future.

A new method of mass taxation that has attracted interest of late is the value-added tax, which is imposed at a flat rate on the "value added" by each firm (gross receipts less the cost of materials purchased from other firms). It is similar to a retail sales tax (if the cost of equipment is deductible), except that it is collected piecemeal as the commodity makes its way through the channels of production and distribution. The value-added tax is now being adopted by the European Economic Community in place of their turnover taxes, and this development has attracted attention in the United States.

Some supporters of the value-added tax have argued that, for competitive reasons in international markets, the United States should reduce the corporation income tax, enact a value-added tax as a substitute, and rebate the value-added tax on exports. The effect of such a change on the prices of U.S. exports depends on the incidence of the corporation income tax. If the corporation income tax is not shifted and the value-added tax is shifted, the switch to a value-added tax would accomplish little. The value-added tax would raise prices on all goods and services, whereas the rebate would return export prices to their former level. Expert opinion is divided on this question. My own view is that the trade effect would be small, if any. In any case, it would be unwise to adopt such a drastic change in the tax system on these uncertain grounds.

Accelerating Tax Action. The most serious drawback of the tax legislative process is that it cannot be used to provide a prompt stimulus or restraint to the economy when needed. Although monetary authorities have full discretion to vary money and credit conditions on a daily basis and the President has the power to control the rate of expenditures within wide limits, Congress jealously guards its prerogative of varying tax rates. The long delays in the enactment of the Revenue Acts of 1964 and 1968, and the delay this year in extending the surtax, are ample evidence that our procedures for raising and lowering tax rates impose serious costs by hindering effective and timely use of tax policy for stabilization purposes.

Many tax experts and national citizens' organizations have recommended that the President be authorized to make temporary increases or reductions in tax rates. This approach would emphasize changes which are relatively simple and uniform throughout most of the income scale. The surcharge enacted last year, which increased tax rates by a flat 10 per cent for all taxpayers except for those with incomes that do not exceed the first two taxable income brackets, illustrates the kind of change that would be involved. More fundamental reforms would be reserved for long-run revisions of the tax structure which necessarily involve lengthy and searching debate.

In general, the proposals would permit the President to change tax rates within prescribed limits for a period of six months, subject to a congressional veto within 30 days. Another possibility might be to persuade Congress to alter its procedures to permit prompt action on temporary tax changes proposed by the President.

Had such authority been available to the President in the past, it would have been possible to raise tax rates as soon as inflationary pressures became evident in 1966. If taxes had been raised, we would have avoided excessive reliance on tight money, which produced a monetary crunch in 1966 and the inordinately high level of interest rates which still plagues the housing industry, small business, state-local governments, and other needy borrowers.

Tax Preferences to Promote Social Objectives

The idea of using tax devices as an incentive to encourage individuals or businesses to engage in socially desirable activities is growing in popularity. The tax mechanism is indeed a powerful device to alter private activity, but it must be used sparingly. Any proposal of this kind should meet two strict conditions: First, the preference must promote a major national objective; and second, the tax mechanism must be the most efficient mechanism for achieving this objective. Most of the recent spate of tax incentive proposals cannot meet these conditions.

I have not made a complete study of all the tax incentive proposals, but an impressive list can be put together on the basis of newspaper accounts alone. The list includes suggestions to promote such diverse objectives as pollution control, manpower training, housing construction, college education, community development, diversion of capital to minority groups, and increases in private gifts to underdeveloped countries. The devices used include tax credits, special exemptions or deductions, accelerated depreciation, capital gains treatment, and tax deferral. The bulk of the cost of most of these proposals would go to reward people or businesses for doing things they would do without the tax incentive. Many would introduce wide-open loopholes that would be exploited by sharp operators. All the proposals would greatly complicate the tax laws. And in nearly all cases there are alternative expenditure programs that would promote the same objectives more effectively.

In principle, there should be no difference between subsidies granted for private activities by tax devices or by direct expenditures of a government agency. Suppose the government decides to pay half the cost of a certain training program if conducted by private business firms. It can allow the firms a tax credit of 50 per cent up to the maximum cost of the program, or it can match the outlays of the firms dollar for dollar up to half the maximum. In the same way, eligibility requirements, minimum program content, and audit arrangements could be made the same for a tax credit and for an expenditure grant.

The tax device seems to be preferred by many of its proponents primarily because Congress ordinarily imposes fewer constraints in the tax law than are required by a government agency in administering a comparable expenditure grant. Moreover, tax returns are not open to the public, whereas government agencies are accountable for their expenditures in great detail. But laxness in administration and nondisclosure are hardly good justifications for allocating public funds via the tax system. Tax incentives should be used only when the activity can be clearly identified in financial statements ordinarily prepared by accountants and when it is more efficient to use employees of the Internal Revenue Service rather than those of other government agencies to administer the program.

The tax law is already riddled with special provisions which should be removed in the interest of equity, simplification, and improved economic performance. Few of them would be tolerated if they were subject to the same scrutiny given by Congress to direct appropriations. Instead of adding to tax preferences indiscriminately, we should insist on an annual accounting to the public of the cost of each of the special tax provisions and an identification of the groups which benefit from them. This information could be provided by continuing the "tax expenditure budget" devised by the Treasury 1968 to show the cost of tax preferences alongside of the direct expenditures in the regular budget submitted annually by the President to the Congress. Annual disclosure of the billions of dollars of forgone revenue would have a salutary effect on tax policy.

The goals of our national tax policy are to distribute the burden of taxation equitably and to promote economic growth and stability. Judgments about equity and about the steps needed to achieve stable growth inevitably differ. We should not hesitate to use tax policy in the interest of promoting national priorities, but we should also be alert to resist the pressures for introducing unnecessary or inefficient preferences and we should close loopholes already in the law in the interest of the same objective. The tax system has served the nation well, but it can be greatly improved to the benefit of the nation and all its citizens.

Printed in the United States
by Baker & Taylor Publisher Services